For eight months in 1975 and 1976, Daniel Patrick Moynihan served the United States as its Ambassador to the United Nations. During a term of almost unprecedented controversy, editorial debate, and front-page headlines, he alerted both his country and the international forum to new forms of assault upon the democratic idea of human rights, which a new majority in the United Nations was trying to distort and which the developed democracies of the West were unwilling to defend. At issue were the principles that underlie all political freedom and are basic to the United Nations itself.

By 1975 Soviet aims and Arab money had stirred up a movement to undermine the legitimacy of the state of Israel by equating (in defiance of history, logic, and language) Zionism with racism. Moynihan battled this lie in the field of ideas and on the floor of the U.N., and the eloquent fight he waged may have proved to be one of the turning points in the history of the United Nations and of U.S. foreign policy.

This fiery and dramatic book is Moynihan's testimony of those eventful days. He begins by telling of his varied service in both domestic and foreign posts under four Presidents. He treats briefly of his two-year ambassadorship to India and what he learned and wrote there. He unfolds the story behind his appointment to the United Nations, and recounts his strategies in the special and regular sessions of the 1975 General Assembly. He tells of the United States' proposal for amnesty for all political prisoners; of his embattled service on the Security Council in 1976 during the Angolan incursion and the fight over seating the Palestinian Liberation Organization; of his agreements and differences with Kissinger.

In the process, he traces the growth of Communist influence in the U.N. and shows how propaganda excited the nations of the Third World to employ the language of freedom in the interests of its suppression. He evokes dramatic scenes in Geneva, Washington, and New York, involving participants such as Jacob Malik, Chaim Herzog,

Previous books by Daniel Patrick Moynihan:

Ethnicity: Theory and Experience (Editor, with Nathan Glazer)

Coping: Essays on the Practice of Government

The Politics of a Guaranteed Income

On Equality of Educational Opportunity (Editor, with Frederick Mosteller)

On Understanding Poverty: Perspectives from the Social Sciences (Editor)

Toward a National Urban Policy (Editor)

Maximum Feasible Misunderstanding: Community Action in the War on Poverty

The Defenses of Freedom: The Public Papers of Arthur J. Goldberg (Editor)

Beyond the Melting Pot: The Negroes, Puerto Ricans, Jews, Italians, and Irish in New York City (with Nathan Glazer)

A Dangerous Place

A Dangerous Place

by Daniel Patrick Moynihan
with Suzanne Weaver

An Atlantic Monthly Press Book

LITTLE, BROWN AND COMPANY   BOSTON   TORONTO

FIRST EDITION

T 11/78

Library of Congress Cataloging in Publication Data
Moynihan, Daniel Patrick
   A dangerous place.
   "An Atlantic Monthly Press book."
   Includes index.
   1. United Nations. 2. United States—Foreign rela-
tions—1974–1977. 3. World politics—1975–1985.
I. Weaver, Suzanne, joint author. II. Title.
JX1977.M68 1978   341.23 78–16473
ISBN 0-316-58694-4

A portion of this book appeared in *The Atlantic* under the title "How Much Does Freedom Matter?" Excerpts from
• Senator Moynihan's "Was Woodrow Wilson Right?" and "The United States in Opposition," copyright 1974 and 1975 by the American Jewish Committee. Reprinted by permission of *Commentary*. • W. Scott Thompson's response to Senator Moynihan's "The United States in Opposition" reprinted by permission of Mr. Thompson. • Senator Moynihan's speech at the *Pacem in Terris* Convocation is from *Pacem in Terris IV: American-Soviet Detente, Peace and National Security* and Kenneth W. Thompson's speech, "Too Much Shouting, Too Little Quiet Diplomacy," from *Pacem in Terris II: American Foreign Policy and the Third World*, copyright The Fund for the Republic, Inc. (Santa Barbara) and The Fund for Peace (New York). Reprinted by permission of the Center for the Study of Democratic Institutions. • Paul Johnson's "The Resources of Civilization" is quoted by permission of the *New Statesman*. • Irving Kristol's "The New Cold War" reprinted with permission of the author and *The Wall Street Journal* © 1975 by Dow Jones & Company, Inc. All rights reserved. • Hilaire Belloc's "On a Great Election" is reprinted by permission of Gerald Duckworth & Co., Ltd. • From Russell Baker's "The Dangerous Case of English," reprinted by permission. © 1976 by The New York Times Company. • His memo to Senator Moynihan on Zionism/racism is reprinted by permission of Charles H. Fairbanks, Jr. • The lead story in *Newsweek* November 17, 1975, and Meg Greenfield's "U.N. Chic," *Newsweek* November 24, 1975. Copyright 1975 by Newsweek, Inc. Reprinted by permission.

ATLANTIC–LITTLE, BROWN BOOKS
ARE PUBLISHED BY
LITTLE, BROWN AND COMPANY
IN ASSOCIATION WITH
THE ATLANTIC MONTHLY PRESS

DESIGNED BY D. CHRISTINE BENDERS

*Published simultaneously in Canada
by Little, Brown & Company (Canada) Limited*
PRINTED IN THE UNITED STATES OF AMERICA

Introduction

This volume, part journal and part commonplace book, seeks to describe certain ideas and events that contributed to the recent emergence of human rights as an issue of American foreign policy. It will, I hope, be of some historical interest, but my purpose in writing, as will be evident from the form I have chosen, is to set forth some of the arguments upon which this initiative was based. Unless these are better understood — and perfected, and improved — it is not likely the initiative will be sustained. I hope the reader will come away with an understanding of why this is so or, at least, why it seems so to me.

My collaboration with Suzanne Weaver began at Harvard University, where she taught in my course "Social Science and Social Policy." She went from there to the faculty of Yale University, from which she took leave to join me at the United States Mission to the United Nations. She was the fullest collaborator in that work, as in this.

We are both of us in the debt of Marcella Barnhart of the Foreign Service, who was with me in India and at the United Nations. Her sense of what needed to be recorded, logged, and filed was that of the true diplomatist, aware of how much subsequently depends on what clearly can be established to have taken place. If it seems simple in the archives, try it in the maelstrom. And Yvonne Lancaster gave us patient and much-valued help in preparing the manuscript of this book.

— D. P. M.

New York, New York
February 14, 1978

A Further Note to the Reader

A short while after this manuscript was completed, several matters appeared in the press that I had not previously felt free to discuss.

On April 11, 1978, it was reported that Arkady N. Shevchenko, the highest ranking Soviet official in the United Nations Secretariat, had "defected from his country." The news, *Time* reported, "caused consternation at the U.N., intense alarm in Moscow, and scarcely concealed elation in Washington." This was the highest ranking defection in the history of the Soviet Union. Shevchenko, Under-Secretary-General for Political and Security Council Affairs, ambassador at forty, aide to Foreign Minister Andrei A. Gromyko before being sent to the U.N., and on most anyone's short list of those who might succeed Gromyko, was not merely the highest ranking Russian at the U.N., he was also the quintessential *apparatchik*. *The New York Times* put it that his decision not to obey a summons to return home simply startled the world organization.

Confusion became disarray when, on April 27, *The Times,* citing "well-placed sources in Washington," reported further that Shevchenko "had written a letter to Leonid I. Brezhnev saying that the country's present leadership had betrayed the ideals of the 1917 Bolshevik Revolution and protesting that the Soviet Union was controlled by the internal security agency, the K.G.B."

On the day after the defection was made known, the Soviet delegation at the U.N. said that in refusing to return to Moscow, Shevchenko had been coerced by United States intelligence agents and was being held "under duress." *Time,* in its issue of April 24, cited Vyacheslav

Kuzmin, one of Shevchenko's aides and "believed to be the K.G.B. officer who was assigned to keep him under surveillance," as saying that Shevchenko "is a sick man who must be sent back to Moscow so he can get the medical care he needs." The usual lies. *Time* also stated that Shevchenko had been secretly talking to U.S. intelligence officers for two years. *The New York Times* published the same information. In these circumstances, I have changed the manuscript in galley in order to touch upon this extraordinary event, which Mr. Shevchenko himself will no doubt one day wish to describe. Before doing so, I reached agreement with the responsible persons in Washington as to what I would write.

On April 13, two days after the Shevchenko defection became known, the Washington *Post*, following up on a story in *Outside* magazine, reported that "the Central Intelligence Agency recruited 14 American mountain-climbers to place nuclear power instruments on two peaks of the Himalayas to spy on Chinese atomic tests and missile firings in the 1960's. One of the power packs was lost. On April 18, Indian Prime Minister Morarji Desai confirmed that this had happened and that these were joint U.S.-Indian operations. In these circumstances I have changed the manuscript in galley in order to expand on the account of my conversation with the then Chinese Foreign Minister Chiao Kuanhua in Peking on my way home from India. Again, before doing this I reached agreement with the responsible persons in Washington as to what I would write.

Finally, in the spring of 1978, more became known of the doomed and absurd United States covert activities in Angola in the latter half of 1975. I have accordingly felt freer to touch upon these events.

The reader may well ask, "What else has been left out that one would wish to know?" The direct answer is that there are intrigues I have left to others to write about, but that, really, they would only get in the way of the *arguments* we try to set forth is this volume. These three particular episodes having come to light, the reader is entitled to have them taken into account. But ours remains, perhaps to its disadvantage, a book about ideas.

                   — D.P.M.

Derrymore
Pindars Corners, New York
May 31, 1978

Contents

For
Leonard Garment
and
Norman Podhoretz

A Dangerous Place

I

A Half-Life

I HAD SEEN STEVENSON humiliated. Goldberg betrayed. Ball diminished. Wiggins patronized. Yost ignored. Bush traduced. Scali savaged. For my part, I had twice said no to the post I was now to assume. And so I said to the Counselor of the Department of State, in that spring of 1975, that there would be two conditions. First, I would not be lied to. That would happen only once. Second, while I understood there would be times when the Secretary, in the interests of policy, would not tell me everything I might need to know, and might even give me and indeed the world impressions that were not strictly speaking accurate, at such moments of great danger I expected to be warned. "You do not understand," replied the Honorable Helmut Sonnenfeldt. Smiling. "Henry does not lie because it is in his interest. He lies because it is in his nature."

———◆———

Thus it began again. I had first gone to Washington with John F. Kennedy and then stayed on with Lyndon Johnson. There I learned as an adult what I had known as a child, which is that the world is a dangerous place — and learned also that not everyone knows this. I was an Assistant Secretary of Labor and had done useful things when, in the winter of 1964–1965, I did something unusual, which was to foresee the urban riots of the second half of the decade and, in various documents, to warn the President of the United States that they were coming.

Washington was then at the height of the euphoria and zeal evoked by the parables of good and evil that the civil rights demonstrators acted out in the small towns of the Old South and that echoed in the great civil rights bills that subsequently made their way through Congress. No harm, it seemed, could come to us now. Our troubles were past. Whereupon I unhappily discovered they had only begun — for I picked up the onset of the instability that was to rack the cities of the North.

How I did it teaches no great lesson. There was method, but not such as could be said to have proved anything. It was one of those leaps. I was thirty-seven, somewhat but not impossibly late for such things. For six months I did the best work I had ever done, or would do.

Lyndon Johnson was at the height of *his* powers, and took my word for it: I wrote the first draft of his speech at Howard University, given June 4, 1965. In it he spoke the famous lines,

> . . . Freedom is not enough. You do not wipe away the scars of centuries by saying: Now you are free to go where you want, do as you desire. . . .
>
> Thus it is not enough just to open the gates of opportunity. All our citizens must have the ability to walk through those gates.
>
> This is the next and more profound stage of the battle for civil rights. We seek not just freedom but opportunity — not just equality as a right and a theory, but equality as a fact and as a result.

The speech was a huge success, but a brief one. Six years later Johnson was to send word telling me that he considered it the greatest civil rights speech he had ever given. But this took six years and the approach of his death. Only nine weeks after the actual event, I had become a general embarrassment. On August 11, 1965, the riot in Watts broke out. A baffled White House press secretary, saying in effect, "See, we saw it coming," handed out copies of my principal monograph to an equally baffled White House press corps. The moment of greatest peril in Washington comes when, at last, one is understood.

From near to anonymous I became seminotorious. But I had already left Washington, having relearned something else I had known as a youth, which is that in a situation growing steadily more dangerous there is a moment when if you don't leave you have to stay.

On Wednesday, July 14, 1965, Adlai Stevenson died in London. On the Saturday morning that followed, Arthur J. Goldberg asked me to come to his house in Washington. I told him I had been offered a place on the Democratic primary ticket in New York City. He told me to take it. He then told me the President had asked him to resign from the Supreme Court and go to the United Nations to succeed Stevenson. I spent the day and the next with him drafting various statements, including the one he finally made in the Rose Garden on the following Thursday, when he was sworn in.

To this moment I tell myself that I did not influence his decision. But this cannot be so. I wanted him to have the job. He was the ablest man I knew, and the one I was most indebted to. *I* had no idea what it meant to be an Associate Justice of the Supreme Court. What I knew was simply that Arthur Goldberg would become United States Representative to the United Nations. To succeed Adlai Stevenson, to wage peace. And that the President of the United States had said to the Justice that he must do this. This, at the time, was enough for me as for many of us.

———◆———

All that changed utterly in the year that followed, and I commenced to find some advantage in the fact that Lyndon B. Johnson was letting it be known that he rather disapproved of me.

After an unsuccessful campaign for New York City Council President, and a year at the Wesleyan University Center for Advanced Studies, I was made director of the Joint Center for Urban Studies of M.I.T. and Harvard. I settled into a dual set of scholarly interests that had been there for some time, I suppose. My doctoral dissertation had explored the relations of the United States and the International Labor Organization: how the trade unions took themselves into international affairs in pursuit of domestic purposes largely conceived as and very much reaching to the defenses of freedom. I'd written the dissertation in three years at the London School of Economics, where I arrived just as Michael Oakeshott assumed Harold Laski's post as professor of political science. I was thus introduced, earlier than most, to the fact that the socialist idea had spent itself as an economic doctrine. What remained, scarcely distinguishable from nineteenth-century liberalism, was the impulse to decency of which Orwell had written. By some law of compensation this came to seem to me even more important. I had left Britain dismayed by socialism and devoted to socialists.

Sixteen years later, settled again at a university, I turned once more to the interaction of domestic and foreign affairs, but in ways that increasingly troubled the liberalism of the time. Ours, to be sure, was an increasingly shaken liberalism, assaulted from the left as it had not been since the early 1930s, and this time with a failing President rather than an ascendant one. One spokesman for the New Left declared that in the summer of 1967 war abroad and revolution at home had contrived to "murder liberalism in its official robes." The problem for liberals was of an awful simplicity. The war was liberalism's war; ravaged Detroit was, as it were, liberalism's city. A kind of intellectual panic spread through the universities and the liberal press. It became a matter of great urgency to demonstrate somehow that our failures were not theirs, but failures of a false liberalism and pretended liberals. The President, of course, was the primary and indeed sacrificial victim.

It seemed to me that such a great untruth as this one would in time exact a great price; and, insofar as I could, I spoke against it. In September, 1967, I addressed the national board, of which I was a member, of Americans for Democratic Action on "The Politics of Stability." The war, I said, "was thought up and is being managed by the men John F. Kennedy brought to Washington . . . persons of immutable conviction on almost all matters we would consider central to liberal belief. . . ." The cities that had rioted were overwhelmingly cities where we governed. "It is this knowledge," I said, "this complicity, if you will, that requires many of us to practice restraint where others may exercise all their powers of invective and contempt."

I proposed first of all that liberals "see more clearly that their essential interest is in the stability of the social order" and argued that we needed to make more effective alliances with informed conservatives who shared that interest. We had to learn the limits of the huge hierarchical structures of central government. Many of the Great Society programs could never have worked, and ought never to have been tried. Far more effective alternatives had been and remained available. We had to learn the limits of legislating social attitudes; to learn to treat blacks as true equals. We had to "prepare for the onset of terrorism." (There was no way, it seemed to me, that this would not finally emerge from the addled left.) Above all, with respect to the war:

> The task of liberals is to make it politically worthwhile and possible for the administration to disengage. This requires that we continue to work within the party system, and to make clear that we do in fact love peace more than we love the Vietcong.

John Kenneth Galbraith, who headed ADA at this time, was more than supportive, knowing well enough whose war it was and already uncomfortable with the amount of untruth filling the air. But the general reaction was not friendly — save from quite unexpected quarters. In his column "On the Right," William F. Buckley, Jr., declared the address as good a day's work as any since Raymond Moley had left the New Deal. More important, Buckley showed he quite understood what I had said, even where he did not agree. Simultaneously, the social democratic left responded with equal comprehension and more support. Bayard Rustin endorsed the speech on the spot, while *The New Leader* hastened into print with the full text. Conservatives and social democrats scarcely knew each other at this time. Yet their concerns were powerfully symmetric, and they were looking, I think, for persons of the center who understood them.

I kept my distance from *The National Review* but for the first time became rather involved with social democrats, even when least aware. On the Vietnam issue I was drawn to Negotiation Now and became national cochairman, the while wondering that I felt so little unease in the company of quite so many Quakers. Only much later did I learn that social democrats were behind the organization. I began to write frequently for Norman Podhoretz, editor of *Commentary,* and became a member of the publication committee of *The Public Interest.* In both settings this symmetry of concerns of a certain mode of left and right was to be encountered. *The Public Interest,* most strikingly, was peaceably edited by Daniel Bell, avowed socialist and regular contributor to *The New Leader,* and by Irving Kristol, even then a professed conservative. Liberty was the first political principle for each of these men; but more than this, each was profoundly *offended* by totalitarianism.

In 1968 I campaigned first for Robert Kennedy, then for Eugene McCarthy, finally for Hubert Humphrey. But it was Richard Nixon who, after the November election, asked me to be Assistant to the President for Urban Affairs. I'd nothing against him, and a certain admiration of the kind called grudging. I always half suspected we'd stolen the 1960 election. He had chosen not to challenge what could not be changed.

Early on in the White House I must have remarked, for William Safire wrote it down, "My half-life will last only until Ehrlichman discovers the Bureau of the Budget and Haldeman produces a telephone directory." This turned out to be nine months and fourteen days — until, that is, November 4, 1969, when I was made Counselor and a member of the Cabinet and took on at most a watching brief until my two years were up. (I had agreed to stay that long.)

I had come to the White House knowing that one thing had to be done, and it was. The summer of 1969 passed without violence, the first since Watts. Of my work on urban problems, I would note only that I did not do what the Assistant to the President for National Security Affairs did, which was to allow the President to become identified with the onset of the crisis he was dealing with, and to contrive to have himself identified with its resolution. I do not ascribe this to finer sensibilities. It came from having worked for the two previous Presidents, and having seen both destroyed.

———◆———

In May, 1970, Cambodia was invaded and I asked to resign. The President asked me to stay just a month to help with legislation establishing a guaranteed income, which had passed the House and looked promising in the Senate when the "incursion" set in motion *this* President's destruction. I did not know this then, of course, but I knew that his enemies had got to him, and that he would waste a good portion of his ascendancy hating those who hated him. I agreed to stay a short while.

A month passed when one morning I was asked to meet with Donald Rumsfeld, John Ehrlichman, and Robert Finch, who had been with the President on the *Sequoia* the night before. The Cambodia storm had seemingly passed; he was shuffling, as they say, the Cabinet. He had decided to send me to the United Nations. "But you don't understand," I told them; "I have resigned."

It was like Nixon not to have told them I'd resigned. On the other hand, it was like him to sense that I might make something of the U.N. After his election he had asked Senator Eugene McCarthy of Minnesota to take the post, and McCarthy had accepted on condition that the Republican governor of that state appoint a Democrat to succeed him in the Senate. The governor declined, and the appointment did not go through, but the President kept looking for a person who could acknowledge our own moral failings and yet make no apologies to our moral inferiors. Nixon understood more about liberals than liberals ever understood about him. He took it as given that we had a role in the scheme of things — a tolerance not always reciprocated.

In the end, I stayed in the White House longer than a month. Summer passed, the second without violence. The Southern schools were at long last integrated. The President asked once again that I go to the United Nations; this time I agreed. In September he took me on a trip around Europe: "To strengthen the structure of peace," as it was billed. In that I was a member of the Cabinet, protocol provided that I step out of Air Force One behind the President and ahead of Kissinger, who was also on the journey. Somehow Kissinger invariably reached the ground ahead of me.

It was his obsession that no one *ever* should appear to be closer to the President than he, while neither should anyone be seen to hold this

President in greater contempt. This was so much a preoccupation as to be, in a way, impersonal. It was not the usual White House style. Presidential aides do not succeed Presidents, and so, in the main, despite the conflicts within any such court, its members do not much conspire. But then, Kissinger did not operate in the usual style of a presidential aide. It was his view, and he did not conceal it, save possibly from the President, that Richard Nixon did not deserve to *be* President.

Kissinger's own style was that of the Politburo, and indeed in time, in a sufficient sense, he did succeed his master. For most of the two Watergate years, during which civil war, as he thought of it and as he described it, raged in the country, Kissinger was able to perform the duties of President in foreign affairs. It was an act of courage and of daring beyond anything seen in our time. One's only reservation is that he helped bring on that civil war, and, had he been in an actual Politburo, would have done so deliberately.

———◆———

In November of 1970 the news leaked that I was to go to the U.N. I had told a friend in Cambridge, who told a friend, who told the editor of the Boston *Globe*. I think now I had not been paying enough attention to the fact that I had agreed to the U.N. job. I spent October in Europe, staying out of the country during the congressional elections, which the White House both debased and lost. The people the nation would come to know in the aftermath of Watergate were commencing to be more in evidence in a White House that I had entered as a colleague of such men as Arthur Burns and Paul McCracken. I returned to the United States in November. Then one evening in Washington, coming home from a dinner where I had asked Stephen Hess to be my U.N. deputy, between the time of getting into and getting out of an elevator, I decided not to take the job but to leave the administration altogether.

Before I could do so, an editorial in *The New York Times* pronounced that I was the "Wrong Man for the U.N." The substance of the comment was that then-Ambassador Charles Yost, thirty-six years in the Foreign Service and unknown to indiscretion, was the right man. Nixon had said so on appointing him. It was incredible, the editorial observed, that no one had even told him he was to be replaced. True enough, but a measure perhaps of Yost's role.

The *Times*'s advice to me was to go back to Cambridge and urban studies or to stay in Washington and help with welfare reform. The editorial continued that I had "exhibited outstanding qualities in public life — but almost never those of a diplomat." It was thought I would be "bored stiff at the glacial pace of United Nations diplomacy." If I thought of it as a way back into New York politics, I "should reflect on Arthur J. Goldberg's fate. . . ." I read the editorial on the way to lunch with the Justice, who had just been badly beaten in his campaign for governor of New York.

Three days later it was announced that I would not take the job. Soon George Bush was chosen. *The Times* did not think him the "Wrong Man" for the job (which indeed he was not). I returned to Harvard slightly ruffled that a Ph.D. from the Fletcher School of International Law and Diplomacy should have been so lightly dismissed as "not qualified." It was hard to imagine, but then so was the editor of *The Times* editorial page, John Oakes.

Before I finally left the administration I found myself one afternoon on a couch in the lobby of the Metropolitan Club bespeaking the somewhat wayward interest of Senator McCarthy in the cause of welfare reform. Given over to the subject myself, I only gradually became aware of an approaching voice bellowing my name in an increasing contraction that approached pentameter. I looked up and it was Dean Acheson. Arms akimbo, mustachios abristle. "Moynihan!" he exclaimed. "My respect for you took a precipitous decline when I learned you even considered that ridiculous job!" And so there were two views.

The following summer, 1971, Bush proposed that I be the "public member" of the U.S. delegation to the Twenty-Sixth U.N. General Assembly, which was to meet that fall. I agreed and was assigned to the Committee on Social, Humanitarian, and Cultural Affairs, known as the Third Committee. This had been Shirley Temple Black's assignment immediately preceding mine and that of an honorable succession of delegates, mostly women, going back to Mrs. Roosevelt. It was where I would have wished to be, although I soon learned how peculiar was my preference.

In the postwar years American diplomacy evolved what has been called a dual tradition of high politics and low politics, with the curious incongruity that the high politics were concerned with death and the low politics merely with life. A kind of male/female principle took hold. High politics were security politics: weapons, wars and rumors of wars. Important matters.

By contrast, low politics, concerned with "social, humanitarian, and cultural affairs," had suffered the ultimate indignity of not being regarded as politics at all by those who mattered. The League of Nations was by now vaguely remembered as having sought to distract attention from the collapse of its collective security efforts — high politics — by busying itself with the standardization of road signs and the suppression of white slavery. The United Nations seemed to be following much the same pattern. The United States had once taken the U.N. seriously in security matters. When we alone had the bomb, we had offered to turn it over to the Security Council. But the Cold War froze the machinery. Scarcely anything of consequence in the world of high politics had happened in Turtle Bay since Korea in the early 1950s, and few could imagine that anything of such consequence would ever happen there again.

When at this point the United Nations itself commenced to grow ever more busy with "social, humanitarian, and cultural affairs," the seeming parallel with the decline of the League into triviality impressed itself on the tough-minded. U.N. affairs in general acquired a social welfare connotation. A succession of Presidents chose liberal men as United States Permanent Representatives. In much the spirit in which we were sending symphony orchestras abroad, Kennedy had sent Stevenson; Johnson, Goldberg; and Nixon had thought to send McCarthy, then me, to the U.N., where we would presumably testify to American concern for social progress and do no great harm.

The huge irony, of course, is that just as the United Nations was being thus written off, its "social, humanitarian, and cultural" committee came to be of enormous moment to its new members, now categorized as the Third World. At issue was nothing less than the legitimacy of Western political systems and democratic beliefs that the U.N. Charter embodied. This is to say, the low politics of the U.N. became the highest, most consequential politics of all.

That in the West no one noticed this reflected not a little on the condition of democratic belief, and the vigor of democratic political systems. Although the League was recalled as having busied itself with trivia because it could do nothing to stop the rise of totalitarian aggression, this is not quite what happened. To be sure, the League could not stop the totalitarians. But it could expel them — and, formally or informally, it did expel them. If the debates in Geneva of the late 1930s had a certain irrelevance about them, they were nonetheless led by democratic statesmen. But by the early 1970s the scene at the United Nations was very different. The world organization was growing in membership and in a certain kind of ideological authority, and this new strength was increasingly deployed on behalf of totalitarian principle and practice wholly at variance with its original purpose.

The American inability to perceive this was based on more than historical confusion. The fundamental problem was a diminishment of liberal conviction, a decline possibly in energy, which brought about almost an aversion to ideological struggle. There was no talent for it in Washington; increasingly no stomach for it either. By 1971 this disposition was much reinforced by the still-continuing trauma of Vietnam. We had failed in our security objectives there, which led those in charge of high politics in Washington to become even more averse to ideological confrontation. Our object at the United Nations became "damage limitation." Like Lyndon Johnson's "jackrabbit in the hailstorm" — an image he would use for himself — we were "hunkered down and taking it."

This denoted, of course, a vast failure of leadership. Faced with the defeat of democratic arms in Asia, we should have commenced immediately to challenge totalitarian ideas throughout the world. Instead we withdrew on both fronts.

———◆———

Having spent much of my years as a graduate student reading the *procès-verbaux* of committees of the League, I had settled comfortably enough into the work of the Third Committee of the U.N. when the *Report on the World Social Situation* came my way. The *Report* had been begun some years earlier as a survey of "social development" in the developing nations, and in time was extended to the whole membership. The draft now submitted to us for final approval had been three years in the making, the subject of a succession of conferences in the pleasanter parts of Europe and of endlessly circulated drafts, the whole presided over by a Finnish member of the Secretariat reporting to a Finnish chairman of the Third Committee.

The result was a totalitarian tract. The nations of the world were assessed in terms of social well-being. The measure of social well-being was the presence or absence of dissent. The presence of dissent indicated the absence of social well-being. Czechoslovakia came out as just about top country. The situation in the United States seemed terminal.

In the committee debate that now commenced this fact hardly escaped the Soviet delegate, the Minister of Education of the Republic of Kazakh, who in particular called attention to the number of times American workers had gone on strike in recent years. I replied that her wonder was not surprising, coming as she did from a nation where the last strike had occurred in 1917.

There was no turning back from this. I grew agitated and commenced to agitate. How could the United States government have passively participated in the preparation of a formal assessment of American society based on totalitarian norms? How could we not have seen? How could we not have protested?

I did protest, in a sharp speech to the committee, and again encountered that curious symmetry of response I had begun to notice in domestic affairs in the late 1960s. The *Wall Street Journal* printed excerpts from my text. Galbraith wrote from Cambridge to say he'd wondered what had possessed me to take the assignment but that he was now well satisfied.

The great event of the Twenty-Sixth General Assembly was the admission of Red China. The U.S. delegation's orders were to stand and die, and down we went. The Tanzanians, in the moment of victory, did a little dance, which it seemed to me they were well enough entitled to. The public reaction in the United States was pronouncedly otherwise.

Bush's position was unenviable. Kissinger had visited the People's Republic in July, and was already planning the President's visit that would take place in February. And yet the assignment of the Permanent Representative was somehow to persuade the General Assembly that the People's Republic, in the diplomatic sense, did not exist. It is not an assignment given to a diplomat whose subsequent credibility is thought to be important.

Just so. From Stevenson on, neither the White House nor the State Department had shown any very great sensitivity on behalf of the U.N. Ambassador. Stevenson had been lied to in order that he would unknowingly spread lies. Perhaps the most honorable man American presidential politics had produced since Al Smith was thus subjected to the worst indecency of public life: to be found in an untruth. Bush was such a man as Stevenson. His humiliation was to be forced to ask others to stand and fight with him when the others knew that his own government confidently expected and quite desired that he should fail.

There seemed no avoiding this, not least because of the disparity between the actual work of the U.N. Ambassador and his Cabinet status, a discrepancy that invited a kind of retribution in Washington, sometimes to the point of cruelty. In the course of the Twenty-Sixth General Assembly President Johnson published his autobiography, in which he told of meeting with Galbraith on Friday, July 16, 1965, three days after Stevenson's death. Galbraith, then Ambassador to India, reported that Justice Goldberg was interested in a more challenging job, and suggested "that he might accept an appointment either as Secretary of Health, Education, and Welfare . . . or as Ambassador to the United Nations. . . ." On Monday, July 19, according to Johnson, Goldberg flew with the President to Stevenson's funeral in Illinois. On the trip the President raised the matter of a new job and offered him HEW. "He replied that the job sounded fascinating but that he had become increasingly interested in foreign affairs." Johnson asked the Justice to think it over. "The next day he called Jack Valenti and told him that the job he would accept was the U.N. ambassadorship, if I offered it to him."

I wrote to *The New York Times* to say this could not be so — that on Saturday, July 17, the Justice had told me of the President's urgent request. And so on, to no avail. Presidents have the last word. And Galbraith had a somewhat conflicted satisfaction. He had feared Johnson would offer *him* the job.

----◆----

The second large event of the Twenty-Sixth General Assembly was the third Indo-Pakistani war. The quintessential conflict of the age: racial, religious, linguistic.

Herewith another duality. Nathan Glazer and I had organized a seminar at the American Academy of Arts and Sciences on the subject of ethnicity. We argued that the single largest theoretical failure of Marxism was its inability to predict or to account for the ever more salient role of ethnic conflict — racial, religious, linguistic — in the modern age. This was something the two of us had worked out together and it was not unoriginal. Yet more and more I was persuaded of the need to fight ethnic issues on ideological lines.

The Indo-Pakistani war offered an occasion. Pakistan, the autocracy, behaved with irredeemable brutality toward its own people in West Bengal. (Glazer, whose wife was Indian, supplied details and urged me to battle. When it comes to providing true motive force, perhaps ethnicity *is* all.) India the democracy had intervened. The United Nations sided with Pakistan, and legality, one supposed, was also on that side. But the United States was supporting the Pakistanis for far more complex reasons. They had done Kissinger the favor of getting him to China in 1971. For Nixon, there was the larger concern of demonstrating to the Chinese — in the first test of a new relationship — that the United States was a reliable ally. Neither argument entirely persuaded me. I could only repeat to the President (who would listen, at least) that *India was a democracy*. At the end of the General Assembly I appeared on *Meet the Press* and went over the argument in public. The

President was wrong, I said, and the United States should be ashamed. The following summer, as I sat out the presidential campaign in a farm in upstate New York, it came to me that Nixon would now begin to see India as the one large, if not great, power he had not really dealt with in his first term, and that he would ask me to go there as Ambassador in his second. This he did, and I did — neither of us knowing he would not really have a second term.

2

Was Woodrow Wilson Right?

INDIA IN THE 1950s and early 1960s, "ex-colonial, nonwhite, developmental, socialist, and democratic," as Thomas L. Hughes has put it, epitomized the liberal enthusiasms of that time. Merely to have been there was to be accorded a certain status on an American university campus. India was going to be like America, and America in turn was going to be like India.

An innocent enough affair of the heart, you might suppose. And yet its end brought great bitterness in India, and there was little for an ambassador to do in its aftermath but wait until the Indians were prepared to settle for a more traditional relationship of diplomacy rather than tutelage.

In my two years there, from 1973 to 1975, I gave four speeches, two of them lectures at the Indian Institute of Management in my next to last month. I held no press conference until my next to last day. Within the channels of the Indian government I sought to state what American policy was, rather than what I wished it to be. The affair of the heart, surely, was over. It was my hope that now that we perhaps liked each other less, we might respect one another more.

I had no great success. Under the rule of Nehru's daughter, the world's largest democracy had, in foreign affairs, become bound to Soviet policy. Worse, it was drifting into an authoritarianism all its own. With my own government collapsing at home, the most I could do was to set about liquidating the extraordinary demi-Raj that the United States had established in India in the nineteen-fifties and -sixties. Rather as the British had, I hoped to march out rather than be driven out.

The great symbol of American intervention in Indian life was the enormous rupee debt to us, incurred in payment for grain shipments, notably in the mid-1960s. The grain was eaten and soon forgot. The debt remained, equal to a third of the Indian money supply, to be paid, if ever, by great-great-grandchildren. Already it was being put about that far from being an act of generosity, the wheat had been "dumped" on India to sustain American farm prices. Soon, surely, it would be "discovered" that the larger purpose had been to injure Indian agriculture. At that point, demand for repudiation of the debt would not be far off. What else was to be expected? The United States ought either to have given the Indians the food or summoned the nerve to let them go hungry. We chose instead to feed them and to humiliate them, although no one thought in these terms at the time, least of all Indians.

In 1966, not six years before I arrived in New Delhi, Mrs. Gandhi had gone to Washington to a White House dinner at which Lyndon Johnson presented a proposal to which the Indians had agreed: that the accumulated rupees should be put into an educational trust, presided over by an American executive director, to finance higher education in India. The Indians soon enough realized what they had done, and the scheme aborted. It was not clear that we ever did. Realize, that is, what we had proposed. To take charge of and thereafter to pay for their culture. Not their army. Nor their irrigation systems. Their very culture.

American liberalism had, in those years, lost a sense of limits. We would transform the Mekong Delta, resurrect Detroit, enlighten South Asia and defend it too, for that matter. (When the Chinese came over the Himalayas in 1962 we almost sent troops to fight them, as the Indians begged we should do.) It was all too much, and invited ruin, which readily enough comes even uninvited.

The one clear task in India was to get rid of that debt. By February, 1974, I had got agreement from Congress to do so, and turned over to the Indians what Guinness records as the World's Largest Check. I had gone back and forth to Washington, up and down the corridors of Congress, explaining the case to men who by now had no trouble understanding that to put a nation in perpetual debt and expect gratitude in return was to invite the ruin of a relationship. There was no great respect for India in the Congress, but there was enough for it to be understood that Indians would have some respect for themselves. After the agreement was reached, response at home was rather like that to the closing of Cam Ranh Bay — an embarrassment put out of mind.

Except for arranging a visit to New Delhi by Kissinger the following year, 1975, during which he declared that the United States accepted the doctrine of nonalignment, the debt settlement was the last thing I would do in India, and the only thing of importance. Kissinger's speech came too late, and was too obviously a bid to settle for what we had long rejected, a true non-alignment, in the face of what was increasingly an alignment against the West and with the Soviets. The United States was seen to be in a profound decline, and history to be moving in other directions altogether.

Those other directions were made clear by the Yom Kippur war and the OPEC cartel that followed. The war was yet another defeat for us, and was judged to be. The Soviet weaponry was seen to have been superior to America's, or such was the view in South Asia. The Israelis had been expected to win and they had not.

That it had indeed been a defeat was promptly confirmed by the quintupling of the price of oil. Tribute. It was soon enough clear that the United States, especially its government, could not see the real politics of the event. The oil price increase was the greatest triumph for state capitalism since the Russian Revolution. Hereafter, the world over, the price of energy would be set by governments, regardless of whether the governments involved wished to direct such matters. The reputation of the free market was, temporarily at least, in ruins. If the market correctly priced resources, how could it have so underpriced the most important resource of all? The answer would have to be that the free market is no less political than any other, that the price had been set low as an act of exploitation. Reparations were accordingly in order, and could be exacted with impunity. This proposition would now be applied to the whole of the world economy.

With work suspended in India — by the beginning of 1974 our relations there were proper once more, and nothing else for the moment was to be expected — I began again to travel and to read, absorbed by the impact of Western ideas on the East. There I was in Hindu India, amidst six hundred million souls who for millennia had been bound to an ethos of resignation, listening every other morning to some member of parliament say that the masses were growing frustrated and inevitably would become aggressive and bring down the whole structure of society.

I began to speculate not so much on what Marx had done to liberalism as on what Freud had done. Marx, for all the talk, had made but a marginal impact on the way persons were thought to behave. Freud, by contrast, had transformed the very image of man. Liberalism, after all, was built on a utilitarian psychology: behavior based on the prospect of future punishment or reward. As a construct this was elementally Christian. It was said to work empirically. The Freudian view, by the sharpest contrast, was directed not to the future but to the past. Behavior was seen to be reactive, determined by events prior to itself. No one knew whether it worked or, for that matter, what it would mean to say of a doctrine that it did work.

Not the least vehicle of Freudian influence was John Dollard, who in the 1930s, in his book *Frustration and Aggression,* had set forth this reversal of direction as a general theory of behavior. Dollard's book, brilliant, allusive, revelatory in so many ways, was the work of the first Freudian social scientist in the United States and, with David Riesman, incomparably the most important so far. Yet his work succeeded so hugely that in short order his role was quite forgotten, while educated and semieducated alike became wedded to a vulgarized and sometimes inane doctrine derived from him. A generation later, nearly everyone held his view and scarcely anyone knew his name. (By the 1960s the worthies of Yale, seemingly unaware that Dollard was still a member of the faculty, came near to caricaturing the infantilism implicit in much of what he had sadly found.)

It came down to a question of autonomy. If persons behaved in anticipation of consequences, they could shape those consequences and be held accountable for them. But if behavior was shaped by events that had already happened, in what sense could behavior be held responsible, or persons held responsible for behavior? If you wished a child to behave, did you give him a candy bar or promise him a candy bar? In the latter view, the child will behave in anticipation of reward. In the former view, the child will behave in consequence of reward. These are not compatible views, although insofar as I could discover, they were generally simultaneously held by those given to pronouncing on the large affairs of life.

A profound confusion had to come of this, especially as this "frustration-and-aggression" doctrine was invoked by liberalism to account for its own failures. Liberalism had assumed that people behave reasonably. It now fell to explaining that this is not so. Few discerned that the doctrine we invoked to explain situations in which our beliefs seemingly had not worked out increasingly supported the proposition that they *could* not.

In the United States, the civil rights movement, a model of autonomous behavior, of hardship and danger and even death endured in anticipation of just reward, had been virtually stripped of its moral authority, by apologies first, and later threats put forth in the name of people looting liquor stores. It was one thing to try to understand the violence, but to welcome it, as James Q. Wilson noticed most liberals did, was to debauch a tradition. For if the mobs of Detroit could not help themselves, how then to blame the orgiasts of the Ku Klux Klan? They had been frustrated, too.

This kind of critique, I knew, was risky. Was I of the view that Dollard ought not to have written? Surely not: I revered him. Did I think him wrong? No. What, then, was my complaint? It came down to the suspicion that there was an element of choice between these competing models of behavior. Mind matters. Up to a point, men *choose* what will motivate them and what they will recognize as motivating them. We were moving, I felt, from a utilitarian ethic to a therapeutic ethic, compelled less by evidence than by desire.*

Nowhere was this more in evidence than in the elite universities and colleges in the United States. In the spring of 1969 the president of Amherst, Calvin H. Plimpton, and a group of faculty and students had sent to the White House a letter addressing that part of the "turmoil in universities [which] derives from the distance separating the American dream from the American reality." Until political leadership brought about social change, the letter stated, "the concern and energy of those who know the need for change will seek outlets for their frustrations." Yale University hastened to endorse the Amherst Declaration. In commenting, *The New York Times* deplored the "young totalitarians" on the nation's campuses, but explained that "great numbers of idealistic and normally moderate students fail to oppose the radical forays, not because they approve of lawlessness, but because they are sincerely troubled and severely frustrated by much of what they . . . know to have gone wrong with their colleges and their country." The greatest institutions of liberal education in the nation were in effect saying that they could not resist totalitarian assaults on *them* because they were frustrated and would remain so until a President in Washington saved them from themselves by transforming American society.

I was still in the White House at the peak of this time, and asked the president of Yale to Washington to discuss the matter. Was it truly, I

---

* See Daniel P. Moynihan, "Social Policy: From the Utilitarian Ethic to the Therapeutic Ethic," in Irving Kristol and Paul Weaver, eds., *Critical Choices for Americans,* volume II, *The Americans 1976* (Lexington, Massachusetts: D. C. Heath & Co., 1976).

asked, in the interest of a university to allow a government to be the arbiter of its well-being? Was it indeed the case that a government wishing to wreck *his* university need only to step up the war in South Asia? Was the war not running down anyway? Were not things getting better? If, alternatively, things were getting worse, was it not all the more important for the universities not to destroy themselves? "You frighten me," the president of Yale had said. No doubt I did, for clearly he frightened easily. In no time Black Panthers had him quite traumatized.

As liberal internationalism seemed more and more to fail abroad, the same corruptions of doctrine appeared in international dialogue. The more a nation mismanaged its own affairs, the greater claim it would be said to have on others — for the reason that it could not help itself. Harlan Cleveland's phrase "the revolution of rising expectations" became a doctrine that justified — by putatively explaining — the most self-destructive behavior. Endlessly frustrated people would become ever more aggressive. Dollard's splendid insights were put to ever more squalid intellectual purposes. The world, it was said, could not survive half rich and half poor, when indeed it could survive very well that way: from the point of view of the rich, perhaps better. With rare exceptions, the economic institutions associated with political liberalism were denounced as the enemy of liberal purpose. When I arrived in New Delhi I had asked the commercial attaché for a list of American businessmen in India. He answered that he didn't have a list, but could tell me who they were, for there were then fewer than three dozen left. The government of India had opted for barter with the Russians. American academics, who in the main were not unsympathetic to the exclusion of Western business, found that their own exclusion soon followed. Far from our running Indian higher education, by 1974 there were left at best a dozen American scholars in the whole vast country.

At the outset of the Second World War there were three great cities on the Bay of Bengal more alike than great cities usually are. Each had been founded by the British East India Company, and each was very much part of an international, trading, English-speaking world. A generation later the first, Calcutta, had become a necropolis, city of the dead and dying. Vast, putrefying, forsaken. The second, Rangoon, had ceased to be a city, and was rapidly reverting to the village it had once been. The law buildings and police headquarters where Orwell had found an inadequate justice now knew none; and the rulers must have known that, for they had surrounded themselves with barbed wire and machine guns. The third city, Singapore, very possibly had the highest urban standard of living in the world. Calcutta, Rangoon, Singapore. Of liberty, Singapore had not nearly enough; but Rangoon had none at all, and what there was in Calcutta was less and less real as the mob grew.

Something had made the difference. And what was it if not a rational liberalism in economic affairs? Singapore had committed itself to the creation of wealth rather than to its redistribution.

Airy thoughts, no doubt. But the half million human beings sleeping on the sidewalks of Calcutta were real. The latest issues of *Vogue* sold at the newsstands in the public housing of Singapore were real. The barbed wire around the law offices in Rangoon was real, as were the soldiers and the machine guns. It was the talk in the Indian parliament that was unreal.

———◆———

February 3, 1974, was the fiftieth anniversary of the death of Woodrow Wilson. I had had to do with the founding of the Woodrow Wilson International Center for Scholars, which was now his memorial in Washington, and returned from India to give the address on the occasion. Norman Podhoretz sensed the presence of a large theme and insisted on an article, which appeared in *Commentary* in May. I find in it, now, most of what I would later have to say. Or, rather, the questions I would ask, having concluded I hadn't any answers. Very well then, questions. Was Woodrow Wilson right? I asked, when he asserted that the task of civilized nations — of the United States — was nothing less than the defense of liberty in the world. There was, I put it, a kind of corrupt Wilsonianism, a false moralism, that carried on as a dominant theme of American foreign policy for years after him, and which we could dismiss. But what of Wilson himself?

> The essential Wilson remains, the Wilson whose singular contribution to the American national experience was a definition of patriotism appropriate to the age America was entering at the time of his Presidency, which is to say patriotism defined first of all as the duty to defend and, where feasible, to advance democratic principles in the world at large. (In this he expanded the original — and singular — American definition of citizenship as a matter not of blood or soil or religious faith, but of adherence to political norms.) Always to defend them — prudently if possible, but at the risk, if need be, of imprudence. . . .

Is it a sustainable vision? Hard to say. . . .

It comes to this: the Wilsonian world view is already half achieved. Most peoples of the world live in independent states demarcated along lines of hoped-for ethnic legitimacy. This very achievement makes for intense difficulties with the remaining internal ethnic divisions. Nevertheless the principle of self-determination has not only succeeded at the level of a norm but has also largely been implemented.

The quality of the incumbent regimes is another matter. Few measure up to Wilson's hopes. Numerically there are not many more democracies now than in 1919 (although [two] of the . . . additions to this short list, India and Japan, are scarcely insubstantial). Even so, most of the other regimes dare not speak of themselves except in terms of Wilsonian ideals. In other words, these ideals — seen widely as American ideals — still establish the internal right to govern, just as, equally, Wilsonian ideals establish the national right to exist. . . . We are a nation of nations and inextricably involved in the fate of other peoples the world over.

———◆———

. . . By the end of the century, given present trends [in immigration], the United States will be a multi-ethnic nation the like of which even we have never imagined. This means at least one thing. There will be no struggle for personal liberty (or national independence or national survival) anywhere in Europe, in Asia, in Africa, in Latin America which will not affect American politics. In that circumstance, I would argue that there is only one course likely to make the internal strains of consequent conflicts endurable, and that is *for the United States deliberately and consistently to bring its influence to bear on behalf of those regimes which promise the largest degree of personal and national liberty.* We shall have to do so with prudence, with care. We are granted no license to go looking for trouble, no right to meddle. We shall have to continue to put up with things obnoxious about which there is nothing we can do; and often we may have to restrain ourselves where there are things we can do. Yet we must play the hand dealt us: we stand for liberty, for the expansion of liberty. Anything less risks the contraction of liberty: our own included.

I see now I had come in that passage to a view of Kissinger. I realized finally that he saw us as a deracinated people, who had lost our political faith much as the English, earlier, had lost their religious belief and "wandered into nothingness." I was not ready to settle for this. ". . . Are we not adopting much the same course at the silent behest of men who know too much to believe anything in particular and opt instead for accommodations of reasonableness and urbanity that drain our

world of moral purpose?" Odd. I'd come out on the side of the Method-
ists. Wesley's text: "A warmed heart and a world parish."

———◆———

And yet my difficulties were as great with those who were just then
trying to drum up a new moral purpose with which to quicken foreign
policy. A somewhat belated discovery of the masses appeared to be
taking place at the Council on Foreign Relations. The implacable fact
of Vietnam was that elites had thought it up, and then pretty much the
same elites had turned against it. For some time an exculpatory exercise
of considerable proportion had been going on among those who had
been in Washington under Kennedy and Johnson, divided roughly
between those who claimed they had only been giving orders, and those
who discovered that all along the orders had been coming from elsewhere. By now, for example, the theory that the war was the work of the
Building Trades Department of the A.F.L.-C.I.O. had won considerable
acceptance.

There was a general disenchantment with the foreign policy leadership
of the past, the "Ivy-League, Wall-Street, Martha's-Vineyard hegemony"
in what were known as the corridors of power. And so, various members
of the hegemonic class commenced to write of the possibilities of "a
large-minded liberal-populist coalition" that would end "the diplomacy
of emergency and the politics of desperation." This coalition would
overcome "the spurious conservative appeal to residual populist Know-
Nothingism. . . ." Serious journals, in this case *Foreign Policy,* edited
by Zbigniew Brzezinski and Samuel P. Huntington, published such
musings. Such posturing seemed to me innocent enough as tactics. The
hegemony had to deplore itself occasionally in order to maintain itself.
But one expected that this group would not pursue its temporary interests to the point of seriously misleading its members along with everyone
else. In the summer of 1974, however, *Foreign Policy* published an
article by Charles W. Maynes, Jr., Secretary of the Carnegie Endowment
for International Peace, entitled "Who Pays for Foreign Policy?" It
contended that "most Americans simply do not understand the totally
disproportionate burden which working people have carried in both
the defense and trade fields in recent years." The distinction between
"working people" and "most Americans" may or may not have revealed
more of the "Ivy-League, Wall-Street, Martha's-Vineyard" perspective
than was specifically useful to Maynes's purpose. It required, in any
event, a reply. Maynes's object was that "the government must find some
way to convince the people that they should believe once again that
their public leaders are acting in the best interests of the ordinary citi-

zen." To this end he charged that public leaders had been doing nothing of that kind. "America's largest corporations . . . ," he declared, were the "major beneficiaries of U.S. foreign economic policy. They exploit . . . tax concessions." The people pay. Rather, that all-purpose minority, "working people," pay.

Were he traitor to his class, that would have been one thing. But Maynes was not. Oxford-trained, he sensed his turn in office was at hand:

> *The accursed power which stands on Privilege*
> *(And goes with Women, and Champagne and Bridge)*
> *Broke — and Democracy resumed her reign:*
> *(Which goes with Bridge, and Women and Champagne).*

Within three years he would be Assistant Secretary of State for International Organization Affairs. His editor, Zbigniew Brzezinski, would be in the White House, the protégé of one Rockefeller brother succeeding Henry Kissinger, the protégé of another Rockefeller brother.

While still in India, I wrote for *Foreign Policy* (at their request) a reply to Maynes, asking what the evidence was that traditional liberal internationalism had lost the support of "the masses" by having proved too costly for them:

> Certainly there are contrary signs. The American labor movement is an authentic spokesman for working-class Americans, and certainly it remains committed to an active and liberal foreign policy. Or at least to a policy that the college-educated once defined as liberal. The view that the labor movement has not caught up with the new sophistication in these matters is simply not shared by the labor movement and in the meantime it continues as a committed and active force in foreign affairs. I will attest that during my tenure as Ambassador to India, labor [has been] the only organized group in the United States which showed any institutional concern for the success of democratic institutions in India.

The problem, I wrote, was not with the "working people." It was with elites who had lost their nerve and were trying to regain legitimacy by forsaking a still profoundly legitimate tradition.

I asked not "Who Pays for Foreign Policy?" but, rather, "For Whom Does Foreign Policy Pay?" and suggested four categories of reward, with the general thought that our problem was not that foreign policy cost too much but that increasingly it paid too little.

The first category was rewards to ideology. Foreign policy had for generations been the domain of liberal ideology, capable of evoking the most intense and proud conviction. But most liberals had ended the

1960s rather ashamed of the beliefs they had held at the beginning of the decade, and few had got it sorted out:

> At the Nobel Prize ceremonies in Stockholm in December 1974, Alexander Solzhenitsyn said that he would like to go to the United States, and that if he did he would tell the youth of the United States that they had fought for freedom in Vietnam. If one considers the confusion which such a statement would evoke, one gets some measure of the decline in ideological rewards.

Thus Tocqueville: "Foreign politics demand scarcely any of those qualities which are peculiar to a democracy" while requiring "the perfect use of almost all those in which it is deficient."

The second-ranking category of reward, only somewhat less venerable, was that to ethnicity. We had gone to war on England's side in 1917. Would we have done so had the President been a Lutheran? Possibly not. By mid-century the number of such claims had multiplied — of Jews on Middle East policy, of Greeks on Mediterranean policy, of Cubans on Caribbean policy. An earlier article in *Foreign Policy* had asked: "Can the blacks do for Africa what the Jews did for Israel?" The author clearly thought they might, and hoped they would. All this was the product of a multiethnic society, but the more such claims that were pressed, the fewer could be fully satisfied. As for the third category, regional rewards, and the fourth, rewards to specific sectors of the economy, much the same applied. Even defense contracts were becoming marginal ventures, and the best-run corporations were cutting back on them. As for "the working people," wartime was typically the period during which democracies paid most attention to social questions. The great increase in the domestic spending of the late 1960s and early 1970s had more or less corresponded with the period of the Vietnam war, a period, in that sense, now over. All this, it seemed to me, accounted for a falloff in public support for foreign policy initiatives rather than any profound flaw in either our values or arrangements: "This and the fact that in the world at large we are losing."

———◆———

There was hardly a better place from which to perceive this loss in these years than India. A great nation with great interests and even greater needs, by 1974 a nuclear power as well, it had for years assumed that its interests were very much involved with the United States, but more and more now sided with those who opposed us, both internally and abroad. Plague years, to be sure, yet from a vantage point in India it was clear enough they would end. What then?

What else? Foch's dictum: *"Mon centre cède, ma droite récule, situation excéllent. J'attaque!"* For in truth our fundamental circumstances were excellent. We had brought a war to an end by the withdrawal of political consent to its continuation, as against the withdrawal of constitutional consent, which was the most common sequence elsewhere. There had been a vast transformation in racial attitudes, under way for a generation; and, for all the alarms of the moment, it had not faltered. Our achievement of political liberty was generally conceded: less understood, even by ourselves, was the extraordinary achievement of equality in American society. In Cambridge, Christopher Jencks and his associates, extending a seminar Thomas Pettigrew and I began in 1966, found a pattern of income distribution in the United States that could only be described as random, which is to say with almost no inheritance of class advantage. (Baffled, the authors proposed socialism anyway.) The degree of ethnic accommodation was extraordinary by any standards, and increasingly so by those of the twentieth century.

By contrast, the Soviets seemed backward in all these matters. They had oil, if you will, but so then did we. Indeed, the day could not be far off when the great majority of nations would awake to find that all they had got from the OPEC quintupling of oil prices was just that: a quintupling of oil prices, to be paid by almost everyone, themselves included. In such circumstances the American achievement would loom in its true proportion, and the present madness would recede. *If* we refused to go along. *If,* instead of defending ourselves in the least effective way against those who attacked us, we attacked instead.

If we attacked. Not to pillage and plunder others, but to establish with those others, true adversaries such as they were, and the great number of nations who merely wished to be on the side of the winner, that *we* would not be despoiled. The problem was that everywhere, but especially in international forums, the United States in these years was under attack and in retreat. A large structural change was taking place in international relations. The East-West issues of the postwar period, which themselves were an extension of the totalitarian-democratic confrontation which had commenced at the end of World War I, were receding, ostensibly to be replaced with North-South issues. Not a little of the initiative for this change had come from the United States itself.

From New Delhi I found myself paying more attention to the United Nations, and became more and more absorbed by the seeming inability of American representatives to deal with ideological argument or even to recognize it. The great delusion of this time, much encouraged by lib-

erals, was that North-South agenda somehow avoided the sterile ideological conflicts of the previous and presumably past era. It appeared to
me that on the contrary, those conflicts would now be, if possible, even
more perilous, for they would be concealed. I came to feel that perception of this delusion was what linked social democrats on the "left" and
conservatives on the "right." I had gone out to India with only the
A.F.L.-C.I.O. still much interested in the place. Academe had turned to
Red China. (Galbraith's *A China Passage* was published at this time:
this newest book of his was, alas, an unfailing mirror of fashion.) But
the old socialists at A.F.L.-C.I.O. headquarters on Sixteenth Street in
Washington still cared about India, still kept in touch, still journeyed
out, and with them Catholic union leaders such as Joseph Beirne. The
likes of Beirne, few enough, to be sure, were the link with the conservatives, who were considerably Catholic, unlike the socialists, who were
mostly Jews.

At their best the conservatives combined subtlety with bluntness.
None so well as William F. Buckley, Jr. In the spring of 1973, Buckley
was asked to serve as the public member on our delegation to the
Twenty-Eighth General Assembly. He arrived as I had done, ready to do
battle. In a first memorandum, he proposed to Ambassador Scali and to
Kissinger the great "strategic gains we would stand to make by an un-
disguised, and undissimulated, constancy to ideals nominally promul-
gated by the United Nations." He was more right in this than even he
perhaps knew. For the United Nations Charter, the work, in the main,
of British and American constitutional lawyers, did not merely pro-
mulgate ideals; in the area of human rights it imposed precise legal
obligations on members, which by this time, 1973, scarcely one member
in four abided by. Buckley was assigned to the Third Committee: Mrs.
Roosevelt's committee, he'd been assured, and mine. His first formal assignment was to deliver the American statement on the occasion of the
twenty-fifth anniversary of the Declaration of Human Rights. The
Swedes were going on about torture, which they were against, while
making clear that it was their "aim not to indict any country," for they
were "guided by a desire to avoid every possible controversy." The East
German delegate was explaining that there was no concern about human
rights in his country because everyone in his country had them. The
Department of State instructions were designed precisely to accommodate to this setting:

STATEMENT SHOULD BE NON-POLEMICAL IN TONE, DELIVERED AS STRAIGHT-
FORWARD EXPRESSION OF OUR SINCERE AND TRADITIONAL SUPPORT FOR AT-
TAINMENT OF GOALS OF DECLARATION THROUGHOUT THE WORLD. THERE

SHOULD BE NO REPEAT NO MENTION OF SPECIFIC COUNTRIES OR SPECIFIC
CASES INVOLVING HUMAN RIGHTS VIOLATIONS.

KISSINGER

Buckley accordingly drafted a brief speech pointing out that the world
was not divided between those nations that say they do not believe in
torture and those who say they do, but rather between those who
practice torture and those who do not. Nor, he judged, was the world
divided between nations who say they believe in human rights and those
who say they do not, but rather between those that observe them and
those that do not. Many articles of the Declaration, his draft went on,
were conspicuously transgressed upon, including Article 13, establishing
the right to leave a country. The United States did not wish to be
censorious. Still,

> . . . that decorum which distinguishes this chamber, and the conduct
> of proceedings within it, would be, I am sure, greatly obliged if, on
> the day of the great celebration, those countries whose own policies
> are not congruent with the United Nations Declaration signified at
> least their abstract respect for human rights by leaving the chamber.

Ambassador Scali summoned him. The speech was out of the question.
There was war in the Middle East. A cease-fire was being negotiated.
Sadat was being reasonable. Buckley recorded the gist of the conversation in his journal: "Anything said by an American that smacks in any
way as a defense of the Jews could throw a monkey wrench into the
whole thing. My statement about freedom of emigration might rile the
Arabs and the Russians."

This was not Scali speaking, but the Department of State and the
Secretary of State, and it was disaster. Buckley could see this: as much
as anything because he could see the ideological dimension. He wrote
of the Soviet Ambassador, Yakov Malik, as "the last of the Stalinists," a
man with "a deeply cultivated propensity for lying," who did not in the
least mind doing so, even in situations where he was sure to be caught.
Buckley saw this to be an ideological trait. Most of his fellow Americans
would, at most, have seen it as a character failing. The result had been a
vast and corrupting avoidance. Buckley wrote, "The United Nations is
the most concentrated assault on moral reality in the history of free
institutions, and it does not do to ignore that fact or, worse, to get used
to it." But that was what we were doing. In August, just before the
General Assembly met, the "Colonialism Committee" (the Special
Committee on the Situation with Regard to the Implementation of the

Declaration on the Granting of Independence to Colonial Countries and Peoples) adopted a Cuban resolution condemning the United States' "colonial" relationship to Puerto Rico — a society with which, whatever the past, the United States was now in fact in a free association, established by and reaffirmed by free and open elections. Scali denounced the vote and from New Delhi I sent a cable cast in terms considerably less elegant than Buckley's, but which he reproduced late in 1974 as the concluding passage of his *United Nations Journal:*

> I SHOULD LIKE . . . TO ADD A PERSONAL NOTE OF CONGRATULATIONS TO AMBASSADOR SCALI FOR HIS STATEMENT IN THE AFTERMATH OF THE AUGUST 30 VOTE ADOPTING THE TOTALITARIAN RESOLUTION, AND TO STATE MY OWN CONCERN NOT ONLY AT THE EMERGENCE OF AN ANTI-DEMOCRATIC BIAS AT THE UNITED NATIONS, BUT AT THE CURIOUS SEEMING ACCEPTANCE BY THE UNITED STATES THAT THERE IS NOTHING TO BE DONE ABOUT IT, INDEED THAT IT IS SCARCELY EVEN TO BE PROTESTED SAVE BY MEN SUCH AS SCALI WHO WILL NOT PERHAPS OBJECT TO MY DESCRIBING HIM AS SOMEONE FROM OUTSIDE THE SYSTEM. . . .
>
> THE MATTER IS TOO FAR DISTANT AND THE WEATHER HERE TOO DISAGREEABLE FOR ME FULLY TO RECONSTRUCT THE FURY WITH WHICH I SAT IN THE [1971] GENERAL ASSEMBLY AND LISTENED TO THE STALINIST SON OF A BITCH FROM CUBA GO ON ABOUT PUERTO RICO. . . . WHAT DROVE ME TO DESPAIR WAS THE COMPLACENCY OF OUR PUTATIVE ALLIES IN THIS MATTER. THE HONOR OF AMERICAN DEMOCRACY WAS BEING IMPUGNED. WHAT IS HONOR? SAID OUR ALLIES. LET US TALK OF MALARIA ERADICATION, AND AID LEVELS. THERE WAS A SAYING AROUND THE KENNEDY WHITE HOUSE: DON'T GET MAD, GET EVEN. IN THE END WHAT TROUBLES ME MOST ABOUT THE PUERTO RICAN EPISODE IS THAT WE SEEM TO BE WILLING TO FORGET ABOUT A CLEAR VIOLATION OF THE CHARTER, A DIRECT LIE ABOUT THE UNITED STATES. WHAT HAS COME OVER US? FORGET ABOUT A SLANDER ON OUR HONOR? WHAT HAVE WE BECOME? ANY, REPEAT ANY, COUNTRY THAT DOES NOT SUPPORT US ON A MATTER OF THIS CONSEQUENCE NOT ONLY DAMAGES THE UNITED NATIONS, BUT MUST QUIETLY BE BROUGHT TO UNDERSTAND THAT IT HAS DAMAGED ITSELF. I LOOKED DOWN THE LIST OF THOSE WHO GO ALONG AND THOSE WHO GO ALONG BY ABSTAINING. IN HALF OF THEM THE PRESENT REGIMES WOULD COLLAPSE WITHOUT AMERICAN SUPPORT OR AMERICAN ACQUIESCENCE. TO HELL WITH IT. SOMETHING SPECIFICALLY BAD SHOULD HAPPEN TO EACH ONE OF THEM, AND WHEN IT HAS HAPPENED THEY SHOULD BE TOLD THAT AMERICANS TAKE THE HONOR OF THEIR DEMOCRACY MOST SERIOUSLY, AND NEVER ISSUE WARNINGS TO THOSE WHO WOULD BESMIRCH THAT HONOR. . . .
>
> BRAVO SCALI! . . .

But the disposition in Washington at this time was to dismiss exchanges in the General Assembly as "mere words." It was the Security

Council that mattered: That was where cease-fires could be agreed to, and why the Department wanted no trouble in the General Assembly, still less with the Colonialism Committee. But Buckley had come to see the truth of Conor Cruise O'Brien's observation that nothing happens in the Security Council that would not happen on its own, which is to say that the great powers will get together if they so wish. It is the General Assembly that is singular as the one chamber where the small nations can speak their minds and be heard in a setting of dramatic force, this being the true consequence of its status as theatre. "[If] this is so," wrote Buckley, "we have something altogether different to concern ourselves with, and that is the order of moral reality. This sounds like a very grand phrase to introduce to a world that would settle for a little practical progress. But it is the only phrase grand enough to convey the importance of the survival of truth." And this, he continued, "is a point that should not separate American conservatives from American liberals, or British or French conservatives from their domestic socialists."

———◆———

Throughout 1974, U.N. assemblies were almost wholly given over to assaults on Western positions by combined Communist and Third World blocs. The United States grew steadily more isolated. In the spring the Sixth Special Session of the U.N. General Assembly, called to deal with the economic crises of the developing nations, adopted a Charter of Economic Rights and Duties of States, which anathematized the workings of the Western economies, and in effect sanctioned the increase in oil prices, devastating though it had been to the new nations. The vote on adoption was 120 to 6. In the summer of 1974 the U.N. World Population Conference, a culmination of years of hopes and planning in the Department of State, met to assail the United States. The capacity of Communist spokesmen to intimidate others was much in evidence. The Indian delegates set out fully expecting to join in resolutions favoring oral contraceptives and male sterilization. Once in Bucharest, they learned from the Chinese that contraception was sheer capitalist imperialism, that there was plenty of room and plenty of food in the world, that the West had simply acquired a disproportionate share. The Maharajah of Jammu and Kashmir found himself denouncing "colonial denudation" of the East and (curious from a man with a swimming pool in his living room) the "vulgar affluence" of the West. In September, the General Assembly met, rejected the credentials of the South African delegation, and welcomed Yasir Arafat of the Palestine Liberation Organization as a head of state.

In November, a World Food Conference met, again a United States initiative within the United Nations system. Once again the scene grew orgiastic as speakers competed in their denunciation of the country that had called the conference, mostly to discuss giving away its own wheat, as ours was almost the only country at the time that had any to give away. Once again the Indian delegation went quite beyond anything that made any sense for India. In Bucharest the Indian Minister of Family Planning, a Cabinet member, had denounced family planning. Now, in Rome, the Indian Minister of Food appeared to denounce farming, at least in his part of the world:

> It is obvious that the developed nations can be held responsible for their [the developing nations'] present plight. Developed nations, therefore, have a duty to help them. Whatever help is rendered to them now should not be regarded as charity but deferred compensation for what has been done to them in the past by the developed countries.

The cumulative effect of all this was ominous. Had the Communists truly formed a permanent bloc with the new nations? This could hardly go well for us, and scarcely better for the new nations themselves. The Communists were not in the business of giving away resources. They would do nothing *for* the new nations — nor could they do much *with* them, save barter bad shoes for cashew nuts, usually getting the better of the exchange. The political and cultural ties of new nations lay to the West — and not to the Russian Empire, the one creation of Western imperialism still intact, and indeed expanded. Where they had choices with new nations, the Communist powers had mostly opted for a policy of immiserization. It was "no accident" that they now called on them to have more babies and grow less food.

At the Sixth Special Session in the spring of 1974 the United States, belatedly but in sufficient time, came forward with a proposal to give $4 billion in additional aid for the poorest countries hardest hit by food shortages and oil and fertilizer price increases. The Algerians, now a hard-line left-wing totalitarian power, dominated the Special Session. A considerable bloc of new nations without oil and without the money to buy it suggested that the American offer be accepted. The Algerians decreed that it be turned down.

Increasingly United States policy was immobilized in the face of events such as this which we seemingly could not understand, much less control. But Gerald Ford had now become President, and the presidency was functioning once more. Just after the Sixth Special Session, in a speech to the opening of the regular General Assembly in the fall of 1974, Ford warned the U.N. against "the tyranny of the majority," and at the close of the session Scali repeated the warning. But the generality of our policy makers could make nothing of our changed situation, and said nothing about it. "Public" delegates and advisors increasingly made do by denying the reality of American defeat, or by transcending it through subtle and not so subtle identification with those who had defeated us. At the close of the 1974 Population Conference, for instance, the American delegation cabled home: "ALL BASIC U.S. OBJECTIVES WERE ACHIEVED AND U.S. ACCOMPLISHMENTS WERE MANY. . . . U.S. DELEGATION UNANIMOUSLY PLEASED WITH FINAL RESULT." (The event might be recorded as the first occasion on which a Rockefeller, in this case John D. Rockefeller II, a man devoted to population control, was led to recant his views before a tribunal set up in a Communist capital. He was not alone.) Writing in the Washington *Post* on December 1, Charles Maynes declared the Special Session of the General Assembly to have been "a disaster for the United States. . . . The main achievement of [the] World Food Conference in Rome," he wrote, was that

> the U.S. Congressional delegates [who] openly revolted against the positions of an unsympathetic administration, may have . . . demonstrate[d] how unprepared we still are for the new challenge placed on a major power in an era of scarcity and starvation.

It was now quite beyond the capacity of such as Maynes to consider that the Conference might have been more a disaster for the developing nations than for us. *They* had got nothing, having declined the American offer; the United States, from a strictly budgetary point of view, had saved $4 billion. Maynes at this point would have found incomprehensible anyone who did not believe that the world was heading for mass starvation, although the world was in fact only a few months away from falling grain prices brought on by bumper crops. For Maynes and for the Carnegie Endowment and that mind set, the point was that the United States had not won the approval of the new world majority, which in and of itself was to be judged a disaster.

———◆———

I spent December, 1974, my last month in India, writing a long paper. I had one principal thought: that the demands of the new nations were political more than economic, that these countries wished a voice in world decisions. There was nothing so awful in their having to ask, as it were. Most of them had not existed fifteen years earlier. But neither was there any reason to refuse them. It was natural that their demands should be couched in economic terms, and not unnatural for them to bloc with the Communist world against the West as an early tactic. But there needn't be anything fixed about that disposition of forces, for the new nations were a distinct *party* in world politics. Something like a party system was emerging. In this context the United States was clearly not a member of the majority, but the U.S. could easily engage that majority in a continued and organic relation of opposition in the parliamentary sense.

My tactical concern was to set forth the ideological bases of Third World politics in terms that would enable American policy both to comprehend the changes that had occurred and to welcome them, and to do so in terms that would command general American support. The modern world, I judged, had been shaped by three great revolutions, of which only the first two were yet widely perceived. The first, of course, had taken place in America and France in the late eighteenth century. Though they may have differed in many things, the political values and forms of government that followed them were strikingly similar, with much emphasis on constitutional rights and individual liberties. That was the liberal revolution. Its antithesis, the Russian Revolution, brought into existence an entirely new political mode, the totalitarian state, more different by far from the liberal state than that state had been from its monarchical predecessor. From the triumph in St. Petersburg in 1917 to the triumph in Peking in 1948, the Russian Revolution was quite the most attended-to movement in world politics.

Then came the British Revolution. This created the huge number of socialist states that had come into being as the British, French, Dutch, Belgian, and Portuguese empires broke up. (I asked to be indulged the term "socialist," for there seemed none better.) Of the then eighty-seven states to have joined the United Nations subsequent to its founding, more than half, forty-seven, had been part of the British Empire. Empire apart, British culture had been in the first half of the twentieth century incomparably the most influential in the world, and that culture was increasingly suffused with socialist ideas and attitudes. Until now the new nations had been seen as candidates for incorporation into one or the other of the older revolutionary traditions that were dominant elsewhere. But, I wrote,

> . . . It was not generally perceived that they were in a sense already spoken for — that they came to independence with a preexisting, coherent, and surprisingly stable ideological base which, while related to both the earlier traditions, was distinct from both. . . . In the Republic of India the United States could see democracy; the Soviets could see Socialism. . . . in synthesis, the Welfare State of the British revolution.

I went on to a huge assertion: that world Communism had about run its course. That it would not overwhelm the new nations. That, to the contrary, the "future" lay in the relation between the old liberal states and the new socialist ones. But for this relation to succeed, there had first to be some understanding of the socialist tradition, especially of British influence.

The first fact about British socialism was that it contained a suspicion of, almost a bias against, economic development. It had emerged in the age of the Diamond Jubilee, and was fixed in its belief that there was plenty of wealth to go around if only it were fairly distributed. Redistribution, not production, remained central to the ethos of British socialism. Profit became synonymous with exploitation. With one or another variant this attitude was to be found throughout the former British world (with further variants in former European colonies). Contrary argument had but little effect, nor did experience, as witness the performance of the British economy itself in "the collectivist age."

My second general point about socialist doctrine as it developed, especially in Britain, was that it was curiously anti-American. More anti-American, surely, than it was ever anti-Soviet. America was both capitalist *and* vulgar. (British socialism was ever genteel.) Russia, for all its faults, was the future. With the coming of the Cold War this attitude became institutionalized and compulsory on the British left. *The New Statesman* had come near to Stalinism in its attachment to things Soviet and its pervasive antagonism to things American.

And so the new nations came into being, adapting their international politics to the modes of the upper-class theorists and working-class parties of their former masters. Independence became a fiercely held principle, as did the belief that they had been subject to economic exploitation and ethnic discrimination, corresponding to social discrimination in industrial society.

Few had noticed this event. Indeed, there was scarcely a vocabulary with which to describe it. The international conferences of 1974, with their wild charges of exploitation and fierce rhetoric of expropriation, were in one sense merely the language of British socialism applied, by perhaps more skillful orators, to the international scene. American diplomacy had yet to recognize this fact.

It seemed to me that if we were to "go into opposition," our first argument must be the economic one. To deny the imperative of growth was to insist on poverty, and we should say so. All across the United States, Hindu and Moslem merchants and manufacturers were setting up shop and manifestly doing well. We welcomed them. If, however, the Indian government preferred to barter with the Russians rather than to do business with Americans, then the government of India would have to live with the consequences:

> For if Calcutta has the lowest urban standard of living in the world, Singapore has in some ways the highest. It is time we asserted that inequalities in the world may be not so much a matter of condition as of performance. The Brazilians do well. The Israelis. The Nigerians. The Taiwanese. It is a good argument. Far better, surely, than the repeated plea of *nolo contendere* which we have entered, standing accused and abased before the Tribune of the People.

But the economic argument was not the only or even the chief one we must make:

> Cataloguing the economic failings of other countries is something to be done out of necessity, not choice. But speaking for political and civil liberty, and doing so in detail and in concrete particulars, is something that can surely be undertaken by Americans with enthusiasm and zeal. . . .
>
> It is time, that is, that the American spokesman came to be feared in international forums for the truths he might tell. Mexico, which has grown increasingly competitive in Third World affairs, which took the lead in the Declaration of Economic Rights and Duties, preaches international equity. Yet it preaches domestic equity also. It could not without some cost expose itself to a repeated inquiry as to the extent of equity within its own borders. Nor would a good many other Third World countries welcome a sustained comparison between the liberties they provide their own peoples with those which are common and taken for granted in the United States.

Finally, I argued that such an approach, moving from apology to opposition, with all the costs it would bring, was on balance worth the risk:

> Such a reversal of roles would be painful to American spokesmen, but it could be liberating also. It is past time we ceased to apologize for an imperfect democracy. Find its equal. It is time we grew out of our initial — not a little condescending — supersensitivity about the feelings of new nations. It is time we commenced to treat them as equals, a respect to which they are entitled. There is a recognizable pattern to the economic and political postures of these countries, of which the central reality is that their anti-capitalist, anti-imperialist ideologies are in fact themselves the last stage of colonialism. These are imported ideas every bit as much as the capitalist and imperialist ideas to which they are opposed. The sooner they are succeeded by truly indigenous ideas,

the better off all the former colonies will be, the United States included.

The Third World must feed itself, for example, and this will not be done by suggesting that Americans eat too much. . . .

In the same way, the Third World has almost everywhere a constitutional heritage of individual liberty, and it needs to be as jealous of that heritage as of the heritage of national independence. . . .

It is in precisely such terms that we can seek common cause with the new nations: granted that they, no more than we, are likely ever wholly to live up to either of our protestations. Yet there exists the strongest possibility of an accommodating relationship at the level of principle — a possibility that does not exist at all with the totalitarian powers as they are now constituted. . . . One may negotiate there as between separate political communities, but to participate as in a single community — even in opposition — would simply not be possible. We can, however, have such a relation with most Third World nations. And we can do so while speaking for and in the name of political and civil liberty.

I finished the manuscript, now grown to huge proportions, by Christmas week and sent it off to Norman Podhoretz, as it was clear that only he could edit it, and, such was the time, that probably only he would publish it.

◆

My last call in India was on Piloo Mody, a member of the small parliamentary opposition to the Prime Minister, and a group of Congress Party members who were commencing to think of forming an opposition within the party. They were worried and so was I. On January 6, 1975, the day before I left, I held my first press conference.

For this I composed yet another tract, declaring my belief that the Indian democracy was in danger. The Prime Minister, I wrote, was running the economy into an ever more rigid state socialism. The consequent economic decline was creating ever-growing opposition, not least from responsible Indians who understood the sources of the decline. Yet she had established a doctrinal position from which to suppress that opposition on grounds that it was a threat not to her, but to the principles she stood for. As the opposition grew, the day of suppression would draw nearer. Unless she could recognize this cycle, the day was not far off when she would try to destroy her opposition, and in doing so she would destroy the Indian democracy.

David M. Schneider, my Deputy Chief of Mission, a prudent and responsible diplomat, argued that if I gave the statement Mrs. Gandhi would have to reply, by which time I would be gone, and what would be the use. I had to agree, and left India in silence. But I was onto something, and I knew it. I was sure she would do what indeed she did do, and had come to think it was possible and necessary to speak about the threat to democracy and personal freedom in the world in new and more urgent terms.

3

The United States in Opposition

AMERICAN AMBASSADORS have the friendly habit of looking in on one another as they travel back and forth to the United States, and George Bush, now head of our liaison office in Peking, invited me to do so on the way home from India. As we did not exchange ambassadors with the Chinese, they had evidently not allowed this before, but for some reason we were given visas.

I arrived in Peking with the two younger children, Maura and John (my wife, Elizabeth, having chosen to return by way of the British Museum to pursue her studies of Mogul gardens). The vast portraits of Marx and Engels, along with Stalin and Mao, in Tien An Men Square somehow confirmed the conviction that it was absurd to let these people, or their like, seize the political initiative from us. When Americans take to sandals and to pasting up posters of Hindu divines, it is understood that adolescence is a difficult phase. But what in the name of God were these half-acre portraits of hirsute German bourgeois doing in the main square of a Mongol capital? Were there grown-ups here? The three-year-olds in the nursery schools sang songs about how they were going to smash Confucius and settle the Western regions. They behaved, alas, as adults. Why not, then, explain to their parents that Marx was a correspondent for the New York *Herald Tribune,* and is someone rather intimately known to us. To us. Not them. Instead, the Americans at the liaison office behaved as if in the presence of a higher civilization than any known at home: ancient, inscrutable, perhaps in the end inaccessible to the one-dimensional Occidental mind.

———◆———

The talk everywhere was of the Fourth National People's Congress, the first in eleven years. It was to revise the constitution, name a successor to Mao, and generally make amends for Lin Piao. Each ambassador I called on had a slightly different view of when the Congress was coming, but all seemed to agree that it could not be far off. After my call on the Minister of Foreign Affairs, Chiao Kuan-hua, Bush's Deputy, Harry E. T. Thayer, cabled Kissinger that the note takers present were of a lower level than they ought to have been, which suggested that preparations for the Congress were indeed much under way. In a fortnight it would turn out that the Fourth Congress was at that moment just about completing its work in the Great Hall of the People, a few blocks away. Which Great Hall gave the impression throughout of a deserted central post office on a Sunday morning. This sort of thing was supposed to impress foreigners.

My half hour with Chiao Kuan-hua was not altogether pointless. I told him I did not think the Indians would soon develop a nuclear capability, and suggested he approach the Indians, at least some of whom were troubled at becoming so openly dependent on the Russians now that they could not ask the Americans to defend them against the Chinese. I said that India had far more to fear from the North than from the East, that this had historically been the case, and that the Chinese should put this to their advantage.

———◆———

Of the various joint Indian-American enterprises, none survived the strains of 1971 more successfully than those directed against China. Indian fear of the Chinese was palpable. As much as the Gandhi government may have desired American defeat in Vietnam, once that became inevitable they could see it would not really be to the advantage of India, and in private became ever more explicit on this point. And so we continued, jointly, to spy on the Chinese from the tops of the Himalayas.

These were routine exercises, but not without drama. In 1965 we had sent a climbing expedition to the top of Nanda Devi, a mountain of 26,645 feet in the northeast, near the border with China, to put in place nuclear-powered instruments which would record Chinese rocket telemetry and atomic tests. A storm came, the instruments, including the power pack, were cached, and the party returned to base. The climbers returned in the spring to find that an avalanche had swept everything away, and the plutonium was lost in the snow pack at the headwaters of the holy Ganges. Our then-Ambassador Chester Bowles went back to Mrs. Gandhi, and the next year a second Indo-American expedition successfully put instruments in place atop Nanda Kot, the 22,400-foot mountain adjacent to Nanda Devi.

The initial mishap, or disaster, as you will, was reported in the American press in 1978, and calmly acknowledged by the new Prime Minister, Morarji Desai. But in 1974 Mrs. Gandhi was still making speeches about the ever present danger of subversion by the CIA, whilst I was meeting with the relevant Indian officials about our common interest in China.

In New Delhi I had pressed the Embassy to go back over the whole of our quarter-century in India, to establish just what we had been up to. In the end I was satisfied we had been up to very little. We had twice, but only twice, interfered in Indian politics to the extent of providing money to a political party. Both times this was done in the face of a prospective Communist victory in a state election, once in Kerala and once in West Bengal, where Calcutta is located. Both times the money was given to the Congress Party, which had asked for it. Once it was given to Mrs. Gandhi herself, who was then a party official.

Still, as we were no longer giving any money to *her*, it was understandable that she should wonder just to whom we *were* giving it. It is not a practice to be encouraged.

———◆———

Any conversation with Chiao was immediately cabled to Kissinger at that time. Had I known this earlier I would have tried to get to Peking more often. And yet, I found myself asking what we were getting out of it all. We went to the Chinese. Hung on their every word. Treated them as persons of superior qualities. And virtually everything they said to us was a lie.

———◆———

After Mogul India, Peking seemed a provincial place, rather like Moscow. Post-and-lintel architecture, and not much of it. The Ming Tombs were the only things to approach the standards of Rajasthan. At the same time the Chinese somehow seemed far the more Western. My first impression, at the railroad station across the Hong Kong border, was of a strange noise, which turned out to be that of a man hammering nails, making a concrete form, a sound not to be heard in Rajasthan. The Chinese are indeed like us in some ways.

I believe now it was the public art that forced this impression on me.

In democratic India, or Hindu India, as you will, government was not
to be *seen* in the literal way it was in Peking. In India, at most a sign
here and there exhorting the populace, in small type, to avoid "com-
munalism." By contrast, the Canton railroad station is given over to a
vast and irredeemably vulgar fresco of Chairman Mao, a Han Chinese,
surrounded by a horde of Uzbeks, Tartars, and whatever, beaming in
subverbal socialist realist ecstasy at their great leader. Where did this art
come from? After Disney, it is surely *the* "popular" art form of the
twentieth century, the *only* public art form in half the world. It flashed:
Courbet! Of course. A corrupted, bowdlerized, vulgar Courbet. If only
he hadn't got mixed up in the Commune. But as we know Marx, we
know Courbet. *We* know where the Chinese get their posters from. What
then is so mysterious, much less wondrous, about the place?

John Moynihan put it that "the people here are color-coded." Green
for army; blue for civil service; gray for Other.

—◆—

I wrote a long "Letter from Peking" for *The New Yorker,* mostly
about public housing, which was hideous but seemed to serve a state
purpose. *The New Yorker* put off publishing it until spring, by which
time circumstances suggested I had best withdraw it.

—◆—

At Shanghai airport there was a long wait and nothing to do. I instructed the children not to move from our wooden bench while I went
to explore what looked like a shopping area on a balcony approached
by a flight of marble stairs done in People's Grandiose. I was halfway up when a Red Guard came down to meet me, fingered his sub-
machine gun, and gestured me back. I returned to explain, "The trouble
with these people is that they don't know who I was." For surely government was behind me now. A man who had worked for Lyndon Johnson
and Richard Nixon.

—◆—

In Tokyo the Minister of Education came by to meet a man he had
heard knew David Riesman. We are the most powerful culture in the
world, I felt; we must somehow get our nerve back.

—◆—

In Pearl Harbor I made my peace with CINCPAC, in the person of
Noel S. Gayler, a magnificent seaman with whom I had continually
squabbled over carrier task forces and Diego García. Carlyle Elwood

Maw, Counsel to the Department of State, was there, and I was invited to a briefing on Southeast Asia. Cambodia, they said, would fall on April 15.

This was wholly new to me. Congress, it appeared, had refused further military assistance. There was thus a finite amount of supplies still to be delivered. These would run out April 15. The Communists would then take over. There was no bitterness about this, although there was a just slightly sharper than usual edge of technical precision to the talk.

Maw was impressive. I had been rather offended by the idea of him: Kissinger getting himself a quarter-million-dollar-a-year lawyer for free. But not for nothing was he a quarter-million-dollar lawyer. We ought never to have got into Vietnam, he said, but this was no way to get out. No one knew we were on the verge of the greatest liquidation of political opposition since Mao swept through China in 1948. But at Pearl Harbor some, I think, guessed.

The Pacific officers had not thought me a friend. In any event, I was now shown the evidence of Soviet bases in the Gulf of Aden and on the Horn of Africa, which were much further along than I had thought. There was no reason not to have made this clear to me earlier. I would have tried to help.

I had once been asked to lecture at the East-West Center of the University of Hawaii, and now did so, presenting the argument of the manuscript I had sent to Podhoretz, which had a better response than I expected. Clare Boothe Luce was present and got it all, perfectly, especially the idea of the British Revolution.

———◆———

I took the children to the U.S.S. *Arizona* so that they too might see the world for a dangerous place. After two years visiting the sites of other peoples' defeats, it was time to visit one of ours. It was spoiled with plaques and gimcrack. The Russian memorial on the outskirts of Moscow, a series of abstract tank traps, is far more impressive, a thought that depressed me.

———◆———

On January 27, 1975, I paid my official farewell call to President Ford, the first time I had seen him as President, and still the most decent man I had known in American politics. For two years under Nixon I would journey regularly to Capitol Hill to explain to the Republican leadership yet another Democratic-sounding proposal which was soon to be coming to them from the Republican White House. Ford, as Minority Leader of the House of Representatives, was unfailing in his courtesy and in his duty. He spoke for every measure, and carried half of them. He had stood with Hale Boggs back-to-back on the floor of the House and twice, by a two-to-one margin, passed a bill to establish a guaranteed income. This time, however, I was not equal to our meeting. He was President now and wanted to know how I thought he was doing. I mumbled about the pardon, agreeing that he had had to do it. I tried to tell him that the most important thing was that he was where he was being who he was. It was as clear as any one thing could be that when he left the presidency, whenever that might be, he would leave it whole again.

Kissinger was cordial. He had, after all, heard from me more than one man's normal quotient of lectures on the importance of the fact that India was a democracy. The man who was to succeed me as Ambassador, Attorney General William Saxbe, was not much interested in my theories.

I had in fact proposed that a career officer replace me. I got on well with the Foreign Service, and in India hugely respected the officers who worked with me. Foreign Service had been my only ambition as a young man, but in 1949 I failed the English composition portion of the Foreign Service examination. I didn't know much about anything in 1949, but I knew I wrote as well as the people who flunked me, and decided it was best to stay away.

Roy Atherton gave me a farewell lunch at one of those small clubs the career men have tucked away in Washington. As Assistant Secretary of State for Near Eastern and South Asian Affairs, he had inherited from Joseph Sisco the Israeli-Arab issue and had to give it all his time. India loomed but little in his thoughts, but we never seemed to differ on anything important, and he paid no attention to things that weren't important. He had opposed the Vietnam war, and had had no great regard for Kissinger's interminable wiggling out. Yet he totally supported the Secretary on the Middle East, and had no difficulty distinguishing between the two commitments.

———◆———

The White House under Donald Rumsfeld, with Richard Cheney second in command, was shipshape and Bristol fashion, as the Navy saying goes, and full of humor again. Kissinger boggled that Rumsfeld sometimes went away weekends and allowed Cheney to take papers directly to the President. He could not understand that Rumsfeld simply didn't care if somebody else saw the President. They would all, after all, be going back to Illinois, or Michigan, or somewhere, someday. It only lasts a little while, which bothered Rumsfeld not at all.

He had already had a singular career and it was only just begun. I wish him the presidency one day, partly because he would be splendid at it, but mostly that I might hang about in my last years telling folk that I gave the Chief Executive his first start, which I did, insofar as the executive branch is involved. In the early months of 1969 I had found myself de facto head of the Office of Economic Opportunity, the agency of Lyndon Johnson's war on poverty, which I had helped to shape, and had been expelled from in spirit at least. The OEO staff were at their worst just then: sour, disloyal, self-righteous. They had been poisonous enough about Johnson and now were hateful about Nixon. The acting director was a civil servant who despised his staff as much as he was despised by them. No Democrat had wanted the job in Johnson's last years. It seemed quixotic to think a Republican with any prospects would want it under Nixon. Yet Stephen Hess suggested a singular Republican: Donald Rumsfeld, a fighter pilot and a Princeton man, with a wonderful wife and a solid Republican seat in Congress. Only an extraordinary person would take the job anyway, and so we asked Rumsfeld. He said yes. He thought it important that the poverty program go on, although, to be sure, he'd voted against it. He thereafter kept an office in the White House but also kept a sufficient distance from the near-conspiracy that the place had turned into by 1971 and 1972. He became head of the Cost of Living Council, which took him out of the White House itself and across Pennsylvania Avenue to Lafayette Square. After the 1972 election he had the good sense to get out of Washington altogether, as Ambassador to NATO. Ford had called him back, and it was a good for the republic that he did.

He had drawn up "Rumsfeld's Rules," for the benefit of his White House colleagues:

> Don't become, or let the President or White House personnel become, one President. Don't forget it and don't be seen by others as not understanding that fact.

> Don't take the job, or stay in it, unless you have an understanding with the President that you are free to tell him what you think, on any subject, "with the bark off" — and have the freedom — in practice — to do it.

> Learn quickly how to say, "I don't know." If used when appropriate, it will be often.

> If you foul up, tell the President and others fast, and correct it.

> In our free society, leadership is by consent, not command. To lead, a President must, by word and deed, persuade. Personal contact and experience are necessary ingredients in the decision-making process, if he is to be successful in persuasion and, therefore, leadership.

Where possible, preserve the President's options — he will very likely need them.

Know that it is easier to get into something than it is to get out of it.

Don't become, or let the President or White House personnel become, obsessed or paranoid about the Press, the Congress, the other Party, opponents, or leaks. Understand and accept the inevitable and inexorable interaction among our institutions. Put your head down, do your job as best you can, and let the "picking" (and there will be some) roll off.

Don't speak ill of another member of the Administration. In discussions with the President, scrupulously strive to give fair and balanced assessments.

Never say "the White House wants." Buildings don't want.

Not a bad approach to remaking the presidency.

———————◆———————

All this was behind me now, and I settled into teaching my seminar on Ethnicity in Politics, the Harvard University Press having finally produced the volume on the subject that Glazer and I had assembled; and, something new for me, a seminar on Ideology and Foreign Policy, it being time, I judged, that someone at Harvard taught the subject, rather than merely exemplifying it.

The condition of democratic belief among the students was unnerving. The youth had learned to hate and to fear their own government, and had almost no standards by which to measure other regimes. I had flown from Hawaii to Boston and arrived on January 20, 1975. As it happened, the first editorial I read at home was in the *Harvard Crimson* of that day:

Vietnam: Good and Bad News

There was some good news from Vietnam last week — and some bad news from Washington. The good news was that the National Liberation Front had captured — or "overrun," as most American newspapers preferred to put it — their first provincial capital since they took An Loc [Phuoc Binh], later destroyed by American bombers, during the spring offensive of 1972. . . . Two decades of civil war have made it plain that the P[rovisional] R[evolutionary] G[overnment] speaks for most of those Vietnamese farmers who are not simply weary of the war, that the PRG is the only force capable of mounting a successful resistance to Thieu and therefore the only real alternative to him, that only the PRG is likely to lead the Vietnamese people in rebuilding their shattered country into a land where it is at least conceivable that freedom and democracy will be more than just words.

The bad news from Washington was that in a feint toward Vietnam Kissinger planned to divert a naval task force sailing toward the Indian Ocean. The Chairman of the Joint Chiefs of Staff "did not specifically suggest" that the Gulf of Tonkin was to have been the task force's destination, but where else? Mr. Seth M. Kupferberg, the *Crimson's* editorial chairman, implied, with the presumed accord of Mr. Robin S. Freedberg, the managing editor. Fortunately, they concluded, President Ford had overruled the plan.

At an earlier time I would have taken it as an essentially ideological statement for the *Crimson* so openly to side with the totalitarians now commencing their final sweep down that peninsula. To state that the Provisional Revolutionary Government was the only hope of the Vietnamese people for a world where "freedom and democracy will be more than just words" was a lie but a familiar lie. Nor was it anything unusual for the elite youth of this time to be repeating Communist lies with various degrees of conviction. But now, with the university quiet and the United States out of it all, this explanation seemed unsatisfactory. It dawned on me that what they were really doing was siding with the winner.

These were not, after all, losers, these young men and women. Life had been good to them, and would be better. Their reaction was nothing so new to the liberal democracies. Following the First World War the elites of the British universities turned against Britain, and there now was a touch of this in our own universities as well, although our youth had none of the bitchiness of the British. I came to feel that the most important fact of them was that they were — youth. Few had gone through demanding rites of passage: being on their own, being threatened, being hurt. Instead they had been put into a near-painless environment, where they were encouraged to play at being adults before they were. The usual naughtiness came out. But it was not the role reversal that now struck me so much as the simple fact of frightened young people identifying with the aggressor.

———◆———

It is a custom of sorts at Harvard to give dinner to members of the British Cabinet as they happen to be in Cambridge, and Professor and Mrs. Daniel Bell did this for Anthony Crosland. He was about the best the British arrangement produces any longer, which was why Harold Wilson had him at the Department of the Environment rather than the

Foreign and Commonwealth Office, which had been given to James Callaghan, a man weaker of mind and heart even than Harold Wilson. The professors who gathered for dinner pressed Crosland for details of the coming referendum on the Common Market. How was it to be worded? Who would draft it? What would be the result? Crosland answered patiently enough, but then said he really wasn't that much concerned about whether to join the Common Market. What concerned him was whether Britain itself would remain a unified nation. The Scots were rising, the Welsh soon would be. This would be the end of the Labour Party, as it had no majority in England itself. Thus it was imperative, Crosland went on, that whatever necessary be done to keep the Scots in the Kingdom, and the Welsh also. He spoke of the Irish, however, as "they," of Northern Ireland as he might have done of British Honduras. I asked: Were the British subjects of Northern Ireland now "they" and no longer "we"? "They," he answered. I asked if he was not the first member of the British Cabinet since 1714 who might have spoken to a gathering of Harvard professors about the impending breakup of the United Kingdom. He was, he agreed.

Once again the duality of all this came to me. Ideology had triumphed in Britain: but was it to be undone by ethnicity? This has been the fate of European socialism, I suppose, since the German Social Democrats voted war credits in 1914. It had got to the point in Belgium where the socialists divided into separate French-speaking and Flemish-speaking parties. Socialism was still a true faith in the higher ranks of the Labour Party, and not just a way of holding on to a car and driver; but for most, how little socialism had touched the heart.

———◆———

February 24, 1975, was the fifteenth anniversary of Norman Podhoretz's having become editor of *Commentary*. In those years it had become, as *The Economist* put it, with just the prudent hedging of a question mark, "The world's best magazine?" I had brought him a piece of silver, and some twenty of us gathered to give him dinner at The Century. Irving Kristol and Daniel Bell and Nathan Glazer were there. James Q. Wilson and Seymour Martin Lipset from Harvard, and Robert Nisbet, soon to assume the Schweitzer Chair at Columbia.

Podhoretz first published an article of mine in 1961, on the New York Democrats, and we had made our way together, on this issue and that, ever since. Always he was in the lead, but with me perhaps writing more. He spoke at dinner of a realignment of political forces. A de facto alliance had formed against the New Left. Men such as Irving Howe, on the democratic left, had sensed the Stalinist cast of mind in the writing and rampaging of the time, and in effect joined the liberal center to resist it. On the philosophical right, the followers of Leo Strauss, far more influential than generally known (possibly because they were so few in number), had also joined with the liberals against the madness of the time. But now the New Left was finished, and so in all likelihood was this temporary alliance against it. The far left would resume its attack on the center. The socialists had already "fractioned." In 1972 the old Socialist Party changed its name to Social Democrats, U.S.A., and acknowledged that its future role would be as an influence on the Democratic Party. This was what its actual role had been for decades, but it was enough to cause Howe and others to split off, forming the Democratic Socialist Organizing Committee. The Straussians would now presumably resume their critique of liberalism, allied with a point of view that was coming to be known as "neo-conservative," a term that had first appeared in Howe's journal, *Dissent,* and was now being applied with no very fine distinction to persons such as Kristol, who was indeed one, to Bell, who demanded the right to remain a socialist, and to persons of the center such as myself, resigned to the fate of personifying, at one and the same time, "neo-conservatism" to Michael Harrington and "left-liberalism" to William F. Buckley, Jr.

———◆———

On February 26, 1975, Podhoretz released my paper, now titled "The United States in Opposition," to a press conference, the first one *Commentary* had held for such a purpose. I did not quite follow his enthusiasm, but then I had been away for two years. Halfway through the questions and answers I began to sense that the journalists liked what I had written, something rarely revealed. *The New York Times* set the tone, printing its story on the morning of the press meeting, thus keeping ahead of the news.

Within days it was clear that it *was* news. I appeared on the *Today Show;* on WGBH-TV in Boston; on Martin Agronsky. *Reader's Digest* decided to reprint the article in a shortened version, the first *Commentary* piece to appear in that journal. For a period I found this distracting, as my real interest at the time was to be back home and out of it all. I had written the paper at the end of a period in my life, and to close it down. Then one afternoon the Secretary of State called to say he had read it through at one sitting and had to tell me straight off that he found it "staggeringly good."

There was something of chance in this. I had sent him a copy; it was put in the reading pile in his limousine. He had glanced at it on the way back from the White House, but then took it to his office, canceled his appointments, read it through, and called me. This was something beyond chance. He, said Henry Kissinger, suddenly felt he understood what was going on out there. He had said to himself, "Why didn't I write that!" He said I would know this was the highest compliment he could pay another man. I did.

He told the Seventh Floor of the Department about the article and the Seventh Floor told the Sixth Floor. In very little time the article was being read throughout the Department as something the Secretary approved, but more importantly as an idea foreign policy could *use*. I was asked to meetings to plan strategy for the next round of confrontations, notably yet another U.N. Special Session on development. The existing documents went on interminably about "damage limitation." I had come along with a different view.

Not everyone in the Department agreed. An eight-page letter from the chief of the population program predictably took issue with my account of the Bucharest Conference. By contrast, Paul Demeney, vice president of the Population Council, who was also at Bucharest, wrote to approve wholeheartedly, sending along the text of comments he had made in Bucharest to the "Population Tribune," an American-financed venture which met in parallel with the official conference to comment on the proceedings in a daily newspaper, and generally pressed the more extreme views. It appeared that Demeney had answered back, saying:

> Western exploitation was held to be the source of undeserved wealth and Third World poverty. But the big income differences, say, between Romania and Ethiopia, are readily explainable by differential productivity. So are wage differentials between Siberia and Northern China. . . . The flow of western capital to the developing world has been repeatedly lamented as a source of Third World backwardness. But, in effect, the single obvious fact that emerges from even the most casual comparisons of statistics is that a grossly preponderant share of the international flow of capital funds is between developed economies, and that the rates of capital flows to developing countries (with few exceptions that invariably resulted in rapid economic growth) are far smaller today than rates of pre-First World War capital imports that supported the rapid industrialization in the United States, Russia or Australia.

All the more valuable, then, was Demeney's report on the reaction to his remarks: "There were about 200 people in the audience and their reaction was very much what you would have predicted — enthusiastic." An audience that might have been thought insensate by this point nonetheless responded to a statement of the complexity of things. I was heartened, as if a hypothesis had been confirmed in a rather nicely controlled experiment.

———◆———

A debate now began, for it was soon evident that if I had heartened some I had appalled many. On March 7, McGeorge Bundy wrote to tell me that he had considerable doubt about the generalization that countries choosing to emphasize liberty would in the end do most for equality as well. Bundy mentioned China and Cuba as two countries in particular that posed a challenge to such a thesis.

Though McGeorge Bundy was in truth a generous man, it was his deaconal practice to greet every proposition put to him by questioning the facts on which it was alleged to rest — to have, that is, "considerable doubt about the generalization. . . ." Persons are easily jarred by this, especially when the question is put in the manner of an examiner who *does* have the facts. It could be devastating to others, frequently too much so. In the early days of the Vietnam war I had seen Bundy at meetings and at dinner tables overrun opposition that had the better case, but that could not rally from this first volley. As he was always in a hurry and usually the ranking official present, he would leave before anyone recovered. McNamara had much the same manner. The weakness of this approach is that it rarely gives you time to find out whether you have encountered a friend or an enemy. All propositions alike are impartially overturned. Hence you often dismiss arguments that are in fact to your advantage. A further weakness for Bundy was that interlocutors, whatever their own disposition, tended to take away the impression that he regarded them as enemies or fools. He did not become Secretary of State.

Kissinger's range in dealing with others was similarly narrow but vastly more elegant. As soon as he could divine the object of any petitioner — and such was his intuition that he could usually do this before his visitors had got through their introductions — he would proclaim that object to be his very own, and proceed to discover a great and possibly unanticipated commonality of purpose as well as a deeply shared mutual respect, now enhanced on his part by gratitude for having been able to share the insights that had come from his visitors' manifestly greater command of the subject. How could they best join forces to advance a common purpose in the face of opposition? Alas, powerful opposition. Certainly at that moment the more aggressive. The question was, how might Kissinger and his visitors defend their shared interest?

No: the question was how Kissinger might do this, for he had taken unto himself that task. There did seem one possibility. If he could concede just a *tiny* bit of the dispute's substance to the opposition, it was very likely they would withdraw their larger demands, or, failing this, would find they had but little support in the community at large, given the manifest reasonableness of those against whom they made demands which were so patently unreasonable.

In this mode a delegation meeting with him from the professoriat, demanding a cease-fire and immediate and total withdrawal of American troops from Vietnam, having been brought to appreciate the extraordinary ominous neo-antidemocratic rumblings in the officer corps, with its Protestant, rural, antiurban complexion, and the prospect of certain ugly charges being made that intellectuals, who were not Protestant and not rural, had subverted the home front during a losing war, would somehow marvelously come to agree and to appreciate that an immediate withdrawal, with the resultant massing of at least three armies, intact and under wartime command, on the West and East coasts of the United States, would probably not serve the long-term interests of peace. That being the case, all could agree on a plan that would provide a phased withdrawal, accompanied by a temporary step-up in the bombing, which would draw attention away from the running down of the war. In much the same manner the leadership of the Armed Forces was persuaded to accept defeat by Communists in Asia rather than risk leftists coming to power in the United States. Kissinger did become Secretary of State.

———◆———

The influence of the London School of Economics had been one of the subthemes of "The United States in Opposition," and I had concluded the *Commentary* article by relating the extraordinary address that Ralf Dahrendorf had given on taking over as director in the spring of 1973. The equality party, he had said, had had its day. The liberty party's time had come once more. I continued in my own voice:

> It is a time to be shared with the new nations, and those not so new, shaped from the Old European empires, and especially the British — and is the United States not one such? — whose heritage this is also. To have halted the great totalitarian advance only to be undone by the politics of resentment and the economics of envy would be a poor outcome to the promise of a world society. At the level of world affairs we have learned to deal with Communism. Our task is now to learn to deal with socialism. It will not be less difficult a task. It ought to be a profoundly more pleasant one.

Marx made much of the fact that a nineteenth-century Manchester bourgeois had a life expectancy of thirty-five years, an intolerable edge over that of the working class. A century later, New York City found itself dealing with the odd question of whether there was not such an excess of (mostly municipal) hospital beds that the health of patients was suffering by their being kept under hospital care for too long a period. The fact of the relative success of liberal societies was unmistakable. But almost nowhere, least of all in liberal societies, was there a rhetoric that would proclaim and, in a sense, substantiate this success. In the United States, for example, progress was more and more seen to depend on an adamant insistence that there had been no progress.

The world did not disagree. The United States was seen to be reeling back in compounded defeat, incapable of retaliation, unwilling even to contemplate retaliation. Thus in the same month the *Commentary* article appeared, a meeting of the Co-ordinating Bureau of the Non-Aligned Countries met in Havana. The Declaration that followed plainly aligned the Non-Aligned with the totalitarians. The Declaration hailed "the people of Cambodia's great and decisive victories over the besieged lackey regime in Phnom Penh. . . ." The United States, anathematized in virtually every paragraph, was enjoined "to cease obstaculizing the United Nations." A kind of Leninist consumerism made its appearance, as the Bureau denounced "the obstinacy of the imperialist powers in preserving the structures of colonial and neo-colonial exploitation which nurture their luxurious and superfluous consumer societies while they keep a large part of humanity in misery and hunger." The official document noted that "delegations from the following countries were also present as Observers." On this list, following the Palestine Liberation Organization, came the Socialist Party of Puerto Rico, which was, in point of fact, the Communist Party of Puerto Rico. The United States said not a word.

There was some perception of this malaise among commentators on foreign affairs. Ronald Hilton wrote me from Stanford of "the absurdity of the official belief that détente means saying nothing which might offend Moscow or the Third World." From my experience in India, he continued, I would surely know that behind the screen of détente Moscow was doing all it could to spread scurrilous one-sided stories about the United States, and that was the least of it.

◆

In June, 1975, the Commission on CIA Activities Within the United States, headed by Vice President Rockefeller, published a report filled with accounts of the Agency's wrongdoings, typically explained as having begun "During the early 1950s, at the height of the so-called cold war. . . ." The Commission concluded there was no "credible" evidence that the CIA had assassinated President Kennedy, but that was about as much as the organization was spared. By contrast, the KGB fared much better. The Commission had learned that the Soviets, from their Washington embassy, from their U.N. mission headquarters in Manhattan, and from a high-rise apartment building they had built in the Bronx, were now systematically intercepting microwave telephone conversations of Americans and sorting them by computer. The most massive illegal invasion of Fourth Amendment rights in American history was being conducted by a foreign intelligence agency on American soil. To its credit, the Commission mentioned this in its draft report, possibly to put the CIA's activities in perspective. The White House, however, refused to allow any reference to the matter.

Were this a secret kept from the country, it would have been one thing. But it was a secret the country was trying to keep from itself. A month after the Rockefeller Commission report was made public, Jeremy J. Stone, in an interview in the Washington *Star*, stated all the details that needed to be known. As director of the Federation of American Scientists, a group concerned at how much the military threat of the Soviets was being exaggerated, Stone spoke of an equal concern that no one seemed distressed by the Soviet telephone interception program:

> In the case of the Soviet Union listening in on our telephone conversations, we see new dangers of manipulation of the stock market, of political forces in this country, possibilities of blackmail.
>
> For example, . . . remember the wheat deal in which they were able to outwit and manipulate grain companies. Imagine how much easier it would be if they were able to listen to the telephone conversations of the wheat dealers preparing their negotiating positions on the prices of the wheat. Or, to take a political example, imagine what the KGB might do if they decided they wanted to destroy one of their political opponents. They could listen in on his conversations in an effort to find something that would be embarrassing to him. Then it would be an easy matter to leak it to the press.

No Congressional committee took up the issue. No wheat trader. Certainly not the Secretary of State. Not many months after this, Adam Ulam, writing of the Twenty-Sixth Communist Party Congress in the Soviet Union, offered as assessment: "The Soviet Union has under Brezhnev achieved — it would be both dangerous and ungenerous for us to deny it — the leading if not yet the dominant position in world politics." Some — Ulam certainly — raged at this. Others, wittingly or no, turned to accommodation.

By midsummer galleys were circulating of a *Foreign Affairs* article by Tom J. Farer, then a research fellow at the Council on Foreign Relations, entitled "The United States and the Third World: A Basis for Accommodation." Kristol and I were singled out as "antiaccommodationists," supporters of the establishment, enemies of the "people." Moreover, we seemed not to know that the West had been defeated:

> Implicit, sometimes explicit, in this line of argument [i.e. ours] is the claim that the developed states still deploy sufficient power to resist the Third World's redistributive efforts. The latter is portrayed largely as a paper tiger, faking it with éclat, to be sure, but still faking it. Precisely why we should regard the Southern bloc in this light has yet to be adequately explained. In the writings of Kristol and Moynihan and other such neo-conservatives one looks in vain for a serious effort to project the costs of the coercive measures required to assure continuing access to the resources and growing markets of the Third World. Seemingly buried in their subconscious is the idea that colonial rule was relinquished as an act of grace. In fact, as John Strachey and other students of imperialism have demonstrated, the colonial retreat was a grudging concession that once the Third World became infected with the virus of self-determination, the price of domination became intolerable. . . .

Maybe so, but the *Commentary* article was taken seriously enough in Moscow to be translated for the Central Committee.

In contrast to Farer, W. Scott Thompson of the Fletcher School not only got my point but half demolished it. In a paper written in response to the article he stated, first, that an anticolonial tradition runs very deep in America, a memory somehow being repressed at this time. "Our foreign policy elite," he reminded me, had, as it were, "lectured Britain and France about the evils of colonialism for a critical generation." We all but forced the Netherlands to disgorge Indonesia after World War II. In Algeria "we supplied the F.L.N. with weaponry through the C.I.A." In Thompson's view, American liberalism reached its apogee in its attitudes toward and success in dealing with the Third World under Kennedy, who built the Volta Dam for Ghana, in the face of the kind of cost-effectiveness judgment that had blocked the Aswan Dam and at a time when the President of Ghana "appeared to try to make his country another Cuba." Similarly, "We cultivated relations with wretched dictators like Sekou Touré . . . with the happy result that, when the Soviets in October 1962 wished to use his airport for refueling planes

enroute to Cuba, Touré refused." But it had all gone awry. "By the
1970s the successors to the liberals were muckrakers who eventually were
to take the Kennedy policy to its ultimate absurdity — the abnegation of
American interests." In part this was the consequence of a general withdrawal: ". . . the liberal intellectual community, preoccupied as it was
with fault-finding in its own government, was relatively ignorant of what
was occurring in an important part of the world." Another, realist,
strand of American policy was prepared to take this part of the world
seriously, for serious interests were seen to be at stake. But by the 1960s
the double standard of the Third World leaders, forever tilting toward
the Soviet Union or China, brought on a "cynical indifference" in these
circles to Less Developed Countries. "From 1969 we almost officially put
the LDC's out of heart and mind," Thompson noted. But,

> If the October war in the Middle East did nothing else for us it
> awakened us to the reality of how much our interests were at stake ·. . .
> the issue was barely drawn until this past spring, when . . . Moynihan
> . . . took pen to hand. . . . He argues that the United States, now a
> minority in world politics, must "go into opposition" in the parlia-
> mentary sense.

Alas, wrote Thompson, it would not work. The appeal to the moral
tradition of socialism would not succeed. The record of the Third World
in the field of human rights was grim, and near to irreversible:

> It is not just the genocide of hundreds of thousands of people born of
> an inconvenient ethnic group or race, in Burundi or Indonesia; nor the
> atavistic totalitarianism in Uganda, Chad, and the Central African Re-
> public; nor the racism so prevalent throughout Afro-Asia, nor the strati-
> fication that characterizes Latin America. To a civil libertarian the ap-
> parent absence of conscience of third world leaderships is what rankles
> most acutely.
>
> Where indeed are the states in which the issue of liberty has any
> standing?

Thompson wrote just as the Indian democracy appeared to have collapsed. The lights had gone out there, and in the Philippines: "And a
new generation of leaders is asserting itself with a very un-Fabian tone,
failing even to mention liberty in the sense that means anything to us."
These new leaders, he summed up, are not interested in liberty, but in
organizing their ethnically fragmented societies. He supported my
assertion that what socialist doctrine in fact provided the new nations
was excuse for collecting in one place enough power to govern with. In
his words, "the drive toward 'socialism' is little related to the economy,

but is related to the drive to state coherence." But his conclusion was glum. We should of course speak out against atrocities, but should expect little dividend:

> Moynihan's strategy is fine, but it doesn't begin to solve the problem. The typical third world leader today has a new model of socialism that differs from classic totalitarianism only in the realm of efficiency. Moynihan would have us save ourselves firstly by recognizing the ideology of the third world states, and recognizing that it is not as such dangerous to us; since it derives from Fabianism, "the prospect now is that the world will not go totalitarian." The sources of such confidence in view of the evidence are obscure.

It is a measure, I suppose, of the demoralization of the elites at this moment that they couldn't get anything straight. They had only been giving orders, they would say of their role in Vietnam. But they weren't giving them anymore. They were no longer policing foreign policy debate, maintaining standards of evidence and of argument. Farer's article in *Foreign Affairs* was ignorant to the point of misrepresentation. He hadn't the least notion what Kristol and I were saying, much less that we were saying different things. By contrast, Thompson got it right, and while friendly enough, argued with considerable force that I was simply wrong. In the months to come, I would have reason to recall his arguments.

4

Ambassador Designate

HENRY KISSINGER'S LUCK RAN OUT on Saturday, March 22, 1975. On that day, at the King David Hotel in Jerusalem, he announced that his Mid-east shuttle had failed. For two weeks he had moved back and forth between Middle Eastern capitals seeking a disengagement of forces, as with the Vietnam cease-fire which he had brought about by a similar feat of personal persuasiveness in early 1973. In the aftermath of that settlement he had acquired a position in world diplomacy unlike that of anyone since Metternich (the subject, as it happened, of his doctoral dissertation). It was a reputation altogether deserved. No one had ever achieved what he had achieved, for the simple reason that no one had ever had combined the personal abilities and political luck that made it possible. His luck had been rather too much the bad luck of others, but this is always a gambler's lot during good times.

Now the luck ran out. His 1975 peacemaking efforts in the Middle East had no sooner collapsed than the entire peace he had negotiated in South Asia collapsed also. The fall of Cambodia proceeded on schedule. Precisely as forecast to me at Pearl Harbor, the Mekong River lifeline to the capital of Phnom Penh was closed by the end of February. On March 12 Premier Lon Nol replaced the commander of the armed forces. On

April 12 the United States Embassy evacuated Phnom Penh. On April 17 the capital of Cambodia surrendered to the Khmer Rouge. Commentators such as Anthony Lewis would soon describe the Secretary of State as the man who would go down in history as the destroyer of Cambodia. Lewis would further say that Kissinger's statement at a press conference on the subject was "the performance of a man so wounded by failure that in the course of blaming others he would exaggerate the damage to his country."

But that was to come later. What Kissinger knew in March, 1975, was that the Middle East shuttle had ended and that in Vietnam the Viet Cong were continuing the successes so welcomed by the *Harvard Crimson*. In mid-March President Thieu suddenly withdrew his forces from the Central Highlands. On March 20 the North Vietnamese regular army crossed the demilitarized zone into South Vietnam, and the end began. The peace for which Kissinger had been awarded a Nobel Prize turned out to have been a ruse. We had been deceived. More than a few persons, though, asked whether this was the doing of the North Vietnamese alone. Luck is like that.

———◆———

The Secretary of State arrived home Sunday, March 23, and went directly by helicopter to the White House.

Wednesday, March 26, at his request, I came to his office for a drink in the early evening. It was not two years since I had first seen him there in a magnificence intended to impress and that indeed was impressive. "On your knees, Moynihan," he had said then as I entered. Not quite smiling. This time he asked me to go to the United Nations. He was right to do so. His center was giving way, his right was in retreat. It was time to attack. The only disturbing thought was that this same idea had first come to him, or to Nixon, the last time both were in trouble in Cambodia. To repeat behavior is to invite ambush. This thought came and went. Kissinger said we had to stand up for ourselves, that I understood how to do this, that the *Commentary* article had pointed the way.

I was without illusion about Kissinger, or without much. I knew he never gave a thought to the U.N. save on the odd occasion it caused him trouble. He never thought about the U.N. Ambassador. No one had told Yost the first time around that I would be replacing him; clearly this time no one would tell Scali. Yet there was at least a chance that the strategy I had proposed would in fact bring some success. Certainly I had written for that purpose. He understood this and was perfectly right that he needed — we needed — some successes and would need more as time went by.

Then there was the truth that I admired and liked him. I knew him as someone of considerably greater ability than my own, largely in the matter of energy, which is what matters most in government. He slept four hours and worked twenty. Thus he was twice the man I was. On the other hand, I was not his inferior and I knew that also. And I had the advantage of knowing the United States better than he did. I said to him on this occasion that he was on the ropes but would spring back. I really don't think he took the allusion. In any event he rejected the notion. I had been on the *Today Show* on St. Patrick's Day, while he was in the Middle East. I had said then that what he needed from us was a little love, that he had Nancy now and that would make all the difference, but still there were the rest of us and we could care a bit also. It mattered to him that I had said this, for I think he knew I meant it.

His problem was that he was dangerous to be close to. It was not as it was with Lyndon Johnson, of whom Eugene McCarthy remarked that no one ever was associated with him who was not in the end somehow diminished. With Kissinger the risk was to end up destroyed. He could not help this.

A few weeks after the Cambodian "incursion" of 1970 he had asked me to lunch in his office in the basement of the White House. We had started out in the White House as equals of sorts, and indeed in 1970 still had equal offices in the basement, but he had quickly eclipsed me. I had no real position; he was head of the National Security Council staff. In any event I had no expectation of remaining beyond my two years' leave, whereas he clearly meant to stay. Yet I had not done that badly. In August, 1969, eight months after I had gone to work, the President sent to Congress three proposals — for a guaranteed income, for federal revenue sharing, and for decentralization of federal manpower programs — that were more sweeping and more liberal, if that is the term, than anything Johnson or Kennedy had ever proposed. *The Economist* judged that Nixon's message on that occasion could rank with Roosevelt's espousal of a Social Security system: "Any one of the three main proposals . . . would rank as major legislation — indeed historical legislation — and here they are combined into one." Moreover, the guaranteed income had passed the House of Representatives by a two-to-one vote, a feat for which the only word is spectacular. Then came Cambodia, and our pace was broken. I had assumed that my small reputation would turn on the fate of these measures and it was clear they were now doomed. And I knew why. Henry Kissinger's damn fool invasion of Cambodia. The same Henry Kissinger, looking straight at me over lunch, explained that the Cambodian disturbance would soon be over, and it was high time the administration got itself a domestic policy.

I asked to think about the U.N. I had been now, since India, only fifty-three days out of government. I had spent twelve of the previous twenty years in government. I had no money and not much left of a profession. My wife, Elizabeth, had taken a very great deal, and the children even more. And yet the nation was on its beam ends, the newspapers and television awash with defeat and failure; it wasn't that clear the country would be able to right itself.

On April 12 I saw the President and agreed. I was afterward glad to have done so. A decent man, he inspired decency in others. A small word, that, but Orwell's term for what had kept the British sane and made them brave when their intellectuals had quite given themselves over to tyrannies of left and right.

The President set few terms. Presidents never do. He asked me to lunch in the Mansion, where Robert A. Goldwyn had arranged a discussion of world food problems. I said little, save that I was not overwhelmed by the likelihood of world famine. I did propose that if the President were to give a speech on the subject, he should do so on a trip to India. I was at this time a bit of a pest on the subject of Indian democracy.

I soon returned to that subject in a lecture sponsored by Freedom House, at the City University in New York, on the theme "How Much Does Freedom Matter?" I asked what had happened in the decade and a half since the inaugural of John F. Kennedy: "We shall pay any price, bear any burden, meet any hardship. . . ." Would we still? Did democracy, other than American democracy, much matter to us anymore? I attempted what was then and probably will remain the near-impossible, which was to distinguish between the Vietnam war and the purposes for which it was fought. I argued that there had been a failure of nerve among the interconnected elites that had shaped postwar American foreign policy, "preceded by a failure of specific undertakings: the failure of arms, the failure to receive support from the regimes those arms were intended to defend, the failure of development, and the failure of our aid efforts to appear supportive rather than exploitative." The same administration that had launched the Peace Corps had sent advisors to Vietnam. (Kennedy said we would go to Vietnam in the same speech in which he announced we would go to the moon.) I made no defense of the way the war had been conducted, nor much of a defense of the American leaders of the period. I allowed that "a great many men one had thought of as good acted in ways unmistakably bad; that men one thought of as sane acted in ways that were not sane. In particular, and unforgivably, the American government, after a time, commenced to lie and to conceal." This deceit had been especially harmful in its effect on the relationship of the foreign policy elite to its own institutions, ". . . and this may be the most devastating loss. For to strip our past of glory is no great loss, but to deny it honor is devastating." I had no solutions, simply a sense of institutions failing: the press, the universities, those who knew better and those who didn't, the Congress, the presidency. I went back to Henry James's essay on Hawthorne and the America of Hawthorne's time, an America without institutions. I suggested that much the same could be said of the institutional landscape of America in 1975. James thought the barrenness of this landscape in his time stemmed from the peculiarly prominent role in America of individual conscience:

> An Englishman, a Frenchman — a Frenchman above all — judges quickly, easily, from his own social standpoint, and makes an end of it. He has not that rather chilly and isolated sense of moral responsibility which is apt to visit a New Englander in such processes. . . . American intellectual standards are vague, and Hawthorne's countrymen are apt to hold the scales with a rather uncertain hand and a somewhat agitated conscience.

I predicted that at this moment this tyranny of conscience would have special consequences:

> What it comes to is that life is tragic for those who are impelled by conscience to pursue objectives which can be attained only through means which conscience finds abhorrent. Whereupon that conscience turns on itself, and a fearsome thing it is when loose. . . . The very conscience that makes us hate what we have done will very likely before long have us hating what we are *not* doing. Freedom concerns us, and will continue to do. But in a world of which we no longer think of ourselves as the natural leader.

The New York Times headline on the talk ran, "Moynihan Assails Role of Liberals." Leonard Sussman of Freedom House protested. The next day's headline ran, "Moynihan Clarifies Views on Liberals."

When Robert Manning published the address in the July issue of

The Atlantic, Dr. Michael C. Latham, Professor of International Nutrition at Cornell, wrote in to the magazine to say:

> It is sad, perhaps even alarming, that Daniel P. Moynihan, our new ambassador to the U.N., should still preach a foreign policy that echoes that of John Foster Dulles. . . .
>
> Does Moynihan really believe that we provided all that assistance to India in the 1950s and 1960s mainly because she was democratic? . . . Surely we gave aid because she was at first anti-communist and later non-communist. Throughout all this period it mattered to us little whether a government was democratic or autocratic. . . . We assisted those governments that were non-communist and we still do.
>
> Moynihan is all for freedom and that is a noble idea. But in using that term he seems to care not a whit for freedom from hunger, freedom from disease, freedom of opportunity, freedom from corruption and so on. To him freedom is living under a non-totalitarian regime, by which he means a non-communist one.
>
> Our failure has been that we have supported governments because they are anti-communist, and not because they were genuinely trying to alleviate poverty and reduce deprivations among their people.

◆

On Monday, April 21, *The New York Times* reported that Communist forces had taken Xuam Loc, a city thirty-eight miles east of Saigon; also that I would replace Scali at the United Nations. On the same day I had been asked by the publisher of *The Times,* Arthur O. Sulzberger, to lunch. This was coincidence, and ought to have been a happy enough one. But no; for I came away realizing I was once again at the mercy of the editor of *The Times* editorial page.

For the longest while *The Times* editorial tradition had been conservative in the sense in which doctors use the term. Advice was proffered in measured amounts and at infrequent intervals. *The Times* itself rarely sought to change the course of events. (Indeed, Adolph Ochs had considered doing away with the editorial page altogether, for fear it might compromise the paper's role as a neutral observer.) Charles Merz had pecked away as editorial page editor from 1938 to 1961 without doing noticeable harm to city or nation, nor yet to *The Times* itself. But John B. Oakes, who succeeded him, quite reversed this policy and commenced to intervene extensively, as it were, in national and international affairs. An early enthusiasm was the Vietnam war. In a representative comment, just after Diem was assassinated in Saigon in 1963, just days before Kennedy himself would be assassinated, the lead editorial of *The Times* observed:

The change of regime in South Vietnam provides the United States with a rare opportunity to redefine its policies in that area.

American recognition of the new regime is amply justified by Saigon's pledges of political freedom and more effective prosecution of the war.

Murder, at this point, was a "change in regime." In time this blindness would be succeeded by an equivalent incapacity to see anything *but* murder.

Oakes's chief characteristic was that he was almost entirely predictable. *The Times* had become, and remained, the greatest newspaper in the world. Its news staff was the most cosmopolitan on earth, and under Sulzberger, who took over direction of the institution in 1963, it was vigorously competitive. But the editorial page retained a distinct New York provincialism. It was as ethnic an editorial page as that of *Il Progresso,* the *Jewish Daily Forward, La Prensa,* or the *Irish Echo.* Its universalist, even deracinated air was its most distinctive ethnic characteristic, the mark of German Reform Judaism of that particular branch that so flourished in, and has so influenced, the City of New York. In city affairs, the greatest achievement of Oakes's tenure was the two mayoral terms of John V. Lindsay. Much as Oakes's enthusiasm for Lindsay was predictable, so, it must be supposed, was his detestation of me. It was not, I think, personal. He was not, to my knowledge, a mean man, but he rarely understood me, and when he did, he did not at all like what he understood.

All this had been harmless enough until early in 1970 *The Times* obtained a copy of a long memorandum I had sent Nixon, summing up the racial situation of that moment. I had something out of the ordinary to report. In the North and West, the income of young married black couples had reached parity with that of young married white couples. In some situations black earnings exceeded white. Nothing the like had ever occurred in the history of race relations in America. It was extraordinarily good news. The educational and social and economic systems were working, turning out equal results for newcomers, much as they had done with previous groups over many generations. There was, however, bad news also. The underclass of black urban slum dwellers, of which, in my view, the clearest indicators were the proportion of female-headed households, and the illegitimacy ratios, was still growing. The developments I had forecast for Johnson had come about, and were going past the point even I would have predicted. A new leading indicator also appeared: urban fires. All these developments were being affected, in my view, and not for the better, by a then-mounting level of racial rhetoric, epithet, and threat (by both blacks and whites). At this time the Black Panthers and their white supporters were spoiling for a confrontation with the federal government. In the general sense, something of the sort was coming, for there were those in Washington who would have welcomed it. I wrote to persuade Nixon that he must not listen to any confrontationist proposals from John Mitchell's Justice Department. The time was at hand to get back to the standards of the Civil Rights Act, the standards of a color-blind constitution. I continued: "The time may have come when the issue of race could benefit from a period of benign neglect. We may need a period in which Negro progress continues and racial rhetoric fades." Glazer and I had by then prepared a second edition of *Beyond the Melting Pot,* in which we warned that ethnicity, which had been a persisting and functional social form, was on the verge of becoming dysfunctional. We had never in any event celebrated ethnicity; we had merely described it. Now, we argued, ethnicity was being exalted to a principle of social organization it had never been, and in our view should never be. It was being celebrated in its most dangerous form, that of black-white confrontation, and not least on the editorial page of *The Times.* (Reality at length imposed itself. By 1977 the same editorial page, commenting on the New York mayoralty primary contest, would speak of the "savage tribalism" that had grown in the city. A lead editorial on the issues of that campaign would assert that "the most delicate issue and most difficult task is the reduction of racial and ethnic rivalries." At the same time, a poll reported on *The Times*'s front page said that 31 percent of New York's Democrats thought the city's near-bankruptcy stemmed mainly from welfare, while another 20 percent said the chief cause had been Mayor Lindsay.)

In 1970, Oakes had the intelligence to see that my argument on reducing the prominence of racial issues was directed against him, and the likes of him on all sides. Unfortunately he did not have the character to represent what I had said fairly and accurately. The phrase "benign neglect," as I recalled — wrongly, it turned out — came from the Durham report of 1839 on the governance of Canada, in which, he judged, the British having left the place alone, the provinces had already in fact become self-governing. William Safire later included the term in a revised edition of his *Dictionary of American Politics:* "A suggestion to allow tension to ease, interpreted as a plot to abandon the civil rights movement." Most newspapers had no great trouble seeing the main point. The Washington *Post* in two lead editorials asked what all the fuss was about. But *The Times* took the view that I had called not for neglect of the "issue of race" but for neglect of the black population. It was a small lie, but a great wrong.

As it happened, the Nixon administration in its first year had not been doing all that badly with black opinion — there had been nothing like the denunciation that would come from every major black organization

in the nation during the first year of Jimmy Carter's presidency. But
The Times now branded the Nixon White House not only as racist, but
as conspiring to bring about racist objectives. My memorandum had, it
was pointedly adduced, been a secret one. (In fact it was so unsecret that
Nixon, after reading it, sent it to all members of the Cabinet.) A certain
kind of liberal conviction fixed on this issue. The administration was
irredeemably damned, and so was I. Next, certain subjects became taboo.
To discuss black progress was to abet racism. Blacks were in effect
coerced into denying what they had done for themselves. Their de-
pendency on white attitudes was insisted upon by whites. The considerable good-faith effort that a Republican administration in fact did
make to continue social programs and devise better ones was simply
denied. History was rewritten even as it took place. Benign neglect and
its variations became fixtures of *The Times* editorial page.

Thus the day before I left for India, in 1973, a column on *The Times*
editorial page headed "Malign Neglect" announced that the administration in its fiscal year 1974 budget would slash the appropriation for
Head Start. I called the government official in charge of Head Start.
Was his program being slashed? Not at all, he said; there would be once
again a sizable increase in the budget, already then in print. *The Times*
editorial page had simply not told the truth — a readily accessible truth
at that. This misrepresentation, it might be added, hardly troubled the
HEW official, whose situation could not have been better. A conservative
administration had increased his budget. The most important liberal
editorial page in the nation had declared that his budget had been
slashed. He and all those associated with the program could take the
money without having to acknowledge receiving it. In 1973 this was the
best possible situation that a director of a "liberal" program could find
himself in, but it was not good for the United States.

———◆———

The Times news columns are impeccable but not infallible, and
something of Oakes's editorial page opinions eventually seeped into the
news reporting. The *Times* report that I would replace Scali recalled
the events of November, 1970, when I had last been offered the post. The
story continued: "Word of the offer leaked out at the time, and there
was some questioning about Mr. Moynihan's acceptability in view of his
often controversial ideas about civil rights and welfare. . . ." This
simply was not true, but it was the mark of a certain mind set.

Rather than cover the press conference held to announce my *Commentary* article, *The Times* had back in February sent its U.N. correspondent, Kathleen Teltsch, to interview me. A first-rate journalist,

she was not without a measure of indignation at the goings-on at the U.N. She told me of a just-concluded meeting of the Human Rights Commission in Geneva which had censured Israel for torturing Arabs. I said of the Human Rights Commission that it was packed with dictatorships whose jails were filled with their own people. We must not stand for such hypocrisy, I said: "We should rip the hides off everybody who presumes to talk about prisoners — shame them, hurt them, yell at them." It was not just the interests of Israel, I went on, but those of the United States that were at stake. Teltsch reported:

> . . . He said he was incensed also at the "obscene lies" uttered in the Colonialism Committee where, at Cuba's initiative, the United States has been attacked for supposedly repressing the political freedom and rights of Puerto Rico.
>
> "There is scarcely a member in the United Nations that is not guilty of far more discreditable situations and yet it would be unthinkable for us to make such charges against third-world countries although they do so routinely against us," he declared.

The celebrated Mr. Bouteflika of Algeria being then President of the General Assembly, I repeated the inquiry I had made in my article as to the health of Mr. Ahmed Ben Bella, the founder of the Algerian nation, now rotting in an Algerian jail. I was, I thought at the time of the interview, leaving government.

The *Times* headline in February read: "Moynihan Calls on U.S. to Start 'Raising Hell' in U.N." The *Times* editorial on my appointment, on May 3, took off from this and did not approve:

> *New Man at Turtle Bay*
> If he becomes Chief United States representative at the United Nations as expected, Daniel Patrick Moynihan will undoubtedly have a lot of fun, score debating points, generate publicity — and perhaps say some things that need saying. With a two-year hitch as Ambassador to India behind him, he is better qualified now than when former President Nixon offered him the U.N. job in late 1970.
> Yet, as Washington must have anticipated, the prospect of Mr. Moynihan at Turtle Bay has aroused among some friends of the United Nations genuine doubts about United States policy toward the world organization, and especially toward third-world countries, which he recently castigated in pungent language: "Shame them, hurt them, shout at them." In short, does Washington still view the United Nations as an essential if limited arena for constructive, collective diplomacy or — wounded by unfair criticism and a cascade of Assembly defeats through the "tyranny of the majority" — is the United States now out simply to respond in kind?

There was no integrity in this. I had not proposed that we go about shaming and hurting other countries. Just the opposite: I had said that we should defend the Jews against defamation, and vigorously if need be. But Oakes chose not to understand. It would go on this way.

Then there was Scali. He had still not been told, any more than Yost, and he was bitter at me. John Osborne of *The New Republic* told me in particular of Scali's conviction that I had wanted his job and had plotted to get it. The *Times* story on my appointment had noted that on the *Today Show,* I had "praised Ambassador Scali for a 'superb job' in making clear that the United States wanted to be part of the United Nations but had to state its position forcefully." Still, this was small consolation for Scali, who liked the job and was good at it.

When I read the *Times* editorial, I called Rumsfeld to say I simply could not take the job. Rumsfeld said he would not take the call, meaning he would not give the President such a message. I called Kissinger and said I couldn't take the job. He said I must. The following Friday, May 9, I sent them identical telegrams saying the same thing: "I MUST WITHDRAW. I WON'T TAKE THE JOB."

When my telegram reached the White House, Richard Cheney of the White House called to say Rumsfeld was in Nassau, but would be given the telegram on Monday. On that day Lawrence Eagleburger, Deputy Under Secretary of State, called to say the Secretary and the President could not accept my withdrawal. The next day, May 13, I called Eagleburger and then the White House to say I would stay in after all.

Later on, in June, *The New York Times* interviewer came around once again, and this time the result was "Moynihan Easing View on 3d World." It was reported that I wished to dispel a lingering suspicion among delegates that I was spoiling for a fight, that I was backing off a bit from my advocacy of "raising hell" at the U.N. and from my *Commentary* article:

> Mr. Moynihan retains the thesis that the United States should respond in kind when attacked, but he clearly thinks there are some wrong impressions around.
>
> The United States is fully aware, he says, that the center of concern for Asia and Africa is their drive to re-order the existing economic relationship between rich and poor.
>
> He suggests that his two recent years as Ambassador to India have given him some appreciation of this position, and his message to third-world countries is a direct one:
>
> "We have heard you. We are listening — listening hard."

This was perhaps no more than I had been saying all along, but it was as well, finally, to have it in print.

In between these events, I gave the Norman Wait Harris Memorial Foundation Lecture at the University of Chicago. The reception given to this lecture, "On Presenting the American Case," as much as any one thing, persuaded me to go to the U.N. The time was at hand, I said, to put our foreign policy purposes in sufficient perspective. In the period ahead there would be much talk about the decline of American influence in the world. This would give pleasure to many and instruction to some, so much so that a case could even be made for holding closely the knowledge that we had been declining ever since the peak of 1919, when the founding of Woodrow Wilson's League of Nations marked an American ascendancy greater than anything ever before or since. The end of World War II in 1945 had been nowhere near such a victory: "There, in 1945, was a world in ruins — or, in the case of colonial nations, still in fetters. Only the Western hemisphere escaped, and we stood astride it. All was humiliation save for us. How could we not be detested?" I recited the now-familiar theme of the Russian Revolution and the British Revolution, with the benefit of further reading such that I could add that in 1865 Charles Francis Adams had written from London: "The progress of the Liberal cause, not in England alone, but all over the world, is, in a measure, in our hands."

All this was changed now by the rise, as David Riesman would describe it, of the intellectual vision of a cooperative commonwealth rather than a competitive one. Save Riesman, few any longer could see that it was precisely the diffusion of ambition and of property in a capitalist society that made inquiry productive and politics possible. Marx, after all, lived off Engels's inheritance. Samuel Beer had helped greatly in sorting these things out, and the lecture reflected the help and the confidence he had given me:

> . . . The emerging international system . . . begins to reflect the bias for equality over liberty that is more and more in evidence in the world. . . . The liberal tradition can be utterly indifferent to equality and see it as quite opposed to liberty. . . . Correspondingly, the socialist tradition has room aplenty for liberty. . . . But as liberty is the first principle of liberalism, for socialism, and of necessity for communism, equality is the prime test. And equality is the great object of collectivist politics, as Samuel Beer has used the term.
>
> In that sense, world politics are becoming collectivist: an enormous change. . . . We have moved beyond the long-established arrangement that Wordsworth described in "Rob Roy's Grave":
>
> Sufficeth them, the simple plan,
> That they should take, who have the power,
> And they should keep who can.

> Which is not to say there are no nations that will any longer act in this way, but such actions (until they succeed?) will be depicted as illegitimate. . . .

Merely to proclaim equality was rarely to achieve it:

> . . . The world is now almost wholly given over to social equality and economic growth. But few have much of the former, and even a good deal of the latter produces only slow changes. In this setting, the temptation of governments is to direct attention to inequalities between nations. . . .

At a meeting of the Non-Aligned Bureau in Havana, Y. B. Chavan, the Indian Minister of External Affairs, had put it that the standard of living of the rich nations was the cause of the poverty of the others, a standard maintained while the earth's nonrenewable resources disappeared. That liberty seemed to be disappearing even faster seemed to matter little. And, at any rate, a ready answer was available: economic inequality has made freedom impossible.

Some further matters seemed equally clear. For one, matters were not likely to change. This made it all the more important for America to present its case, that case being no longer self-evident. Further, we were going to be much hampered by our own lack of confidence:

> We do not wholly believe our own case. There is the nub of it. If the influence of "American" political ideas in the world reached its high point in 1919, and has declined generally in the world ever since, that influence has declined in America also. . . . In the meantime, subsequent waves of doctrine have broken on these shores also, and have had their impact. Thus the Russian Revolution had an enormous, and after a point quite visible, impact on American intellectual life. . . .
>
> It would not quite be accurate to say that the wave of collectivist influence came next, as it did in the world at large. In reality, it came first. The American encounter with both socialism and communism has been greatly influenced by immigration, so much so as to be in some ways as much an ethnic phenomenon as an ideological one. Immigrants brought their doctrines with them, or were waiting when the doctrine, as it were, followed on the next ship. But socialism was a doctrine not only of continental Europe and suchlike regions of emigration, but of Britain also. Indeed the most prestigious and influential of all socialist movements — the least Marxist, by far the most liberal, and the most brainy — was British socialism, especially Fabian Socialism. . . . The time came in postwar America when avowedly communist ideas had become once again sectarian, at most a marginal influence on the culture. But socialist ideas had by then gained the widest currency, al-

though rarely with socialist labels. . . . Expenditure in the public sector, largely for the provision of social services and myriad forms of redistribution, rose to a third of the GNP. But somehow the point was lost as successive national administrations denied they were engaged in any such social transformation. . . .

So, I thought, a certain reeducation was necessary:

We must learn socialism as we once learned communism. There is, after all, a respectable record of our having found ways to comprehend, and eventually to interact with, Marxist-Leninist leaders. We have not much engaged the new nations at the level of ideology. . . . To meet the challenge so presented, low politics are going to have to be elevated somewhat. The United States government now has more than its share of intelligence and energy within its bounds, and more is yet available. But such talent will not be directed to this range of matters unless it is known that the issues are seen to be important. . . . It is an honored maxim of folk medicine that cures are found where maladies arise. Something similar holds in politics. The American response to communism in the world, and within America itself, was enormously informed, even fashioned, by persons who had been near to or even involved with that doctrine. In the present not so very different situation, it is on the Democratic Left that we are most likely to find both informed and unintimidated advocates of a vigorous American role in world-affairs and equally unashamed partisans of American performance. In the clamor of recent years, with so many newer voices and shriller ones raised in protest of one form or another, the social democrats of America have had difficulty being heard. . . . It is not that the labor movement and the social democrats like what we have, so much as that they are aware of the alternatives, and acculturated, if the term may be used, to the realm of ideology in which the American case must be presented. In time a foreign service might be trained to this task, but it will be difficult. . . . For the moment we should look to the defenders we have. As in point of fact we are not likely to do this, we must accordingly not expect to be well defended.

There were lighter moments, the sails beginning to fill. Limericks came readily. Extempore on the occasion of Catholic sociologist Andrew Greeley's forty-seventh birthday:

With countenance awesome and steely,
The Cardinal Archbishop said, "Really!
In the name of proportion,
I'll go with abortion,
But must I endure Father Greeley?"

Greeley in truth had given little pleasure to the hierarchy, certainly not that of Chicago, but much comfort to the faithful. He was among the best sociological minds in America, and through all the madness of the 1960s kept reporting that Americans were a liberal-minded people and growing more so, and in fact not at all ashamed of themselves or their country. Speak up for us, he said as I left for the U.N. (Theodore H. White quoted Danton's more refined but not less bold version of the same sentiment: *"De l'audace, et encore de l'audace, et toujours de l'audace!"*) Saul Bellow came to the Chicago lecture and was equally rallying. I knew what I had to say now, and people who mattered to me were telling me to do so.

I had talked throughout these spring weeks at Cambridge and in New York with Podhoretz and Wilson, Kristol and Bell, but with none more than Leonard Garment. He had been a partner in the law firm Nixon joined in 1963, and, although a Democrat, in turn joined Nixon's 1968 presidential campaign. He went to Washington and remained to the end, faithful alike to the President he worked for and the standards of personal honor he set for himself. He was far my closest friend in my two years there. With Nixon gone, Garment was at last back in New York, saddened but not diminished. Ford had appointed him the United States Representative to the Human Rights Commission and he felt entirely as I did about that body. He urged me to take the U.N. post. As I went through the indecision of May, he kept urging. Finally he said that if I went, he would go with me. This made it possible to think both of taking the job and of surviving it, for no one knew Henry Kissinger better than he. Knew every mood and every device, and most of the secrets. Perhaps *two* of us would be his equal!

One evening in New York it came to us. We would make human rights the theme of the next General Assembly.

There was one other man we would need for this: Clarence M. Mitchell, Jr., Washington director of the National Association for the Advancement of Colored People. I had known him longer, though Garment perhaps better. Every civil rights initiative by the federal government for two decades had Clarence Mitchell's mark on it. He was perhaps the most skilled parliamentarian and effective advocate of human rights in the United States, and it was time he took on the United Nations. I had published an article in the April issue of *The Crisis*, the journal of the N.A.A.C.P., and was in touch with him. He came to lunch in New York and agreed to be the public member of the delegation to the Thirtieth General Assembly.

If I could leave Harvard there was no reason Suzanne Weaver could not leave Yale, which she did. And that was our merry band.

It wasn't all disapproval from *The Times*. I had called James Reston on the morning of May third, to say, as I was saying to everyone else that day, that I was just not up to taking any more such editorials. "Who reads them?" he asked, and on May 23 he did his best to make up:

> President Ford's appointment of . . . Moynihan to be his ambassador to the United Nations is being attacked on the ground that Pat is too blunt, too dramatic and combative to represent the United States at so delicate a time in world history. . . .
>
> Like all other institutions, the United Nations is changing, redefining its rules and its mission in the world. It has a limited but important role to play in a hungry and divided world that is already in the middle of a class war between the rich and the poor nations — and doesn't quite know it.
>
> The coming session of the United Nations General Assembly this autumn, however, will bring this issue between the industrial nations to the fore, and while Mr. Moynihan will not determine U.S. policy, he will be its spokesman — and the guess here is that he will be the most effective ambassador we have had at the U.N. since Adlai Stevenson.

When I finally decided to take the U.N. job, on May 13, I called Lawrence Eagleburger, Deputy Under Secretary of State, to say so. I added that I felt the nomination should go forward promptly and that I should be on board July first. He called back the same day to report that "Fat Heinz," as he was pleased to refer to the Secretary of State, agreed. He added that he had told Scali that he must leave and must not talk. There are gentler callings in this world than the higher reaches of the American public service.

The President nominated me on May 21. The Committee on Foreign Relations, or more accurately, Senator Percy, held a hearing June 4. Galbraith on his own sent a wonderfully warm letter on behalf of, as he put it, "my fellow Ambassador to India; my fellow faculty member; my next-door neighbor; and though I have no wish to damage him in the eyes of any of the Republican members of the Committee, my fellow Democrat."

This was a new development. I had never in any way ceased to be a Democrat, but now was being claimed as one. In Washington, the Women's National Democratic Club had me to lunch. On June 4 the Coalition for a Democratic Majority presented me a scroll for my work on behalf of "a strong America in national defense, international affairs, human rights and economic life." Bayard Rustin made the presentation, Senator Henry Jackson presided, and Senator Hubert Humphrey, scheduled to be present but three functions behind, cheered from somewhere across Washington.

———◆———

On June 10 the "Notes on People" column of *The New York Times* reported that I had been confirmed by the Senate, "without debate or even objection. . . ." Thus I was sworn in June 30 in the Rose Garden. President Ford invited Elizabeth and me and the children into the Oval Office before the ceremony. He asked my view of events in India, where four days earlier Mrs. Gandhi had suspended civil liberties and canceled the forthcoming elections. "Mr. President," I replied. "Look at it this way. Under your administration the United States has become the world's largest democracy."

———◆———

5

Geneva

THAT SAME EVENING, June 30, the A.F.L.-C.I.O. gave a great dinner in Washington for Aleksandr Solzhenitsyn. It was a political event of consequence, and this was clear even at the time. Those who went to the Solzhenitsyn dinner and those who did not thereby divided.

The speech was like nothing anyone present was likely to have heard. Long and, throughout, passionate. Yet detailed and argumentative; an historian's speech, almost. Solzhenitsyn reminded us that it had been Alexander Shliapnikov, a worker, a lathe operator, and not the émigré intellectuals (certainly not Lenin) who had headed the Communist Party in Russia; who had brought about the revolution and been destroyed by it, for he saw the Communist leadership betraying the workers and oppressing the proletariat and forming itself into a bureaucracy.

The speech was also, somehow, that of a professed Christian, a Russian Orthodox Christian. It shared little with the Russian and Polish Jews who could well have been half the audience at the Washington Hilton. There was evident discomfort as Solzhenitsyn went on about the perfidies of Franklin D. Roosevelt, who had recognized Stalin's regime; some unease when he asserted that the British unionists had disgraced

themselves by visiting so-called trade unionists in Russia and receiving
visits in return. Most discomfiting of all — for it was not an easy evening
— the speaker somehow was someone who knew about *us*. He appeared,
his first time ever in the United States, bearded and speaking Russian
and scarcely able to know where he was, much less to whom precisely he
was speaking, and yet he knew what was going on here. He knew secrets,
and the knowledge gave him a stunning strength.

His message, for all this foreignness and all this secret knowledge, was
simple enough. The Soviet system was fundamentally evil, and had been
from the first, from Lenin. "When many lies have accumulated over the
decades," he said, "we forget the radical and basic lie which is not on the
leaves of the tree but at its very roots." Almost alone of American institutions, he allowed, labor had shared his own perception that the
totalitarians had been advancing for three decades: "China and the
Soviet Union, both actively participating in détente, have quietly
grabbed three countries of Indochina." And at this very time, ". . . you
have some hysterical public figure who said: 'I will go to North Vietnam.
I will stand on my knees and beg them to release our prisoners of war.'
This isn't a political act — this is masochism." And more: "You had an
instance in the United States where a bugging caused an uproar which
lasted for a year and a half. For us it's an everyday matter." And still
more:

> . . . The United States of America has long shown itself to be the
> most magnanimous, the most generous country in the world. Wherever
> there is a flood, an earthquake, a fire, a natural disaster, disease, who is
> the first to help? The United States. Who helps the most and un-
> selfishly? The United States.
>
> And what do we hear in reply? Reproaches, curses, "Yankee Go
> Home." American cultural centers are burned, and the representatives
> of the Third World jump on tables to vote against the United States.

But — Solzhenitsyn did not relent — our responsibility was inescapable:

> . . . this does not take the load off America's shoulders. The course
> of history — whether you like it or not — has made you the leaders of
> the world. Your country can no longer think provincially. Your politi-
> cal leaders can no longer think only of their own states, only of their
> parties, of petty arrangements which may or may not lead to promotion.
> You must think about the whole world, and when the new political
> crisis in the world will arise (I think we have just come to the end of a
> very acute crisis and the next one will come any moment), the main
> decisions will fall anyway on the shoulders of the United States of
> America.

Introducing Solzhenitsyn, George Meany spoke simply and well of his guest, and then, with a glance at me, seated between A. Philip Randolph and Melvin Laird, said:

> We need echoes of his voice. We need to hear the echoes in the White House. We need to hear the echoes in the Congress and in the State Department and in the universities and in the media, and if you please, Mr. Moynihan, in the United Nations.

Meany said of his own labor movement what his espousal of Solzhenitsyn had made clear: "The American trade union movement, from its beginnings to the present, has been dedicated to the firm unyielding belief in freedom. Freedom for all mankind, as well as for ourselves."

The three members of the Cabinet present, myself and John Dunlop and James Schlesinger, were half of the six professors in Gerald Ford's Cabinet. As for the others, Edward Levi stayed out of politics, and Earl Butz wouldn't have been expected to go. It was Kissinger whose presence might have been expected, and who did not go. Worse, when it was proposed that Solzhenitsyn meet with the President at the White House, Kissinger had said no.

Kissinger knew his mind, but at this point he did not know the country. His tactics at home were largely mechanical: a blow to the left, a blow to the right. In April, for instance, as the end was at hand in Vietnam, he suddenly began blaming the Congress, or, rather, getting the President to do so. (Which — this was wholly reflexive by now — would enable him to say to Congressmen that they should help him protect them against the President by giving him something that would make the President feel better.) On April 17, Carroll Kilpatrick began a Washington *Post* story: "President Ford yesterday refused to blame Peking and Moscow for the debacle in Vietnam and asserted that if the United States had maintained its aid commitment, 'this whole tragedy could have been eliminated.'" Michael Janeway wrote that this was "in effect saying to Congress, 'OK, if you guys want to play in this game, you've got to do what we want, or we get to say that you lost Vietnam, betrayed our allies, rolled over for the dirty reds.'" In Schlesinger's view, Kissinger had risked compounding the disaster of the fall of Saigon by keeping the Embassy there to the very last moment, gambling with lives, hoping for one last deal. The North Vietnamese could have stormed the Embassy compound days before we finally left, but did not. A favor to be cashed in later? Or did they think it better that Americans should spend their evenings in April watching televised Marines club South Vietnamese trying to get over the walls to be on the American side? This was the price the President paid for keeping the Secretary of

State. It was worth it, but there was even so a price, and the White House staff knew this. Kissinger, after becoming Secretary, had at first insisted on remaining Assistant to the President for National Security Affairs and keeping his White House office. Rumsfeld had finally got him out of the building, but Gerald Ford had not yet taken hold of foreign policy, and people knew this. In a national poll taken at the time by the Chicago Council on Foreign Relations, "leaders" were asked who was currently playing a very important role in determining U.S. foreign policy. Ninety-seven percent named the Secretary of State: 51 percent named the President.

The White House staff knew this also, and were not above a certain maneuvering. They took some care that the President associate himself with the position I had staked out. At the June 30 Rose Garden swearing-in ceremony, he had declared that the United States would resist efforts of the Third World countries to "exploit the machinery of the United Nations for narrow political interests." That became *The New York Times*'s lead on the story, which continued: "Mr. Ford in effect endorsed a statement earlier this year by Mr. Moynihan that it was 'time for the United States to go into the United Nations and every other international forum and start raising hell' with its critics."

———◆———

The American labor movement remained in ways the most internationalist of any of the great institutions of American political and economic life. Only the oil companies and the banks (and of these only a few) were more involved in international affairs. The internationalist roots of labor went back to its beginnings in the 1880s, and had been preserved by an extraordinary continuity of leadership. The Americans were from the first quite at home with the socialist unions of Europe — there were hardly any other kind — and were ever at odds with the Communists. Here the American unions had an experience unique to American institutions: Communists had seriously sought to infiltrate and take them over. Irving Howe has estimated that at their height, in the 1930s, Communists controlled a third of the C.I.O. The institutional and personal memory of this was strong. In his long apprenticeship as Secretary-Treasurer of the A.F.L., Meany had become deeply involved in the international labor movement of the postwar years, and in the struggle against the Communist forces in both Western and Eastern Europe. Solzhenitsyn in his Washington speech could refer to an amazingly accurate map of the *Gulag* which the A.F.L. had published in 1947, at a time when few persons in the West knew anything about Stalin's prison camps; and of those who did, fewer spoke. This anti-Communism, arrived at in part through the American connection with the social democracy of Europe, was deep-rooted in the A.F.L.-C.I.O. Washington headquarters, and deep-rooted as well in Meany's Secretary-Treasurer, Lane Kirkland, a man of intellect, integrity, and, in these matters, zeal. Others came and went in Washington; the labor people stayed. Year in and year out their pronouncements, and their resources, were unsparingly directed to international affairs. A month after the Solzhenitsyn dinner, the A.F.L.-C.I.O. Executive Council held its semi-annual meeting in Chicago. A third of the resolutions adopted there concerned foreign affairs: the I.L.O., the Helsinki agreements, "India, a democracy in chaos," "Portugal and détente," "Russian grain purchases." Last, an appeal for funds for the *Jewish Daily Forward,* the Yiddish-language publication of the Russian socialist immigrants of the turn of the century: ". . . Over the years, it generously gave substantial material assistance to strikers on the picket lines, to unionists defending their organizations from Communist attacks, to countless labor, liberal and humanitarian causes at home and throughout the world."

Yet when the Council on Foreign Relations poll asked "leaders" which persons or institutions played a very important role in determining American foreign policy, only 6 percent picked labor unions. This surely reflected in part the elite cast of foreign policy decision-making. In part also it reflected the growing distance between the way in which the labor leadership continued to view the world and the changing perceptions of others, brought on by events, most notably the Vietnam war.

At about this time, William Watts reported an extraordinary turn in public opinion in a study he entitled "What Kind of People Are We?" In 1964, Americans asked to express the level of their concern about a broad range of domestic and international issues gave emphatic priority to international affairs and defense. By 1974, in a similar poll, the first international or defense issue ranked seventeenth in a list of thirty. In Watts's term, a "vast turnabout" had occurred. Isolationist sentiment had doubled in a decade. By 1975, 71 percent of the population agreed that "we shouldn't think so much in international terms but concentrate more on our own national problems. . . ." This change did not come about from any special surge of concern for welfare issues, which had also fallen back on the list of priorities. What had occurred was a displacement of one set of upper-class concerns with another. "Environmental degradation" now came ahead of military defense.

On July 1 I stopped by the U.S. Mission in New York to fly my flag, then traveled to Geneva, where the annual meeting of the Economic and Social Council was opening. A message was waiting from McGeorge

Bundy. The meeting of the World Food Council in Rome had fallen apart. The Non-Aligned nations had demanded the departure of John Hannah, who had come out of retirement to be executive director of the new council that the World Food Conference had established the previous year. Hannah was quite shaken, and the situation a ruin. Food was an intensely symbolic as well as real issue at this time. A succession of events — the Soviet grain purchases of 1975, the Club of Rome report on the limits to growth, continued bad weather in the African Sahel — all combined with the general clamor for a new international economic order to make for an intensely emotional atmosphere whenever the issue was discussed in a forum that included the United States. The famine widely predicted in the early 1970s never came to pass. The one exception occurred in 1973 when there almost certainly was a major famine in Ethiopia, with as many as half a million persons dying; but the government of Emperor Haile Selassie chose not to say anything about it, indeed to deny it. There may well also have been famine in Nepal that year, but it is not clear that the government of Nepal knew about it. For the rest, world food supplies steadily grew. It was world food conferences that were ruinous.

The conference at Rome in 1974 had created the World Food Council to see that the agenda of action agreed to at the meeting actually got carried out. An Egyptian, Sayed Marei, who had been Secretary-General of the Conference, became president of the Council. Hannah, formerly head of the Agency for International Development and president of Michigan State University, had served as deputy to Marei at the Conference, and thereafter agreed to be executive director of the Council. Its first meeting convened in Rome in June, 1975. The Non-Aligned countries, led by Mexico, Bangladesh, Senegal, and Guinea, stormed in, charging that the new Secretariat was unrepresentative of the new nations, and demanding in effect Hannah's resignation. Whatever the true objective of the Non-Aligned leaders, they achieved what they had achieved with earlier conferences, which was to have the whole effort depicted as a failure. A typical press report read:

> World Food Parley Offers Little for the Hungry
> Millions of hungry and undernourished people in Africa, Asia, and Latin America drew scant encouragement from the first meeting of a new United Nations body, the 36-member World Food Council, which ended in disarray here last week.

I asked that Hannah come to Geneva.

John Hannah had three qualities which seemed to me of the first importance. He was an American official in a world organization. He was an old and admired friend of the President of the United States. He was a supremely well qualified and dedicated man. The Secretariat whose control was being contested consisted of nine persons, all of them borrowed from other U.N. agencies. For this, Bangladesh — Bangladesh! — would break up the first meeting of the World Food Council!

In his opening address to the Economic and Social Council meeting, its president, Iqbal Akhund of Pakistan, spoke directly and graciously to the new American, and particularly to the *Commentary* article. The role of the opposition in a parliamentary system, he said, was an honorable, necessary, and constructive one; a well-led opposition could look forward one day to becoming a majority and should do so. A promising start.

There are fifty-four members of ECOSOC, so that a good portion of the U.N. Permanent Representatives were on hand in Geneva. Of them all, Akhund was quite the most impressive. British without the fatuity that had come over the British. As president of ECOSOC he contrived to represent the institution itself more than his own nation, but without the least disservice to Pakistan's national interests. The one thing he did make certain was that India was not elected to ECOSOC while he was president. Neither was India at this time a member of the Security Council, although it had been assumed that the second most populous nation in the world would always hold a seat on one or the other of these two U.N. bodies. The Indian Ambassador was simply outclassed, and it made a difference.

There were four ECOSOC vice presidents. Mills of Jamaica, an economist and evidently a good one, was much given to reassuring homilies about the North-South conflict. It was, he would say, a trade union dispute. It would be protracted, and the language would grow heated, but in the end there would be a settlement, for management simply cannot do without a work force. Smid of Czechoslovakia was said by Westerners to be a liberal, and he hinted at this. (He was not.) Ake of the Ivory Coast had no noticeable views. Longerstaey of Belgium, true to the genetic confusion of that estuary, had neither views nor features.

Clarence C. Ferguson, Jr., was on hand as the U.S. representative. He was to return to the Harvard Law School at the end of August. Robert W. Kitchen, Jr., head of the ECOSOC Affairs Office of the U.S. Mission, and an old acquaintance, served as Ambassador Ferguson's deputy. Blacks, both had surrounded themselves with black secretaries and black Foreign Service officers. This symbolism was presumably meant to be a substitute for ideas as to what to do with or at ECOSOC.

Good men both, neither, however, had any ideas of his own on the subject, and, more important, neither had any instructions.

They had been sent with nothing to do, to Geneva, and so busied themselves with luncheon parties, a sensible response.

———◆———

It was by now common to hear the world described in images that suggested it was growing smaller: a global village, a Spaceship Earth. All manner of writers were discovering that the world had become interdependent. (Marx and Engels used the term in the *Communist Manifesto*.) Less common, but nonetheless recurrent, was the observation that while the world might be growing smaller, there was also a sense in which it was becoming more complex. The number of states that were recognized members of the international community had grown very considerably in only half a century. Forty-one states started the League of Nations, with a handful of defeated powers temporarily excluded. Fifty-one states started the United Nations, again with a handful of powers temporarily excluded. But by 1975 membership in the U.N. had reached 144, and seating arrangements were being worked out for 165. It was becoming necessary to revise Orwell's forecast for 1984. Orwell lived at the very last moment of a period of world history, some three to four centuries in duration, in which political units, in the main, grew larger, the Turkish Empire being the one exception. This was immediately followed by a period in which they grew smaller, the Russian Empire being the present exception. The world had not, after all, evolved with a relentless logic into three vast sovereignties locked in desultory but permanent conflict. Rather the opposite case could be made: that something closer to regression has been taking place, that the world has been relapsing into the timeless mode of tribal fragmentation and strife; that in man's future lay anarchy, not dominion. On the other hand, the possibility emerged that these seemingly contradictory movements, a global village of ever increasing distinct sovereignties, were resolving themselves by the emergence of coalitions which served in effect as world political parties. In the experience of Western politics, parties have been tolerated more than welcomed. James Madison was more tolerant than most, but almost alone Burke argued that party would give stability and longevity to ideals and standards of public conduct that a political order must have. These ideals and standards might reside in great men, but great men being no less mortal than others, they could not in that way endure very long. Party was needed to institutionalize them, and party in time became a defining institution of modern politics, both of the idealistic and the not-so-idealistic varieties.

The beginnings of party made their appearance fairly early at the United Nations with the founding of the "Non-Aligned" group, led by Nehru, Sukarno, and Tito. This survived the first leaders, as theory would have had it do. American policy was never friendly to this development. There was to be one party in the United Nations, we thought, and that was ours. It was not until 1974 that a Secretary of State, on a visit to India, declared, "The United States accepts non-alignment." Those had been my words, or in any event my proposition, for it seemed to me that the new nations had every reason to organize if they were to manage their affairs in a coherent and instrumental fashion. Party arises with the advent of representative institutions and the expansion of the suffrage. Neither the League nor the U.N. had evolved out of representative impulses, but the principle of representation made headway nonetheless. I rather approved the Non-Aligned and the "Group of 77" in the General Assembly, and reassured myself that in opposition our function was to oppose. I felt there were votes to be gathered to our side in these forums and influence to be had. And so with some serenity I waited about in Geneva with no instructions myself, especially after I realized that the developing nations had no instructions either. They would meet in Lima in August. They would put together there the program with which we would deal after Labor Day. In the meantime there was lunch.

On July 4 I met at breakfast with the Secretary-General, Kurt Waldheim. I knew him slightly from the Twenty-Sixth General Assembly, when he had been chosen. Our candidate had been Max Jacobsen, of Finland, whom the Russians wouldn't have. Waldheim, who had served on the Eastern Front during World War II, was then put forward. Faced with a choice between anti-Semitism and antifascism, the Russians came down on the side of enduring values, and Waldheim won. I remarked to Bush at the time that our candidate had been a Jewish socialist but we had settled for a German infantry officer.

Waldheim's term would expire in 1976. Kissinger had told him he would have our support for a second term, and I now repeated this to Waldheim, hoping to make clear that Kissinger told me such things.

An entirely decent man, the Secretary-General functioned as a post office, a somewhat antique but reasonably efficient public service run along Austro-Hungarian lines. As one sat down with him, he would be mentally sorting the mail while making small conversation. The Africans, he would say on this particular occasion, simply do not understand the demands on his time. The Chinese deputy had agreed with him on this, and had remarked that the Chinese, by contrast, had been "civilized for centuries." So it would go, until finally: Here is a Special Delivery for *you*. Again, on this occasion: The United Nations will have to deal with the forthcoming independence of Spanish Morocco. Algeria does not want it to be divided between Morocco and Mauritania, as seems in prospect. Accordingly Algeria wishes Spain to hold onto her colony for yet a bit. Next a postcard from Vietnam. It had been difficult, but it was over. Nothing else that day.

I then turned in the various items we wished him to deliver elsewhere. First, a general circular that we mustn't be pushed around anymore. We were very much committed to the U.N., and that was *why* we could not any longer allow it to present such an unfavorable image to the American people. As a mark of our commitment we would be nominating William B. Buffum, Assistant United States Secretary of State for International Organization Affairs, to succeed Bradford Morse, then Under-Secretary-General of the United Nations for Political and General Assembly Affairs. Mr. Morse would then succeed Mr. Rudolph A. Peterson as administrator of the United Nations Development Programme. Waldheim thereupon turns up another letter. The West Germans hope Peterson can stay on for another year. I say I will find out.

As to the "unfortunate" events at the recently concluded meeting of the World Food Council, Waldheim goes on, this surely would not have occurred if the various monies pledged had actually been paid. (For which read: You and I know that you haven't paid up, but you will no doubt at some appropriate future time remember that I chose to think of this as an administrative matter, and not one tending to cast doubt on the good faith of your great nation.) I say this interpretation is unacceptable. John Hannah will stay on as executive secretary for one more year, and if there is to be any more money there are to be no more such incidents. Message complete.

◆

Not to know the spirit of Geneva — nor know something of the League of Nations — is a handicap to anyone who would understand the United Nations in New York, from the uniformed *commissionnaires* waiting to transport visitors in the elevators to the blond wood furniture and baskets of peaches in the delegates' dining room overlooking the East River, to the politics of the place itself. Those who knew the parent organization still think of the U.N. in terms of the League. *"La Société des . . ."* comes out easily in small exchanges. An institution took root on the shores of Lac Léman in the 1920s and 1930s, and it has merely continued to grow on the East River. To this moment the largest number of U.N. employees is to be found in Geneva, and the organizational spirit of Geneva both informs and haunts the successor. This is the spirit of a civil service as an elite class. In the European experience, the emergence of such an elite was a bridge between the aristocracy of preindustrial society and the bulging undifferentiated bureaucracies of the collectivist era. The status of the higher civil servants was, ostensibly, an achieved one, but the achievement came before the career began. Which is to say, it lay in education and the taking of examinations: not quite a matter of birth, but something inherited from a prior period of life, a partly aristocratic principle. Thus there was an era when *The Times* of London would routinely report both the births of younger sons of peers *and* the Oxford and Cambridge "double firsts." This was of the age of the *haute école* and the *inspecteurs des finances*. Once achieved, status became *as if* ascribed.

American civil servants, striving from one grade to another, no sooner breaking out of the low reaches than to face sudden death by "up-or-out" selection boards, could never fathom these organizations and had little success in them. Waldheim, by contrast, was wholly at ease. He was head of an organization whose qualities perforce were to a large degree his own qualities, its disposition his own disposition. None of the institutional influences bearing on him were responsive to American interests or styles. Thus by 1975 there was no American influence of any kind in the Secretariat. It was understood that certain posts — to be precise, within the Secretariat, one post — would be ours, and this was given as a retirement benefit to a succession of persons: a Congressman such as Morse, a Foreign Service officer such as Buffum. As long as we raised the money for the development fund, we could have directorship there as well. This would have been tolerable if the League system had actually been preserved. It had been a system uniquely fashioned to serve parliamentary nations where party governments could safely come and go because of the continuity provided by the permanent government of the bureaucracy. In addition to the intensely meritocratic selection process, this League Secretariat had two decisive characteristics. First, it was small — tiny, in fact. In these circumstances pay and conditions could be quite favorable, and commonly were. Young men from the civil services of Britain and France who came to work for the League or the I.L.O. in 1920 were given twenty-year contracts, and it was assumed that at the expiration of this period of service most would simply retire — in their late forties, not an unusual age in the nineteenth century — and would have quite a sufficient pension on which to do so. A second characteristic of the League bureaucracy was that it was loyal to the system, but otherwise neutral. But now, with respect to both size and neutrality, the United Nations system had become profoundly corrupt. Envision the British Home Office of 1900 enlarged five hundredfold, teeming with the incompetent appointees of decadent peers and corrupt borough councillors, infiltrated and near to immobilized by agents of the Black Hand, Sinn Fein, and the Rosicrucians (some falsely representing themselves as devotees of Madame Blavatsky). That approximates the United Nations Secretariat three quarters of a century later.

Of all of Waldheim's principals, only Brian E. Urquhart, Under-Secretary-General for Political Affairs, could be said to carry on the tradition of the great generalists; only Erik Suy, the Legal Counsel, measured up to the professional standards which his rank entitled the world to expect. Arkady N. Shevchenko, Under-Secretary-General for Political and Security Council Affairs (the United States "got" the General Assembly, the Soviets "got" the Security Council) was the leading Soviet representative within the Secretariat, and a striking representative both of the totalitarian principles at war with the principles of the Charter, and of the far greatest success of the Soviets in making their way within the corrupt U.N. Secretariat. Shevchenko was a man of *authority*. Important enough to have a KGB agent of his own keeping an eye on him. (So important, indeed, that he could afford to be charming.) Possibly a future Foreign Minister of All Russia. And, in any event, for the present, authoritatively the *voice* of Russia. The Russians and the Chinese made no pretense of abiding by the old League of Nations rules of an international civil service. Secretariat members and members of the diplomatic corps lived together in the now-familiar compounds, and related to one another in terms of respective rank in their own civil services. The Russians were known on occasion to complain at having to turn over their U.N. salary checks in return for the smaller stipend paid Soviet diplomats, but then, Russians generally complained a good deal. For the rest of the Secretariat, if there were complaints, they were hard to take seriously.

As with most matters concerning government, architecture told most. The buildings of the League had reflected the purposes of the organization. The I.L.O. got a start on everyone else, and by 1920 opened its office at the edge of Lac Léman. It was a sensible building — not entirely an office. It was both a monument of sorts to the international labor movement *and* a place where work got done. The Palais des Nations, not finished until 1937, was verily a palace: a palace of entrance halls and receiving rooms, of vast corridors and great assembly rooms and grand terraces with spectacular views. The representatives of nations were to be seen there, conducting the affairs of state. There were servant quarters, to be sure, and these were typically at the top and in the back. The United Nations building complex in Turtle Bay had quite a different symbolism. There was a General Assembly hall, the entrance for the public being far grander than that for the delegates, who arrived on a lower level, rather like performers for the evening's opera or ballet. In an effort at socialist realism, or some such thing, air conditioning ducts and the occasional I-beam were left exposed. All suggested a vision of the delegates as a work force. By contrast, the Secretariat was apotheosized, its shimmering glass stele towering forty stories over assembly hall and meeting rooms alike, reducing delegates and delegators to the insignificance of tiny markings on the plaza far below. In the 1960s in Geneva there had been a great building boom by the specialized agencies. Here delegates were dispensed with altogether. On great Nervi poles the bureaucracy fashioned their dream world and retired into it. The new International Labor Office, high up on the slope now, was luxurious to the point of sensuality. The restaurant was of an *haute cuisine* decor such that there cannot have been a workman in the world who would have felt free to enter there, save to fix something.

The qualities of the League Secretariat ought not to be forgotten. It could harbor persons with great capacity for work. Thus in the 1930s Simon Kuznets was a member of the League Secretariat, in consequence of which the League's economic papers were the best the world had known. Forty years later all this had disappeared, or almost all. The mode of the Secretariat was indulgence, and the talk was of retirement settlements: all in Swiss francs and in six figures.

In New York the United Nations building boom of the 1960s almost aborted. It had been judged that owing to the shifting focus of U.N. activities to areas such as hunger, malnutrition, famine, disease, fire, and flood, and above all poverty and disadvantage, a second Secretariat building would be necessary. But the United States Congress balked and would not put up the necessary funds as it had done for the original. In New York, however, a group of citizens, headed by John J. McCloy, persuaded Governor Rockefeller and the state legislature to enact legislation establishing a public corporation that could sell moral obligation bonds with which to construct this new building. Kevin Roche, who had designed the memorial to the Ford Foundation around the corner, was accordingly engaged, and a thirty-nine-story building went up on United Nations Plaza. For the convenience of the functionaries who would use the building, six stories in the middle were reserved for a hotel. At the dedication ceremonies in 1975, a brochure describing the new facility was included in the press kit. The cover carried the plain announcement: "United Nations Plaza Hotel. New York's Newest Refuge for the Privileged."

I paid diplomatic calls in Geneva, first on Gamani Corea, Secretary-General of the United Nations Conference on Trade and Development, an engaging Sri Lankan. His problem was that the entire rationale for UNCTAD rested on the assertion that terms of trade for the developing nations have been steadily deteriorating. He had appointed a committee of experts headed by Henrik Houthakker of Harvard to press this assertion further. Unfortunately they had come up with the finding that the terms of trade had *not* deteriorated for the new nations. The Houthakker committee was made up mostly of representatives of the Third World, or more accurately the Fourth World, as that term is coming to be understood. But it was also a committee of *economists,* and they had been faithful to their profession. I had picked up a copy of the report from Houthakker in May, after the press had reported the findings, and realized it would affect the coming debate, even if no one acknowledged it.

The International Labor Organization was constituted as a body of representatives of government, business, and labor. Delegates of business and labor were and are presumed by the I.L.O. charter to be independent of government. But what was to be done with the delegations from Bulgaria, or the Central African Republic, in which such distinctions did not exist? In 1965 I had proposed to Arthur Goldberg that he take the initiative in calling for an I.L.O. constitutional convention on its fiftieth anniversary, which would be in 1969, to see what changes could be made to accommodate a liberal constitutional charter — drafted, for all practical purposes, prior to the advent of the totalitarian state — and the new realities that followed. Nothing of the sort happened, and the I.L.O. in consequence was near to paralysis by 1975.

Amadou M'Bow, Director-General of UNESCO, was also in Geneva at this time, lamenting that the Congress had withheld the U.S. contribution to his organization. He had no English, and seemed not at all to follow my discourse on the significance of the fact that the sponsors of the legislation withholding UNESCO funds were Congressman Jonathan B. Bingham of New York, who had been our ambassador to ECOSOC under Adlai Stevenson, and Senator Clifford Case of New Jersey, both committed liberals and normally supporters of the United Nations. The trouble in UNESCO arose from a resolution condemning

Israeli archeologists for "desecrations" in the course of their excavations of the Wailing Wall in Jerusalem. I was willing to entertain the possibility that the Israelis had been high-handed in these matters. Even so, UNESCO had behaved outrageously. M'Bow had appointed a Belgian archeologist to investigate the dispute. Evidently the report exonerated the Israelis. In consequence, M'Bow would not release it. He attempted to explain this to me. I had as little success understanding his explanation as he did my attempts to tell him nicely that he was lying.

———————◆———————

Dr. Abd-El Rahman Khane of Algeria was a francophone also but of a very different order from Mr. M'Bow. Dr. Khane had fought the French in the great Algerian insurrection, and had beaten them. He thereafter went abroad for his new nation, and served for some years as head of the OPEC office in Vienna, before he was made Director-General of the United Nations Industrial Development Organization. This was the man for me, or so I thought, and so I was assured. If the U.N. were to do anything in development, the single greatest task was to break out of the steel-mill fixation and develop along the lines of natural resources and comparative advantage. Khane and I dined at the Intercontinental Hotel in Geneva on July 8. I brought the subject around to Calcutta, the greatest industrial city of the developing world. We got nowhere. I pressed on until at length it came to me: the Director-General of the United Nations Industrial Development Organization had never heard of Calcutta.

It would be a profound mistake to take this to be a measure of Khane's personal qualities. To the contrary, he was clearly a man of the first abilities. It was merely that he had other interests. His interest was Algeria, his focus was Europe, and his constituency was the producers of oil and gas. He asked at dinner whether Calcutta was a place on the way to the Taj Mahal. When told it was not, he showed no further interest in just where it might be. It was not in Algeria.

———————◆———————

On July 3, I met with Sigvard Eklund, head of the International Atomic Energy Agency. He was everything you would want such a man to be. His agency is the one U.N. institution the world could not very well do without. It is accordingly, I suppose, an argument for all the others. At the Stanford commencement I had spoken of the great, all-but-unnoticed consequence of the OPEC oil price increase. Atomic energy does not become economic until the price of oil (in 1973 dollars) passes three dollars or so a barrel. In 1973 it looked as if it would take a generation for this to happen, and accordingly the world had a generation to deal with the proliferation of plutonium. Then the price of oil went to twelve dollars in one afternoon. Two dozen nations that were thinking of atomic power in the next century suddenly needed it the next day.

———◆———

Prince Sadruddin Aga Khan, United Nations High Commissioner for Refugees, entertains well at his palace across the lake. In the Twenty-Sixth General Assembly Bush and I had talked with him about the Secretary Generalship, when Jacobsen was being blocked. He gave the air not so much of breeding as of having been bred, rather like one of his father's horses: beautifully muscled, lovingly groomed, and fast as hell. For two years in India I had made my dutiful way through the forlorn palaces of assorted Nizams and Maharajahs of the old realm. Their privy purses had been taken away soon after independence, and all that was left unsold was unsellable. I had begun to doubt that it had all been real. But no, here it was in Geneva, only slightly altered by the change of air. Half Surrey, half Hyderabad. The large fireplaces and small boxes and photographs in silver frames; women and horses; horses and women; the occasional monarch; *many* Queen Mothers. A furlong of candelabra led from the sitting room to the dining hall. I am not sure how much he would have enjoyed being Secretary-General.

———◆———

On July 10, Kissinger arrived in Geneva for talks with Gromyko and sent immediately for me. I was in trouble, this was clear. Into the bedroom, away from the aides: "Listen, how *could* you have gone to that dinner for Solzhenitsyn!" He was more angry than I had ever seen him; surely more than he had ever been with me. Angry no doubt with himself for what he was saying; doubly angry that he was saying it to me and knowing that it would have no effect and that anyway it was he who'd made me take the job. There I'd been at the dinner, next to Schlesinger. There I'd be, in the Cabinet, next to Schlesinger. What had he done?

None of this was calculated, as his anger sometimes was. It went on until it was over. Then he was confiding, and truthful, or so I chose to believe. My notes on the occasion are brief:

> . . . reads Sol. /Thinks more like him than anyone save me. /Israel tragedy. Jews. /Force immediate settlement — communities. 200 km wide on our terms. /Dulles — Peace Movement — Vietnam. /I agree with Sol. on Vietnam. /Admires Meany. /I will be gone. Meany gone. Already Congress cool on I.

"I will be gone; Meany gone; already Congress is cool on Israel." This was the man. Passionate. Tormented now that the world might not get out of the trouble he had got it into in order to get it out of trouble that had seemed worse. In the end he kept coming back to Israel and the Jews.

It was his tragedy never to be believed, save by people with dull minds. And yet he frequently told the truth; and when the truth did come out it was never ignoble.

———◆———

Israel. This was, of course, the center of the political life of the United Nations. The one issue in the world over which the U.N. could claim jurisdiction and not be disputed by the parties. The state had been created by the U.N., and its future turned intricately on the interpretation of Security Council pronouncements. One might have thought it was a British problem, but what could the British do about it? So was South Africa a British problem, and Rhodesia, and for that matter Kashmir.

Further, from the first day to the present, as Solzhenitsyn had observed, it had been America's problem also. At the United Nations, on the subject of Israel, the disjunction in American foreign policy between security issues and all other issues was to be encountered in its most pronounced form. Leon Gordenker of Princeton had written me on the subject: "International security involves the simplicity of danger and violence. It therefore gets priority as an understandable and unavoidable short-term issue." I had sat in the Roosevelt Room in May of 1970 while Henry Kissinger briefed the White House staff on the Cambodian invasion that had been launched a few moments earlier, halfway across the globe. He spoke with sexual excitement. He was going to smash the faces of those sons-of-bitching-no-good-bastards. On the subject of Israel, security matters aroused the same excitement and jealousy. They were handled by Kissinger and a small circle, primarily Roy Atherton, Assistant Secretary for Near Eastern and South Asian Affairs, and Joseph Sisco, Under Secretary for Political Affairs, and no one outside the circle. Other issues concerning the Middle East, issues that did not involve security, were handled by persons the Secretary had mostly never heard of and had certainly never met.

I never overcame my wonder at this arrangement. What were, after all, the security issues involved? A handful of tiny-to-medium-size countries testing other people's weapons in six-day wars. And "other issues" in the Mideast? They involved merely the symbols of progress for mankind in the last decades of the twentieth century; the future of freedom and human rights; the idea of independence. Merely all that Jerusalem had meant to mankind, and much that Athens had meant. Yet no one seemed to object, and I certainly would not, for the arrangement left the initiative on "other matters" to the rest of us, and on such matters I could with some confidence accept responsibility. In the months that followed there was a succession of deadlines and crises, mostly manufactured, involving security issues in the Middle East. On each occasion, without the least friction or, to my knowledge, the slightest mishap, I asked for and received, usually through Sisco, explicit instructions from Kissinger. I very occasionally offered advice; I once queried a semicolon. Otherwise I did precisely as instructed, having sought instruction. The problems of my U.N. tenure rose only as the "other issues" in the Mideast acquired an unexpected saliency owing in part to initiatives the U.S. Mission had taken because we thought such matters to be important, regardless of their lack of prestige in the Department of State. I did not do anything I hadn't tried to do as the public member of the delegation to the Twenty-Sixth General Assembly. But this time I was head of the delegation, and the nation this time was in a mood to listen.

◆

There was a further difference this time. It became clear to me from that first interview with Kathleen Teltsch of *The Times* in February. It was she who told me that the U.N. Human Rights Commission had condemned Israel and hence that the politics of human rights was being linked to the politics of the Mideast.

In April, 1975, Gordenker had sent me an article he had written for the Washington *Post* the previous July, concerning an incident in the closing days of the 1973 General Assembly:

> That great hall of winds, the General Assembly of the United Nations, gets less attention than it should. Last December, for instance, the General Assembly elevated the anti-Zionist doctrine promoted by the radical Arab states into a full-blown recommendation on apartheid in South Africa. But the incident went unnoticed in the news and unprotested by the U.S. government. Thus was injected an unnecessary and harmful symbol into United Nations doctrine. There are signs it is coming into greater use.
>
> The episode began with Burundi asking for approval to insert two paragraphs into a proposed recommendation asking governments to put more pressure on South Africa. One of the new paragraphs emphasized ". . . the collusion between Portuguese colonialism, the apartheid regime and Zionism"; the other condemned ". . . in particular, the un-

holy alliance between Portuguese colonialism, South African racism, Zionism and Israeli imperialism."

Everything about this language has significance for the United States — its symbolic quality, its origin and the procedure by which it became a recommendation of the General Assembly by a vote of 88 in favor, seven against and 28 abstentions. It stands for the needless Arabization of international pressure on South Africa.

In short order the doctrine of "collusion" between Zionists and racist colonialists was showing up in Soviet pronouncements around the world and at the U.N. What troubled Gordenker was the ease with which the doctrine attained the status of an international judgment. It was never debated in the committee phase. It was left for Burundi, a nation given to murdering dissenting citizens in genocidal proportions, to bring the issue to the General Assembly. The American representative present at the time, Gordenker wrote, "neither entered a heated procedural wrangle nor explained his vote." The U.S. was content simply to vote against Burundi's amendments, which passed by two-to-one majorities, with a third of the members abstaining. Only Canada and Barbados joined Israel in protesting. Israel warned that "behind these attacks on Israel and Zionism lurks a basic, primitive anti-semitism." When the final vote came on the full resolution as amended, the U.S. was joined in opposition by only six other votes, two of these Portugal and South Africa, and the third Israel. Gordenker despaired:

> The United States cannot influence a body in which it takes a re-tiring role. Yet this has been its normal reaction during the last five years when an unpleasant subject was dealt with in the U.N. symbol factory. . . .
>
> Surely a government that can negotiate with China and the Soviet Union can organize enough persuasiveness to reduce the production of pernicious symbolism and to win support from sensible regimes for human rights.

In any event, the movement of opinion at the U.N. was not to allow us the luxury of a "retiring role" on such matters much longer. At the General Assembly of 1974, the credentials of the South African delegation were rejected, and South Africa was effectively expelled. At their March, 1975, meeting in Havana the Non-Aligned nations indicated that this might now be done to Israel. Arthur Goldberg had declared that if this were done the United States should freeze its funds and suspend its participation in the General Assembly. That question was put to me at my confirmation hearing in the Senate on June 4. I was inclined to agree with Justice Goldberg, but added that it would be folly to wait until one-hundred-forty-odd instructed delegations arrived in New York and thereupon try to get their instructions changed. The real decision would be made *before* the General Assembly, at the Lima meeting of the Non-Aligned in August, and we should bring our influence to bear even before that.

Kissinger had agreed to this. On June 6 a cable went out stating that the United States would "strongly oppose" any effort to suspend Israel. Before too long reports began coming back that Egypt wasn't that enthusiastic about expulsion, as Israel could then claim not to be bound by Security Council resolutions calling for the return of occupied territories. The reports suggested that our initiative was having an effect. The 1974 General Assembly, presided over by the Algerian Foreign Minister, Abdelaziz Bouteflika, had been more turbulent than perhaps anyone expected. Perhaps a certain calm was returning. Some forty Moslem states were said to be talking of "disaccreditation," but somehow it began to appear that nothing too serious was afoot on this score. We were all quite blind to what actually would happen.

6

Washington/New York

ON JULY 9, a reporting cable arrived in Geneva from Barbara M. White of the U.S. Mission to the U.N., who was in Mexico City as the chief Department representative at the International Women's Year Conference there, which the United Nations had sponsored. It had already been reported in the press that the United States, along with Israel, had voted against the final declaration, owing to a passage in it calling for the "elimination of . . . Zionism, apartheid, [and] racial discrimination." Oblivious to this, or indifferent, the Ambassador's cable bubbled with enthusiasm:

> THE U.S. ACHIEVED ITS PRINCIPAL OBJECTIVE: PASSAGE OF A WORLD PLAN OF ACTION. . . .
>
> AS WAS INEVITABLE, THE CONFERENCE WAS POLITICIZED TO A DEGREE . . . BUT NOT TO SUCH A DEGREE THAT IT FAILED TO TAKE ACTION ON THE WOMEN'S ISSUES. THERE WERE A HALF DOZEN STRICTLY POLITICAL RESOLUTIONS (ON SUCH SUBJECTS AS CHILE, PALESTINE, PANAMA CANAL) WHICH REITERATED FAMILIAR POSITIONS. . . . OUR "NO" VOTE WAS BASED ON UNACCEPTABLE REFERENCES TO ZIONISM. . . .
>
> WHILE REGRETTABLE THAT THE "NO" VOTE WAS NECESSARY, AND PARTICULARLY UNFORTUNATE THAT WE WERE ISOLATED IN COMPANY ONLY

WITH ISRAEL, I DO NOT CONSIDER IT OF GREAT IMPORTANCE TO THE OUT-
COME OF THE CONFERENCE.

I cabled back to say I did not understand how, if the Declaration was
so inspiring, we had voted against it, and alternatively, if we had voted
against it, how it could be so inspiring. I closed with the line of Disraeli's
that Gertrude Himmelfarb had resurrected in her *Victorian Minds:*
"Few ideas are correct ones, and which they are none can tell, but with
words we govern men."

———◆———

My cable was received with puzzlement at the U.S. Mission in New
York; no one could understand what I had in mind. What I had in mind
was that the Declaration of Mexico, as it was known, was a totalitarian
tract. In a now-recognizable pattern, a nominally apolitical issue had
been set up; the widest range of support was mustered for it; but when
the final pronouncement came, the substance involved other issues altogether. The persons who drafted the Declaration were not necessarily
totalitarian, but their language was. It was the language of a wholly
politicized world, of a permanently mobilized society in which all interests were subservient to and ultimately placed in the service of the
political objectives of the state and the "New International Economic
Order," or whatever. But there was no one at the U.S. Mission who
seemed to have the vaguest perception of any of this. To the contrary,
they had persuaded themselves that their job *as diplomats* was to get
along with other diplomats. And so, like Ambassador White, they made
their way from one conference to the next, painfully anxious to please,
willingly associating themselves with the most outrageous assaults on
principles they should have been defending, eagerly sending off the
proposals to Washington where someone important, busy with SALT
talks or a Sinai disengagement, would eventually get to it and cable back
that the delegation was to vote "No." There would then follow a cable
such as arrived in Geneva.

The Mission in New York was surrounded by institutions and organizations which survived and flourished in public life by seeing, hearing, and speaking no evil about the United Nations. Such groups were
ever helpful at filling out delegations. The United States could, for
example, have included in its delegation to the Mexico City conference
articulate intellectuals of national and international stature who would
have instantly sensed the manipulation of women's causes that was taking place and who, as women and as intellectuals, would have been
devastating in their counterattacks. But there had been no such persons

on the American delegation; and there had been no apparent reaction among our delegates to the wording of the Declaration or to the fact that the delegation had been instructed to vote against it. In Mexico City a formal declaration of a United Nations conference had called for the elimination of "Zionism," which at the very least entailed the destruction of the State of Israel, and in effect equated Judaism with the nastiest forms of racial and group oppression. This evidently made no impression on the Americans present; certainly none on the fifth-ranking officer of the Mission I had just taken over.

———◆———

I returned to New York July 12, and scheduled a press conference for July 17. As is the practice of the Department, questions and answers were prepared for me. The following came in from Ambassador White:

QUESTION: Was the International Women's Year Conference a success in your opinion? What did it accomplish?

ANSWER: The Conference was never intended to change age-old patterns of discrimination against women in two weeks. Its primary objectives were to call international attention to the situation of women and to stimulate action to eliminate the discrimination and exploitation from which they suffer to varying degrees in all countries of the world. The conference did that. Whether or not it achieves lasting success will, of course, be determined by the extent to which governments, non-governmental organizations and individuals follow up on the proposals — the Plan of Action — that emerged from the conference.

Of course, the governments represented in Mexico City differed on political and economic issues and the press emphasized these differences. What has not been sufficiently understood is that the women there realized that they had a community of interests that cut across the ideological and economic policies of their governments. I don't think that women can ever again be taken quite so much for granted as they were before Mexico City. That is what the conference accomplished.

———◆———

Two of the five ambassadorial posts at the U.S. Mission were empty when I was appointed. In Geneva I had asked Albert W. Sherer, Jr., who had just completed the Helsinki negotiations, to represent us on the Security Council, and Jacob M. Myerson, who had been at Brussels, to do the same in the Economic and Social Council. Both were superb officers, with Myerson enjoying the further distinction of being an economist. W. Tapley Bennett, Jr., was the Deputy Permanent Representative and had been for as far back as any could remember. He was an experienced man and an unfailing indicator of whether one's own stock was rising or falling. Anyone who could maintain sufficient objectivity could learn a good deal about his situation merely by keeping an eye on Tap Bennett. I asked Ambassador White to stay also.

It was immediately clear that I would have problems with the Mission. On July 15 I held my first staff meeting; the next day it was all over the press, something which would have been unthinkable in, say, New Delhi. Columnist William R. Frye reported that "more eyebrows were lifted than in the Elizabeth Arden beauty salon on New York's Fifth Avenue." His image, on reflection, was an apt one, for there was a certain superciliousness in all this. These were not, after all, embattled politicians wiping the dust and sweat of the arena from their brows, nor yet were they gifted and aristocratic amateurs who might disdain the excess of enthusiasm I may on occasion have displayed. They were Foreign Service officers making a living carrying out the policies of the President. Abroad they do this with admirable fealty; but something about the U.N. changes this, or had done so with this cadre. Frye captured their dismay: " 'It was the *Commentary* article plus 4000,' one astonished staffer remarked later. . . . 'The liberalism is draining out of American policy,' another middle-ranking United States official said."

———◆———

As it happened, two days later Irving Kristol published in the *Wall Street Journal* an essay on precisely these issues. It had been worrisome, Kristol observed, to watch State Department officials reformulating American foreign economic policy in the hope of achieving a more amiable dialogue with the Third World. It was true that the Treasury was balking somewhat, and that I had been chosen as Permanent Representative at the U.N.; but nonetheless the State Department's "instinctive approach to this issue has been little less than frightening." The Department did not seem to see that any effort to establish a New International Economic Order would entail basic changes in our own domestic economic order, nor did the Department seem to understand the political realities that lie beneath our controversy with the Third World. Kristol went on:

> It is not simply a question of "world poverty." It is much more a question of one's attitude towards liberal political and economic systems, and towards liberal civilization in general. This explains why those "less developed" countries are always attacking the United States

and never say an unkind word about the Soviet Union — not exactly a poor country. Nor do they show any animus toward Saudi Arabia, now fabulously rich as the result of the exorbitant price demands for its oil from *both* rich and poor countries alike. Indeed, the very definition of "the Third World" entails a hostility toward liberal capitalism. Otherwise, how can one explain why Saudi Arabia and Cuba and Algeria are fully-accredited members of the club, whereas Israel, Taiwan, South Korea, and Turkey are not?

In truth, he continued, this "new cold war" between North and South was not really about economics at all. It was a conflict of political ideologies:

> What the "Third World" is saying is not that it needs our help but that their poverty is the fault of our capitalism — that they are "exploited" nations while we are a "guilty people." And, to the degree that the United States officially accepts the terms of the debate set down by the nations of the "Third World" it also accepts moral responsibility for their poverty.

Yet, many Americans, he concluded, and even more Europeans, seemed inclined to appease rather than repudiate this claim:

> . . . The State Department itself is very much a non-ideological institution, and never fully appreciates the ways in which words and ideas ultimately shape world politics, and always prefers negotiation to confrontation. It cannot get much excited over the principle of expropriation (without due compensation) of American business overseas; it cannot see the ideological significance of setting up various "world authorities" to stockpile commodities and rig the international markets so as to "help close the gap" between rich and poor nations. It cannot even see the practical implications of such arrangements — i.e., that you cannot "collectivize" and "plan" the international market economy without at the same time intervening massively in domestic market arrangements.
>
> But what it cannot see, others can. . . .
>
> There is always a good case, in both principle and prudence, for the more affluent being charitable toward the poor — even to those whose poverty is largely their own fault. Nor is there any reason to expect, much less insist on, gratitude: Such benevolence is supposed to be its own reward. But when the poor start "mau-mauing" their actual or potential benefactors, when they begin vilifying them, insulting them, demanding as of right what it is not their right to demand — then one's sense of self-respect may properly take precedence over one's self-imposed humanitarian obligations.

I sent the essay to all Mission officers, asking what they thought of Kristol's assertion that the State Department was "very much a non-ideological institution." Joseph Meresman, the administrative officer, replied in terms that made clear that if he did not wholly agree with Kristol, he fully understood him. The rest of the replies ranged from incomprehension to "respectful dissent." Ambassador White sent a four-page response that could well stand as the average perception of American career diplomats as to what they were up to in those days:

> I agree that the State Department is not an ideological institution. I do not think it should be. The whole thrust of our foreign policy since 1969 has been that we can co-exist with countries of different ideologies, so long as they do not threaten our national existence and vital interests. The business of the Department of State is to help to work out the problems of coexistence (or if you will, interdependence).

These were decent people, utterly unprepared for their work. Earlier in the year, after the *Commentary* article appeared, I had been asked to meet with a group from Social Democrats, U.S.A., headed by Bayard Rustin. Most of the article they approved; some parts troubled them. Why, they asked, was I so hard on socialist countries? I replied, the countries on which I was hard were not in fact socialist; they were state-capitalist regimes of a most depressing order. In such regimes the privileged classes lived off rents collected from government licenses. (Thus in India a license was required to import almost any product. In consequence the price of imported products was artificially high. A person might receive a license to import one million rupees' worth of steel. This steel would then sell in India for two million rupees, the license being worth one million rupees.) This kind of "socialism," I said, simply deprived people of freedom. Rustin's group had no difficulty understanding this, and agreeing with it. But it was incomprehensible to the U.S. Mission. From rather an opposite pole of opinion, the July/ August, 1975, issue of *The Humanist,* journal of the American Ethical Union and the American Humanist Association, entitled its lead editorial "Wanted: A New Commitment to Freedom." With the Vietnam war over, its editor, Paul Kurtz, wrote, it should be clear that the principal cause of our defeat was that we had waged only a technological struggle, while our adversary waged an ideological struggle:

> Thus if there is any lesson to be drawn from the Vietnam debacle, it is that we failed to make the case for a radical commitment to freedom and democracy. We failed in the ideological struggle.

Socialists understood the point, and humanists understood the point. My difficulty would be with Foreign Service officers convinced that "the liberalism is draining out of American foreign policy." There was no near-term solution save to stop presiding over staff meetings.

———————◆———————

On the same day that I sent Kristol's essay around, I presented my credentials to the Secretary-General. He had batches of Middle East alarums for me. The Egyptians were not ready to extend the mandate of the United Nations Emergency Force, which maintained the truce zone in the Sinai. He had come reluctantly to the conclusion (a rare event, a conclusion from the Secretary-General!) that the Israelis were resorting to "dilatory tactics." There would have to be a meeting of the Security Council.

After presenting credentials, I held a press conference, as is the custom. The U.N. press corps was large, but not at this point especially influential. The wire services were there; William Oatis of the Associated Press did a specially incisive job. But of American newspapers, only *The New York Times* and the New York *Post* maintained regular correspondents, and of the television networks only CBS, which kept a full-time correspondent, Richard C. Hottelet. Happily there were not half a dozen correspondents in American television with Hottelet's experience and capacity. Apart from *The Times,* and for many purposes more important, CBS was the U.N.'s one outlet to the American world. I said little at that press conference save to recall the French couplet:

> *Cet animal est très méchant,*
> *Quand on l'attaque, il se défend.*

This, I said, would be our policy.

———————◆———————

I was not looking for a fight; I wished to make this clear. Yet we would not back off from one, and might even relish one if someone else chose to start it. It was all very well for the Foreign Service to judge that "the business of the Department of State is to help to work out the problems of coexistence . . . ," but in the face of continued disappointment and defeat, the willingness of the American public to support such initiatives had near to disappeared. Whatever one's personal inclinations, anyone who cared to help with the problems of coexistence was at this point going to have to look first to the morale of the American people.

There had been a startling decline in public support for anything the United Nations might do. The Chicago Council on Foreign Relations poll found that only 28 percent of the public and 3 percent of "Leaders" thought the U.N. played a "very important role" in determining U.S. foreign policy. The Watts survey found virtually no support for U.S. involvement in a New International Economic Order. Providing economic aid to less developed countries, and contributing to the work of the United Nations, were ranked twenty and twenty-one in importance on a list of twenty-three major national issues.

Few things ought more readily to have commanded public support than providing food to hungry people, if only American diplomacy made it seem even marginally appreciated. But at this time, American diplomacy seemingly could not do so, and didn't much try.

Thus John Hannah and the World Food Council. Waldheim had quite ignored my first representations on behalf of Hannah. At our July 4 meeting in Geneva I had insisted that Hannah was not going to be driven out, and must stay through the next Council meeting, in March, 1976. On July 7 a spokesman for Waldheim said merely that Hannah would serve out his one-year term — *and* that there would be changes in the World Food Council Secretariat. No demand from the new Third World majority for Secretariat jobs would be taken lightly by Dr. Waldheim. This was perhaps to be expected. But neither, it seemed, would any insult to an American arouse the concern of the State Department bureaucracy. On July 10, the Department sent instructions to Geneva that when the World Food Council report came before the ECOSOC meeting, our "delegation should take a positive approach regarding the future of the WFC." Thereupon I went to Kissinger. He had put a great deal of effort behind the World Food Council and I reasoned that if I could not get his support on this, I would never do so. I asked that protests be made to the countries whose representatives had disrupted the meeting in Rome and demanded Hannah's resignation. On July 12, he directed that protests be made in Dakar, Dacca, and Conakry (none, however, in Mexico City). Kissinger was a terror to his bureaucracy, and normally an instruction *direct* from him produced tremors, especially when it indicated displeasure. Save on U.N. issues.

On July 16, I was in Washington for a Cabinet meeting, and inquired in the Department how the Secretary's protest was coming. It was being drafted. I took the matter up with assorted Assistant Secretaries and Under Secretaries. Finally, on July 18, the cable did go out, but there was no life in it when it left the Department. All cables from Washington are signed with the name of the Secretary, or whoever is the ranking officer in Washington at the time; with an explicit directive such as this one, it was normal practice for the cable to read: FOR AMBASSADOR FROM SECRETARY. But this particular cable carried no indication that the message was actually from Kissinger, or that he was the least interested in it.

In my original proposal on the matter, I had suggested that each of the countries to which we protested should be made to pay some small cost for what their representatives had done. I had especially suggested that we should seek the recall of the representatives from Rome to the more prosaic surroundings of their home capitals. Most capitals had not the least idea what their representatives were doing, and a discouraging number of representatives were doing whatever it was the Arabs or the Soviets were paying for. But the United States did not have to give food to nations whose representatives insulted our international officials. It was as simple as that.

To my mind. To the Departmental mind it was a fuss about nothing. And so that cable went out with the lowest classification, Limited Official Use, which is exactly what it received. In Dacca, for example, where an ambassador might hope once in his tour of duty to receive a message actually *seen* by the Secretary of State, the U.S. protest was delivered by our Deputy Chief of Mission to a third-echelon civil servant, who promised to "look into the issue." In each capital the government claimed no knowledge of the episode. Neither, save for the curious cable, would the U.S. Embassy in the place have known about it.

This latter point came to me now with some emphasis. From time to time when I had been in New Delhi, a cable would arrive asking that the Embassy lobby the Indians on some U.N. issue, usually concerning Korea. These were at most desultory requests, and our responses were hardly greater. On going to the United Nations, however, almost the first thing I heard — no one briefed me, it wasn't written down anywhere, it was just something everyone knew and for obvious enough reasons mentioned to me — was that it was an Indian resolution in the Security Council in the summer of 1973 that led to the Yom Kippur war.

It seems that in July, 1973, their Ambassador to the U.N. had put together Draft Resolution S/10974, which deplored Israeli occupation of Arab territory, rebuked Israel for a lack of cooperation with the Secretary-General's peace-making efforts, and stated that Palestinian rights must be a basis for any Middle East settlement. The United States vetoed the resolution. War came in October. Two years later, on July 28, 1975, I dined in New York at the home of Egyptian U.N. Ambassador Ahmed Esmat Abdel Meguid, an exceptionally patient and thoughtful diplomat. Could the Indian resolution really have led to war? I asked. Yes, he replied, it had: the American veto of the Indian resolution had forced Egypt to the conclusion that there was no alternative to war. I raised the matter with Kissinger. He was prepared to say only that the

American veto was *one* of the reasons why war came; but he would not discount the contention further.

I had been in New Delhi all that time, aching for something to do; no one had told me the Indians were up to anything, much less starting the Middle East on the road to war, the oil embargo, and the OPEC price increase. No cable from the Department ever arrived asking me to ask the Indians what they had in mind; telling me to find out whether this was something the Prime Minister herself had ordered. Or the Minister of External Affairs or whosoever. No cable instructed me to tell the Indians that we would veto the resolution. No cable asked me to ask them whether there was something they had in mind that we might help with. We now searched the files in New Delhi, New York, and Washington. It turned out that the Bureau of International Organization Affairs in the State Department had gone through its accustomed panic as the prospect of a veto approached, but its concern was with the impression our veto would make with others, not with our effect on what those others were doing. No one in Washington ever asked us in New Delhi to try to stop the Indians, and for all we knew, even the Indians in New Delhi didn't much know what was going on in New York.

———◆———

The system was not working well, an observation that hardly escaped the notice of the Commission on the Organization of the Government for the Conduct of Foreign Policy, chaired by Robert D. Murphy, which had submitted its final report to the President in June. With respect to United Nations affairs and multilateral diplomacy generally, the Murphy Commission had two substantive recommendations. "Recommendation 63" called for the creation of a full-time U.S. representative to the Human Rights Commission with ambassadorial rank and "a broad responsibility for human rights considerations inherent in all U.S. participation at the United Nations." If necessary, this ambassador should be provided with additional staff. "Recommendation 78" proposed pretty much to abolish the Bureau of International Organization Affairs.

In July, the Bureau sent these recommendations to the U.N. Mission along with copies of its own reaction, and instructions for us: if we had any thoughts in the matter, we should have them back by the end of the day on which they had been received. A one-page option paper had been prepared for the Secretary on each recommendation. The "background/analysis" on Number 63 noted that the Commission "criticizes the lack of continuous high level coordination and follow through in human rights matters." It noted also that the principal duty of the U.S.

human rights representative at the current time was to lead the U.S. delegation to the annual Human Rights Commission meeting in February and March. If the Murphy Commission's recommendation were adopted, "he could also follow human rights issues at ECOSOC and the UNGA,* still not a full-time job." Following this analysis, the Bureau of International Organization Affairs offered the Secretary three options. The first was to "support the recommendation." The second was to "reject the recommendation." Then there was Option 3:

> 3. *Respond partially by recommending that the U.S. representative be given ambassadorial rank and be regularly made a part of the U.S. Delegation to the U.N. General Assembly (perhaps as a Senior Advisor).*
>
> *Advantages:*   a) *Would show our responsiveness to the Commission and signal greater attention to human rights.*
> b) *Would not create a new position but simply assign on a permanent basis one of the existing slots in the U.S. delegation to the U.N. General Assembly.*
>
> *Disadvantages:*   *Might look like a cosmetic response to a substantive recommendation.*
>
> *Recommendation: That the Secretary approve Option 3.*

In response to Recommendation 78, that the Bureau be abolished, the Bureau produced four options for the Secretary, of which the fourth was that the Bureau be enlarged. The Bureau recommended the fourth option.

All this was both familiar and still somehow painful to Suzanne Weaver, whose field was American public organizations. Our responses to the Bureau were brief and not altogether polite. We proposed that the proposal for a human rights ambassador be supported in its entirety. As for the proposal respecting the Bureau itself, we commented that the Bureau's opinion that it should be enlarged seemed to us greatly to reinforce the Commission's recommendation that it be abolished.

———◆———

The Department of State simply could not grasp the significance of the issue of human rights at this time. On the other hand, Gerald Ford could. It was clear enough to him in part because he chose not to have too complex a view of things. The Conference on Security and Cooperation in Europe had reached agreement, and accords were signed at Helsinki on July 30/August 1, 1975. In his address to the conference,

---

* United Nations General Assembly.

the President could not have been more forthright on this issue. He
began by asserting that détente "must be a two-way street." That
tensions could not be eased on one side alone. With respect to the
Helsinki agreements, he pointed first to the provisions on personal
liberty: "They affirm the most fundamental human rights: liberty of
thought, conscience, and faith; the exercise of civil and political rights;
the rights of minorities."

This would have seemed a clear enough signal, but it was not received
by the State Department, which was the essential clue. If a bureaucracy
can't hear something a President says, it is because it is not listening. The
U.S. Mission in New York and, rather more unusually, the Bureau in
Washington had become clients of the institution to which they were
accredited. It was not likely that this would change until a wholly new
set of influences was brought to bear. We would never handle our multilateral diplomacy well until it was integrated into the bilateral networks
that dominate the life of the State Department and the careers of its
officials. The Murphy Commission had sensed enough of this to have
proposed that multilateral issues, one by one as they came along, be
handled by the Department bureau which had substantive responsibility: hence the proposed abolition of "IO." In this way, if the Security
Council were meeting on, say, British Honduras, the European bureau
and the Latin American bureau would handle the matter between them.
If the matter concerned nuclear weapons, the Bureau of Politico-Mili-
tary Affairs would pick the delegates and write the speeches. Missing
from this prescription, though, was a means for enabling country officers
and ambassadors to see their own stake in what was going on in the
arena of international organizations.

In August, Weaver and I responded to this latter problem with a long
paper entitled "Bilateral Traditions and Multilateral Realities: A New
Approach to Relations with Sixty-four Countries." I sent two copies to
Kissinger with a note that he had made his mark on history and that it
was now time for him to do something truly epic, which was to make an
impress on the Department of State. Our proposition was simple. We
tried to show that for some half the countries in the world — a number
we kept deliberately low, by tight definitions — the United States' multilateral relations were distinctly more important than bilateral relations.
If this was so, our argument went,

> . . . it follows that American relations with these countries should con-
> centrate on their multilateral actions. In practical terms this means that
> the American Ambassador in Ouagadougou, instead of being only
> vaguely aware that there is to be a ministerial meeting of the non-
> aligned in Lima at the end of the month, would at this moment be

furiously busy seeking to influence the actions of Upper Volta at that meeting. He would know that the meeting will determine a number of matters of critical importance to the United States, as for example, whether Israel is suspended from the General Assembly, with all the incalculable consequences that follow; or whether American forces in South Korea, after a quarter-century flying the United Nations flag, will be branded imperialist aggressors and summarily called upon to withdraw from the peninsula.

An attraction of the proposal to be made in this paper is that it gives the Ambassador in Ouagadougou something to do. What is more, it allows him to treat the government to which he is accredited as important in the principal respect that it is important. To wit, the fact that its vote in multilateral forums is counted equally with that of France from which it was once ruled.

Clearly, an argument such as this rests on the premise that events in multilateral forums *are* important. But it is not even necessary to think that they are *very* important — simply that they are, on balance, more important than any other influence which Conakry or Dacca or Dakar routinely exerts on matters of interest to the United States. This is not to argue that our bilateral relations are unimportant. From time to time, with most countries, they will have moments of great saliency. But over the decades, year in and year out, as monsoons come and go, or fail to do so, how these particular countries vote in international forums will have the larger effect upon us.

These countries know this about themselves. They have made themselves important — to the degree they are important — by acting in concert in international forums. If they have understood this, so should we.

American diplomacy put overwhelming emphasis on seeking friendly direct relations with individual other countries. The institutional arrangement for this was the ambassador and his embassy. To get an embassy was the great goal of the career officer; having achieved it, his final object was to be judged a successful ambassador by maintaining friendly relations, or indeed improving relations. Anything that interfered with this goal was resisted by the system. In recent years, and notably in the new nations, the one aspect of foreign policy that could most interfere with this object was the voting behavior of so many of the small or new nations in multilateral forums, behavior hostile to the United States. In consequence the "bilateral system" resisted, and usually with success, the effort to introduce multilateral considerations into its calculations. In a section of our paper entitled "Toothless in Dacca," we recounted the story of what had happened when the Secretary had sent out his cable on the breakup of the World Food Council. We told how it had been all but ignored, and then asked: *"Why is this problem such a difficult one?"* elaborating on Kristol's argument:

. . . The Department of State is a notably non-ideological institution. It is pragmatic, business-like, and rather uneasy with ideas, its own or other people's. . . .

And nowhere has ideology been more to be seen, more on display, than in multilateral affairs, especially those of the United Nations. Hence, nowhere has it invited more hostility from a widening range of American opinion.

There have been two phases of this history. At first the U.N. was seen as the instrument of American ideologues, much given to pronouncements about the parliament of man and to forking over American resources, even secrets. In 1946 we even proposed to give the U.N. the atom bomb. More recently the U.N. has been seen to be under the control of anti-American ideologues, and distrust has become even more widespread. . . . American interest in the United Nations affairs has more or less steadily declined.

What Is to Be Done?

The Commission on the Organization of the Government for the Conduct of Foreign Policy certainly sensed this situation. It has proposed all but abolishing the Bureau of International Organization Affairs and assigning lead responsibility for any given multilateral question to the appropriate functional bureau, the theory being that multilateral concerns ought to be an integral part of the work of, say, the African Bureau, and not something set apart as somehow special and different. . . .

But the Commission does not make the more important argument, which is that *for a third to a half of the countries in the world, America's most important relations take place in multilateral forums.*

This assessment arises from two basic facts. On the one hand, there is simply a very large, and still growing, number of countries, most of them former colonies, many of them scarcely inhabited, with which the United States just doesn't have much business. Or any business at all. Whilst they were part of the British or French or Portuguese or Dutch empires, we were scarcely aware of their existence. We have *become* aware of their existence mostly because of a second fact, which is that each of these new nations has one vote in the General Assembly, in UNCTAD, in UNESCO, in the Non-Aligned Conference, in the NPT Review Conference, in the Security Council, and so on almost *ad infinitum*. Serious issues are dealt with in these forums. It is not necessary to establish that they are *immensely* serious issues.

It were enough if they were only somewhat serious. We tried to establish with some rigor just who the "multilateral countries" were. From our list of candidates we excluded the following:

A. Any single nation from which the United States imports a significant amount of oil — e.g., Kuwait, o.1 percent of current consumption. . . .

B. Any nation from which the United States imports a significant amount of a critical material other than fuel, as defined by the Council on International Economic Policy — e.g., Gabon, which provides 29 percent of our manganese consumption, or Liberia, which provides 2 percent of our iron ore. . . .

C. Any nation to which the United States exports have a value of at least $500 million a year — e.g., Singapore. . . .

D. Any nation from whom we import at least $500 million worth of goods a year — e.g., the Bahamas. . . .

E. Any nation where our investments at book value exceed $100 million — e.g., Guatemala.

We further excluded some nations — Cuba, Pakistan, Yugoslavia, the Vietnams, Syria, Lebanon, Jordan — as our bilateral relations with them were, at the moment, important for other reasons.

We were left with sixty-four countries, participants in various forums of the Non-Aligned, that did not meet *any* of the above tests of bilateral significance.*

We realized, we said, that we were proposing to change an organizational habit of two centuries. It would be comparable to a basic change in strategic doctrine by the military. It could take twenty years to bring off, and would have to begin with a decision by the President, carried out by the Secretary. A basic list of "multilateral countries" would have to be drawn up and a procedure established for keeping it up to date. Analysis of voting records would become a key management tool. This was one of the few things political scientists did well; a thorough system should be put in place, with data going back the whole of the U.N. system's thirty years.

Finally, we tried to make the case that the change would be worth the trouble:

> *What are the advantages of the new concept?*
> Clearly, the first advantage is to our multilateral diplomacy. Over time, the new practice should produce better results for us. If it doesn't, it will have failed. If it is thought that it will not, it shouldn't be tried.
> But there are further advantages.

---

* Afghanistan, Angola, Bahrain, Bangladesh, Barbados, Bhutan, Bolivia, Botswana, Burma, Burundi, Cambodia, Cameroon, Cape Verde Islands, Central African Republic, Chad, Congo, Cyprus, Dahomey, Democratic Yemen, El Salvador, Ethiopia, Fiji, Gambia, Ghana, Grenada, Guinea, Guinea-Bissau, Guyana, Haiti, Ivory Coast, Kenya, Laos, Lesotho, Madagascar, Malawi, Maldives, Mali, Malta, Mauritania, Mauritius, Morocco, Mozambique, Nepal, Nicaragua, Niger, Oman, Paraguay, Qatar, Rwanda, São Tomé and Príncipe, Senegal, Sierra Leone, Somalia, Sri Lanka, Sudan, Swaziland, Togo, Tanzania, Tunisia, Uganda, Upper Volta, Uruguay, Western Samoa, Yemen.

We added that special considerations of the moment might lead to excluding Bahrain, Ethiopia, and Morocco also.

First, it gives those American Embassies a full time task. Each nation involved has an equal vote with China and the Soviet Union. The Secretary of State can in good conscience tell the Ambassador that the vote matters.

Second, *mirabile dictu,* it provides an unambiguous record of ambassadorial performance, and for that of the desk officers at home. Has the voting record got better or worse? From 2 percent "right" has Upper Volta gone to 4 percent right? or down to zero? Obviously this need not be a crude judgment. Nor need it be a cruel one. But in the end some kind of quantification is needed, if any true standards of performance are to be achieved. In any event the voting record is a hedge against the Ambassador and the desk officer who seek to maintain the appearance of friendly and successful relations by avoiding any unpleasantness about voting in the Non-aligned Ministerial meeting or the NPT review conference. . . .

Third, the concept of the "multilateral country" will serve to clear away what is left of our illusions about our relations with much of the world. It will be seen that in international forums about eighty percent of the countries in the world consistently act in ways hostile to the United States. It is at least possible that many of these countries do not fully realize it. Or if they do, assume that we don't. Nothing but good could come from the American Ambassador making his monthly call on the Foreign Minister with his monthly printout in hand. The United States is increasingly isolated in a dangerous world. The danger is obviously compounded by concealing it from ourselves.

Fourth, if multilateral relations are seen to have been given priority with respect to half the nations in the world they are likely to be given somewhat more attention in the other half. The next time the Indian Ambassador sets out to start a war in the Middle East, the American Ambassador in New Delhi might be informed.

It is, further, just barely possible that some small part of our growing isolation is to be accounted for by our own behavior. Just possibly, a close accounting of the judgments others make of us might lead to some improvement in our own behavior, as well as theirs. To persist in ignorance is to invite calamity.

———————◆———————

The remark about "our own behavior" was directed to Kissinger, who two days earlier had instructed me to veto the admission of North Vietnam and of South Vietnam to the U.N., our eighth and ninth vetoes respectively, and the first ever cast by the United States on the admission of another country.*

———————

* See Chapter VIII.

Paul Hofmann of *The New York Times* described the Security Council session on the Vietnams as "marked by an abundance of rhetoric and an absence of any real drama." The votes were decided well in advance, in capitals far from New York. We were alone in our negative vote; Costa Rica abstained; every other Security Council member voted against us. The case for working harder in the capitals was clearly enough made, and a second opportunity came along forthwith. Early in August the U.N.'s Decolonization Committee made it known that it would once again take up a Cuban resolution reaffirming "the inalienable right of the people of Puerto Rico to self-determination and independence." (Four years earlier the United States and Britain had withdrawn from the Committee in the spirit of "damage limitation." Thereupon the issue of Puerto Rico became a fixture of the Committee's proceedings.) This year's resolution called on the United States to abstain from "any act of political persecution" against the liberation movement of Puerto Rico, and provided for a fact-finding mission to be dispatched to the island. Some African members of the Committee, in a move that was supposed to placate us, had "softened" the measure, which no longer called, as it first had done, for representation of the Puerto Rican liberation movement at the U.N., and did not denounce the United States for the forced sterilization of Puerto Rican women.

This was my chance. Kissinger called one afternoon to complain about something or other; I agreed with his complaint and then put it that it would be intolerable, after our defeat on Vietnam, to lose on Puerto Rico. I proposed that we inform the members of the Committee *in their capitals* that we would regard voting against us on this matter to be an "unfriendly act." No small matter. He agreed, and so at last we took the initiative on a U.N. issue. Cables went out: Puerto Ricans had been freely exercising their right of self-determination ever since 1952; in the referendum of 1967, 0.6 percent of the voters opted for independence; elections took place routinely on a fixed calendar; the Independence Party of Puerto Rico was a legal party free to contest any seat it wished; we were not about to have dictators lecture us on democracy.

No such thing had happened before. The Cuban delegate, Ricardo Alarcón de Quesada, complained that "a great imperialist power" was resorting to every weapon to defeat his resolution. I offered the private comment that this was not true, for we had not said that to vote against us would be a "hostile act," in other words a *casus belli*. At one point in the proceedings an Indian diplomat approached a member of the U.S. Mission and asked, "Are you threatening us?" The American called for instructions; I told him to tell the Indian "Yes." The governor of Puerto Rico, Rafael Hernández Colón, a singularly forceful and attractive man, came to New York and invited any delegate who wished to come back with him and see for himself what went on in Puerto Rico.

The vote to put off the resolution for a year carried eleven to nine in our favor. The debate on our behalf was led by Australia, which voted with us along with Afghanistan, Chile, Denmark, Fiji, India, Indonesia, Iran, the Ivory Coast, Sierra Leone, and Tunisia. Voting against us were Congo, Iraq, Mali, and Syria, co-sponsors of the resolution, along with Bulgaria, Czechoslovakia, the Soviet Union, and Tanzania. Yugoslavia and Trinidad and Tobago abstained; China, citing the sharp division of Third World opinion, did not vote; Ethiopia was absent. I issued a brief statement citing the "unassailable fact of the free condition of the people of Puerto Rico" and calling the Decolonization Committee's decision "a responsible action." I happened to be at lunch at *The New York Times* when the vote came. A call came to me there, and with that early notice, there was an editorial the next morning:

> This victory for common sense represents an important first dividend for a tough but reasoned stance by the United States and its partners against the hollow rhetoric and mindless majorities that have brought the United Nations into disrepute and eroded its support.

The Times news headline ran:

U.S. Wins a U.N. Victory on Puerto Rico.

7

The Seventh Special Session of the General Assembly

UNGASS. THERE IS NOTHING quite so unlovely as the acronyms of the U.N. United Nations General Assembly Special Session. UNGASS was our task for the summer, and a critical one for me. Whatever anyone chose to think I had written or said on the subject of the U.N., the outcome of the Seventh Special Session would be the first concrete measure of whether I was right or wrong. From the day I was sworn in, I had eight weeks to get ready.

———————◆———————

As we began planning, the paper from Thompson of the Fletcher School arrived with its observations on the *Commentary* article; it stayed in my mind, a source of more confusion than probably I realized. I had returned from Asia with a simple thesis, however difficult some had professed to find it. The new nations, I had said, shared our principles. Accordingly, we ought to share their aspirations, but in the way that would both respect the principles and best fulfill the aspirations. Thompson saw plainly that this was my position and, he said, I was wrong. The new nations did *not* share our principles, he said, and *that* was why we ought to share their aspirations.

He had taken his argument back to the creation of the U.N. Conference on Trade and Development, or UNCTAD, as it was known. The organization was the child of the Argentine economist Raúl Prebisch, founded on the proposition that the world economic system had a systemic bias against developing nations. A more equitable relation could be achieved by bargaining between the two blocs. Once UNCTAD was under way, the world, including the United States, had by default or otherwise agreed to a form of political and economic bargaining. But then, in Thompson's view, we had never really bargained.

He had been in Geneva in the spring of 1964 for the first UNCTAD meeting and had been astonished there by the speech of the chief American delegate, then Under Secretary of State George W. Ball, who "lectured his audience on the importance of foreign investment to them" while the rest of the American delegation reminded the delegates from the developing countries that they accounted for only a tiny proportion of world trade, and could have no greater bargaining power than that, regardless of what pronouncements passed with paper majorities. As Thompson saw it, Ball's arguments were not taken as good advice, but as a slap. The nadir of the conference, he recalled, came when a Soviet delegate promised to end all tariffs on goods from the less developed countries entering the Soviet Union. As a state trading country, the Soviet Union has no need for tariffs to control foreign access to its markets. Nonetheless, the proposal brought "prolonged applause and cheering."

"Small wonder," Thompson wrote, "that the George Balls of this world would be cynical. But the object of the game is, after all, to win, not just to be right. And so far, the Third World has done the winning, for they proved . . . that their resolutions passed by 'paper majorities' in time could mature into real policy." And this was surely so. Shortly before the Seventh Special Session, Harlan Cleveland wrote in the *Saturday Review* that the approaching meeting was a "coming crisis"; in 1964, whatever his own views, he had been part of a Department of State that had let UNCTAD form but then didn't take it seriously.

In more general terms, over the thirty-year life of the U.N. system, we had, first, imputed great powers to the General Assembly, powers that it didn't have. Next we had gone along with the notion that a majority bloc in the General Assembly might be recognized as legitimate for the purposes of bargaining with a minority bloc. *Then* we found the majority bloc wishing to use the imputed powers of the Assembly to legislate agreements that could never be reached by bargaining as such. At this time Waldheim was quoted as saying that "some people were shocked to see the U.N. reflect the 'entirely new balance of power in the world,' as compared to the founding days of 1945."

But in truth nothing much had happened to the true "balance of power" since 1945. The change to which the Secretary was referring was the emergence of the notion that a majority of votes in the General Assembly in itself conferred a certain kind of power, which now "they" had and "we" didn't. This, of course, was a notion that the United States had originally helped create, and now didn't want to live with.

Thompson's view, like mine, was that we surely needed a new strategy — but his would be a very different strategy. He laid down three guidelines. First, for us to take a "realistic" approach to these questions was not realistic. For us to ask what would *really* help development, as I proposed, was quite to miss the point. The point was to ask what would be *thought* to help development. It had been foolish, in Thompson's view, for us to refuse to help build the Tan-Zam railroad merely because it was not "cost-effective." As a *symbol* it would have been worth the money to *us*.

His second guideline was that, except on the highest matters, it was better to concede on principles and then haggle on details: "The Third World at this point feels, and nothing will change this, that history is on its side." His third guideline, which he allowed to be a "tricky" one, was that in shaping policy toward the Third World, "form is more important than substance." What the leaders want, he wrote, "is a form of understanding of their aspirations." He proposed that we set out to understand their aspirations, "and identify with them, in ways larger than life that cannot be missed."

I found all this persuasive; certainly the only good tactical advice I had gotten. The United States had to get along in the world, and that meant, in the first instance, getting along with governments. We had refused to finance the Bokharo steel complex in India because it was to be government-run and would lose money. All true enough. And so the Russians put up the money. The result ten years later was that the Russians practically controlled Indian foreign policy, at least so far as it concerned the United States. If the Indian government hadn't really wanted steel, but wanted the political power that came from owning a steel mill, why then should we give a damn?

As for principles, some surely were less than immutable. I had lunched with Wassily Leontief in May. He was then leaving Harvard to take on an econometric project for the U.N., a world input-output model. Such analysis was indispensable, he argued, because the free market simply couldn't set comparative prices efficiently. It might, in his words, do a good enough job at setting the price of powdered sugar as against granulated sugar, but it could never efficiently set the price of oil. It was an argument now difficult to refute. In September, 1973, after all, the free market had set the price at $2 a barrel. The governments of the OPEC

countries then raised the price to $11 a barrel. With the result that in
the United States, demand for imported oil proceeded to double. With
what ultimate conviction could an American, then, any longer insist
that free markets were good for poor countries? One might think so,
but one could not insist on it, nor hold it forth as a principle.

And what of free enterprise, and of transnational business? I had written of the multinational corporation that it was "arguably the most
creative economic institution of the twentieth century." I knew enough
of the workings of business to know it has a trifling influence on American government as compared, say, with trade unions. (I had even heard
Henry Kissinger try to persuade an after-dinner group of Indians, intellectuals and journalists, to this effect!) But this was absolutely not the
view in the developing nations, or indeed in almost any nation. At the
failed Sixth Special Session of the General Assembly in April and May
of 1974, the transnational corporation had been nearly universally held
to be the source of many of the economic, financial, social, and military
ills of the world.

But what of it? United States delegations had been assaulted for a
decade now by ritual assertions at virtually every U.N. conference, the
International Women's Year being only the most recent, that each
nation had full sovereignty over all its resources and all economic activity within its sovereign borders, and could nationalize at will. "Their
rights and our duties" was the wry formulation in Washington. The
poor nations wanted us to acknowledge both their right and their disposition to expropriate foreign wealth. But envision the worst that might
come of this: a world in which investment capital was safe only
in the United States, Western Europe, and Japan. How awful would
that really be? What if the Saudis had no other place to put their money?
We would get back not only the extra dollars the Saudis were charging
us for oil; we would get the extra dollars they were charging Bangladesh
and Tanzania as well.

In the aftermath of the OPEC price increases, commodity agreements,
another precept of the new order, were all the rage among the new
nations. Although a new category of poor countries had recently come
into being — "MSA," for "Most Seriously Affected," meaning most bru-
tally punished by oil price increases from fellow members of the Third
World — the value of commodity agreements was nowhere questioned.
Third World delegates vied with one another to extol the rape of their
economies by the sheikhdoms of the Persian Gulf. In the meantime,
there was the finding of Houthakker's group — appointed by UNCTAD
— that commodity prices, contrary to the fundamental raison d'être of
that organization, had moved in directions *favorable* to commodity producers. Thus commodity agreements were, at least potentially, a means

to reverse the natural movement of prices, which favored the developing countries, and transfer wealth instead to the already wealthy! The plain probability was that a great many things the developing nations demanded were probably not likely to be good for them at all. But what would be the reward of trying, in *their* interests, to talk them out of what *they* wanted? I was six months out of India now, and considerably more relaxed, but somehow less friendly. Kissinger had been genial, and like a good loser had asked only for a decent interval. What had we got but humiliation and defeat?

It came to me that we could make use of the deviousness of others.

What if we used the uncertainty about all these issues as a tactic? What if we pleaded with the majority not to impose commodity agreements on us — but were perceived as knowing that when we favored a proposal the majority would turn against it? Thus we could obtain anything we wished merely by opposing it, and far from being demoralized, feel we had absolute control of the General Assembly.

There was a level at which all this was merely the game of nations. Thompson had noted Kennedy's great style in these things. John F. Kennedy, who invaded Cuba (and was defeated), whose agents sought to assassinate Castro (and failed), and who started up the Vietnam war that would lead to utter debacle — John F. Kennedy had perhaps made the greatest impact on world opinion of any American since Woodrow Wilson. John F. Kennedy, whose photograph was to be found hanging next to the Sacred Heart of Jesus or Mahatma Gandhi or whomsoever in wooden shacks and mud huts across the world. It was not what he did, but what he had said. Or seemed to say.

When all this was thought through, though, there remained one wrenching contradiction between my thesis and Thompson's, a disagreement that went well beyond tactics, that went to the most fundamental of my assertions. I was naive, he said, to think that the leaders of the new states were interested in liberty. He, too, had once thought this, but had been forced to change his mind. What they were interested in was ruling. Their drive to socialism was related not to the economy, but to coherence.

Thompson's experience had been with Africa, mine with South Asia; and this was turning out to be a significant difference. The newest of the new nations were hardly Fabian. Thus the legacy of Portuguese fascism was a cluster of Stalinist dictatorships in its former colonies. Nothing very good was going on in Africa, and it was there that the numerical majority of the Third World would be found. Historical accident had produced a total of five nations in South Asia — including Bhutan, six — although these six accounted for a quarter of the world's population. Africa, by contrast, emerged from its European period as fifty-one nations, although all combined had only half the population of India, much less South Asia. This was a world I knew little of.

◆

As I prepared to deal with the economic issues no one seemed to understand, it was becoming more clear that economic issues might be the least of the conflict to come. What was this talk about declaring Zionism to be a form of racism? The idea reeked of the concentration camp and the gas chamber. No person sensitive to the idea of liberty in the twentieth century would want in any way to be associated with such language. Surely not the nations I had written about for *Commentary*. And yet it was just these nations that did just this. On August 30, at Lima, the Fifth Summit Conference of the Non-Aligned agreed to a massive agenda for the Special Session and the General Assembly to come. The first substantive paragraph declared:

NON-ALIGNED COUNTRIES HAVE BECOME THROUGH THEIR STRUGGLE AGAINST IMPERIALISM, COLONIALISM, NEOCOLONIALISM, RACISM, ZIONISM, APARTHEID AND ANY OTHER FORM OF FOREIGN DOMINATION ONE OF THE DECISIVE ELEMENTS IN THE SIGNIFICANT CHANGES THAT ARE TAKING PLACE IN INTERNATIONAL RELATIONS. . . .

This was hardly the substance of economics — and certainly not the language of liberalism. Had I got it wrong? Was there no "good news" after all?

Then came a further doubt. Might we have to settle for a Third World such as this one as the only way to keep a balance with the Soviets? In April I had appeared on a panel at the annual meeting of the American Society of Newspaper Editors with Zbigniew Brzezinski, who put it that for years the dominant struggle in the world had been between the United States and the Soviets, and that the Third World nations had generally benefited by playing one of us off against the other. Now, he said, the dominant struggle in the world was between the West and the Third World, with the Soviets the principal beneficiaries. Thompson in his paper had gone further. Even the most seasoned skeptic on the question of the U.N.'s relevance would recognize our isolation there. We were everywhere on the defensive. This had "epochal consequences," Thompson wrote, "because, for better or worse, the third world position redounds to the advantage of the Soviet Union at a time when we are also on the defensive in our relations with her." Did it follow then that we would have to accept the Third World as it revealed itself in Lima, as against the world I was coming to think I had simply dreamed up in my study in the garden in New Delhi? I never resolved the matter in my own mind while I was at the U.N., and I have not done since.

But there was one thing I was clear about. Podhoretz and I had agreed that, come what may, we would not plead guilty. If that is what the others really wanted, they would never get it from me. It was not perhaps that much of a principle to work with, but it saved me from sheer incoherence.

———◆———

This was the New York end of it. In Washington a different set of calculations was at work. Kissinger wanted a victory. If no longer at the height of his influence, he was still formidable. No one, now, knew the government better than he, and he now moved with great energy. Three discernible concerns prompted him. The Special Session would be the first world assembly at which the United States would appear in the aftermath of the defeat in Vietnam. If we were routed here also it would signal something ominous indeed. Alternatively, if we gained the initiative, established ourselves as the dominant force in world development, and brought the session to an American vision of the future, a good deal might be recouped.

A second consideration had to do with the developed countries — "DC's" in the new lexicon of interdependence. There were signs everywhere that our erstwhile allies, far from merely defecting on the occasional vote, were in the process of negotiating something very like a separate peace with the developing nations. In February, 1975, at Lomé in Togo, the European Community had negotiated with forty-six new nations an innovative and integrated set of arrangements on aid, trade, and commodities. Even the United States Treasury took notice. Were the Europeans reconstituting the old colonial system, minus the bother of maintaining a navy? At a Commonwealth meeting in Kingston, after Lomé, Harold Wilson had proposed bold new approaches to commodity problems. None of the Commonwealth or European countries would wish to lose the prestige they appeared to have gained from this. The United States might easily find itself, as an early State Department position paper put it, in "a situation in which we are completely isolated and appear to be the lone defender of status quo policies." Kissinger would have thought even beyond that. The oil price increase had staggered the economies of Western Europe and Japan. The Special Session would meet in September, 1975, at a time of rising unemployment, declining production, and a generally anxious, even fearful mood. The world was in the midst of the worst recession since the great depression of the 1930s. No matter what had brought it on, and no matter what would have happened anyway, there were limits to what the industrial democracies would put up with before they began to say that the trouble had come about because of American policies in the Middle East, and that our policies in the Middle East were dictated by internal American politics that had nothing to do with the interests of Europe or Japan and ought not to interfere with those interests.

A final consideration was that internal political pressures were building in the United States to make some effective response to the demands of the new countries. There were partisans of the new nations in Congress who called for such a response. More important, and especially in the Senate, there was a growing impatience with stalemate and recrimination. Everyone wanted a success.

———————◆———————

Kissinger had called a general meeting at the Department of State on June 18 to organize his campaign. In such matters he was not so much a master of detail as of preparation. At any given moment, while one set of writers was finishing the sixth draft of the next day's speech, another team would be at work on the first draft of the speech to be given six weeks hence, and the Secretary of State would be equally impatient with both. He denied himself nothing in the way of staff, and there was indeed a viceregal quality to the vast establishment that moved with him in stately progress from one capital to another, back and forth across the world. But he got the best, and in Winston Lord, his head of Policy Planning and chief staff writer, one of the most incisive and energetic minds of the Foreign Service.

The June meeting began with an account of a meeting the previous day with a group of Senators to whom the Secretary promised the most progressive program we could contrive for the Special Session, a program which we could hope would avoid a confrontation. He had scheduled a speech in Milwaukee on July 14. It would be a U.N. speech. He wanted a bellicose section, which would express sorrow over the opportunities being destroyed and speak of procedural reforms. He wanted right away a tactical plan for dealing with the key powers. The United States would have two objectives at the Special Session. First, to keep the industrial nations together. Second, to split the Third World. He would speak early. His speech would be sweeping and progressive. He had no illusions that much would come out of a U.N. conference, or indeed out of the U.N. But the European Community was different. It could provide effective channels for multilateral efforts to aid development. We must join. We would avoid issues that could be encompassed in slogans. We would say to the developing countries that we had heard them. We would say to them: "We have understood your concerns and matched them with our own."

I asked whether we would deal with commodities and the new demand that prices be indexed against industrial prices so as to maintain purchasing power. He said we would. At this point Thomas O. Enders, Assistant Secretary of State for Economic and Business Affairs, spoke. He had entered the planning exercise in a way that would have been applauded by the Murphy Commission. The Bureau of International Organization Affairs had begun work on UNGASS the very day the previous UNGA had closed down. The Bureau's first paper, a general policy memorandum, had gone from Buffum to Kissinger on February 3. Alas, the papers prepared for the June 18 meeting noted with the sad candor of a bureau resigned to a low place in the scheme of things, "We have not yet received comment on this memo from the Secretary." Good men had been at work, from the Bureau, from the Agency for International Development, from Policy Planning, but none of them controlled resources, least of all those directly responsible for U.N. affairs. Enders did. He was in charge of the international economic policy of the world's largest economy. He could give and take within that economy, and between it and other economies.

But more. Enders was also the most impressive man in his forties in the Foreign Service. Whatever he touched, he marked. In a world given to blurred distinction, fuzzy grammar, and collective decisions, he strode about, six feet eight inches tall, like an Elizabethan adventurer. He was preparing, he told the meeting, a large-scale income stabilization scheme — for the world. It would be "breathtaking." The U.S. would be receptive to the concerns of the less developed countries, but from a posture of strength. A genuine approach to development must begin with an attitude that these matters can in fact be dealt with effectively, and even solved. We would display this attitude, and would do the solving. We did not mean to ostracize anyone on political grounds. We looked to the Less Developed Countries as the growth area of the future. Their prospects, in increasing degree, would be our prospects. The U.S. Permanent Representative should let others know that this was coming.

This was indeed breathtaking. It was, further, precisely what I had hoped for from a United States in opposition. The developing nations had been coming up with one stereotyped bad idea after another. First, commodity agreements. London, which specialized in failure in these decades, was already the site of three dozen defunct commodity agreements, each presumably still with an office and a secretary somewhere along Leadenhall Street. Now indexing, an idea straight from the *Bureau du Plan* of two dozen defunct tropical economies. Here instead was a concept from *our* experience that we could fairly claim had worked: income stabilization. This was the heart of the social legislation of the New Deal. Social Security, unemployment compensation, and, for that matter and with whatever implications might follow, the minimum wage. Dazzling. I had not the least idea what would be the details of Enders's proposal. I didn't need to.

There were three other matters which it was generally understood we would have to deal with at the Special Session of the General Assembly. There was much talk then of "restructuring" the U.N. to deal with North-South questions. In effect this meant giving the LDC's yet more opportunity to use the imputed powers of the General Assembly for their purposes. Kissinger agreed without interest that we should assent in principle. Food aid would come up, and this Kissinger agreed, even insisted, should be part of our own initiative. Finally there were the multinational corporations, the "MNC's." The U.N. had appointed a Committee of Eminent Persons to look into the question of the conduct of the great world corporations. Senator Jacob K. Javits had been a member of the Committee, and was disposed to the development of a code of conduct of some sort that would allay some of the fears and calm some of the agitation on this issue. Again, Kissinger agreed. Charles W. Robinson, Under Secretary of State for Economic Affairs, Enders's superior, was quite bestirred by the issue in the way one might expect from a man whose considerable fortune came from extracting mineral wealth from less developed countries. He likened the multinational corporation to the giant corporations in the United States at the turn of the century, which were state chartered but becoming nationwide and in need of national standards. He was wholly in favor of an international code of corporate conduct.

Kissinger assigned the work and summed up. The proposals would have to be negotiated through the bureaucracy. (Treasury had been traditionally negative on most of these matters.) We were to leave that to him. He had done it before; he knew where he wanted things to come out. Ultimately he would take it all to the President. In the meantime we were to work with James Lynn, who was the Director of the Office of Management and Budget. Lynn was against grain reserves. It was his right to be.

This was a typical conclusion to a Kissinger meeting. *We* had enemies. He would go now and negotiate with them on our behalf. Later we would learn what he had to give up to ensure our safety. On the other hand, one could sympathize already with the Director of the Office of Management and Budget. Within days he would be hearing that the Department of State — Robinson, Enders, whosoever — was quite out of control, had been taken over by rampaging levelers intent on looting the Treasury and carrying off the presidential plate, but who might, just possibly, if everyone was careful and kept their nerve, who might just be bought off by conceding them a grain reserve.

———◆———

I commenced speaking to the press about the Less Developed Countries in the terms of our meeting, saying, "We have heard you. We are listening — listening hard." But we would not be so polite as to be misunderstood. We would take no nonsense on Israel. The Secretary, I hinted, would be giving a major policy statement in mid-July. This came on July 14 in an address to the Institute of World Affairs, University of Wisconsin, in Milwaukee, which — unusual for any topic and probably unprecedented for an address on the United Nations — was shown on "prime time" network television. As he later remarked, "We showed our teeth." "Kissinger Warns Majority in U.N. on U.S. Support" was the *Times* headline. He was reported as warning the Third World majority that its "arbitrary tactics" in the General Assembly were alienating the support of the American people for the United Nations. In what was taken as a reference to calls for the suspension of Israel — a clearly specified prerogative of the Security Council — he said: "We fear for the integrity and survival of the General Assembly itself and no less for that of the specialized agencies." The United States had been by far the largest financial supporter of the U.N., "but the support of the American people, which has been the lifeblood of the organization, will be profoundly alienated unless fair play predominates and the numerical majority respects the views of the minority." As for world economic issues:

> Never before have the industrial nations been more ready to deal with the problems of development in a constructive spirit. Yet lopsided, loaded voting, biased results and arbitrary tactics threaten to destroy these possibilities.

I had written a portion of the speech, and now for the first time Kissinger and I emerged as of one mind on this issue. Even so, there was a distinction. He, far more than I, was aroused on the subject of the abuses of the General Assembly. Far more than I, he had had to put up with them. But it was I who was seen as the more combative.

For the moment — Egypt having announced she would not renew the mandate for the United Nations peace force in the Sinai — I was shuffling about from one meeting to another, assuring the press that the peace force was likely to remain to "do its role" and that there would be no war. For our part, we were genuinely thinking peace.

———————◆———————

Summer passed in a succession of luncheons and dinners, a legacy of Geneva. Always two wines, always thereafter champagne. Always, seemingly, the Secretary-General thanking the host. I began to know the diplomatic corps, where there were few surprises, but some pleasant, such as H.E. Dr. Edward Wilmot Blyden III, Ambassador Extraordinary and Plenipotentiary of Sierra Leone, "Ed" from our days at the Fletcher School. Radha Krishna Ramphul of Mauritius was still on hand; "No fool like a Ramphul," George Bush used to say.

The best of the lobbyists contend that about one third of the members of the House of Representatives know what they are doing. This is not said in derision, but as a statement of fact about a complex institution which takes time to understand, where there are many players, with something like a random distribution from the quite bright to the quite dim, and with a high turnover. So with the U.N. Whatever the occasion, many delegations would sit in frank bewilderment — and how could they not? It was not likely that more than half the missions received regular and detailed instructions from their governments. Coups at home were not infrequent. Many ambassadors in New York had been sent by previous governments, some going back through several overthrown regimes. In these circumstances, groups such as the Organization for African Unity and the Non-Aligned acquired great influence. As these groups worked by consensus, a kind of forced unanimity, an ambassador called on at home to explain a position could explain that it was the position of almost everyone else and he had had to go along. There were leaders within these groups, some impressive, such as Salim Ahmed Salim of Tanzania, who had some of Julius Nyerere's gentleness mixed with genuinely radical views, and a touch of Nyerere's willingness to board the political prisoners of other regimes, as Tanzania was then doing for friends in Namibia. T. T. B. Koh of Singapore was probably the most gifted ambassador at the United Nations at this time. I had known him in Singapore and looked to him for advice whenever we had any real range of choice. The Scandinavians were — Scandinavians, the exception being Ole Ålgård of Norway. He had spent time in North Vietnam, where he was confidently told the war would end through an uprising in the United States of blacks and trade unionists. He did not seem to like the North Vietnamese. Peter Jankowitsch of Austria was young enough, and interested enough in intellectual politics, to have some sense of the United States. He knew of my social democratic connections, and even ventured out into that world himself.

The strongest disappointment was the Canadian ambassador, Saul F. Rae. He was a career officer of perfect manners and unfailing courtesy, but he represented Mr. Trudeau, and we could never count on Canada to be with us on hard choices where the totalitarian tendencies of the U.N. system were involved. Trudeau seemed to admire Fidel Castro more than Gerald Ford. In quite a different way, the Japanese also disappointed. Their ambassador, Shizuo Saito, was accomplished and subtle but no help. The Japanese foreign policy of avoidance of conflict was compounded here by a profound unwillingness to take sides. When Japanese interests were immediately involved, as with the case of Korea, there was considerable diplomatic competence to be called on. But only then. The West German envoy was no help in a different way: the Baron Rüdiger von Wechmar seemed to spend most of his time in Southampton. When he *did* help, he was superb, but this was rare. There were times when Fernando Salazar of Costa Rica, which, praise God, was on the Security Council, seemed the only ideological support we could count on in all one hundred forty-three other members.

The French Ambassador, Louis de Guiringaud (later Foreign Minister), was firmly of the view that only a dozen or so other ambassadors really much mattered in New York. The five permanent Security Council members, and leaders of blocs such as Salim of Tanzania, and an occasional energetic man from an important country, such as Fereydoun Hoveyda of Iran. This was one of the few of his observations de Guiringaud would have wished taken seriously. Otherwise his deepest concern seemed to be that no one should think he believed anything said at the United Nations, including anything said by the Ambassador of France.

Yakov A. S. Malik was still on hand in 1975, prevaricator-at-large. He had mellowed some by this time, and on occasion would tell stories of Stalin. A complex double game, one had to think: when he gave an account of Stalin lying, was *he* lying? Huang Hua of the People's Republic, who would succeed Chiao Kuan-hua as Foreign Minister, was quite a bit more comfortable than when he had first come down from Ottawa in 1971. He had been Mao's secretary and so was presumably the most powerful individual serving at the U.N. At this time Malik held a party position also, but his time had passed. (It was impressive, though, the Russian's staying power. He was said to have gone on a three-day drunk when Gromyko was chosen Foreign Minister in 1957, but otherwise he had been almost thirty years at this post. By contrast, there had been eleven Americans before I came, some whose tenure was measured in weeks.)

The British Ambassador, Ivor Richard, son of a Welsh mines inspector, was a hugely fat, thoroughly likable, rather cynical politician. He had lost his seat in the House of Commons and was sent to New York as there was nothing else to do with him. For him, the United Nations was the last outpost of empire, the one place on earth where Britain was still

formally a major power. He enjoyed it all immensely, but with the air
of a man who regarded duty-free liquor as the difference between happiness and the real world.

————◆————

In New York we awaited the end of the Non-Aligned Conference,
which had convened in Lima August 25. Their final session came on
the thirtieth. The conference pronouncements, which arrived in New
York by cable on Sunday morning, August 31, put an end to such illusions as I still held about a "British revolution." The political communiqué from the meeting was an endless and at times exuberant document, and what it was exuberant about was the decline and the defeat
of democratic principles and societies across the globe, and, most especially and viciously, the decline and the defeat of American purposes.
The language was unfailingly totalitarian:

> THE FOREIGN MINISTERS EXAMINED THE INTERNATIONAL SITUATION AND
> NOTED THAT THE CONTRADICTIONS BETWEEN THE EXISTENCE OF LARGE
> CONSUMPTION ECONOMIES BASED ON AN UNEQUITABLE STATE OF CRISIS, AND
> THE SOCIAL AND ECONOMIC MARGINATION OF VAST MASSES, IS BECOMING
> MORE ACUTE AND GENERATES A RADICALISATION OF THE REVOLUTIONARY
> POTENTIALITY IN DEVELOPING AREAS WHICH, IN TURN, MANIFESTS ITSELF
> IN THE IRREVERSIBLE PROGRESSION OF AN HISTORICAL CURRENT LEADING TO
> ECONOMIC AND POLITICAL LIBERATION, STRENGTHENING OF NATIONAL
> IDENTITY AND CULTURES AND THE ATTAINMENT OF FAIR SOCIAL ORDERS
> WHICH ALLOW THE MASSES TO PARTICIPATE IN THE DEVELOPMENT PROCESS
> AND IN ITS BENEFITS.

With the defeat of the United States in Southeast Asia, the war was now to
be taken directly to us. The North Vietnamese at the conference condemned United States troop maneuvers in the Canal Zone. The Ministers
at Lima reiterated their support for the demand of the "Cuban Revolutionary Government" that the United States return the base at Guan-
tánamo. Solidarity was declared with efforts to accelerate the process of
decolonization of the Puerto Rican people. (Among those accredited to
attend the Conference was the "Partido Socialista Puertorriqueño.")
The government of the United States was called upon to "CEASE ALL
POLITICAL OR REPRESSIVE MANEUVERS INTENDED TO PERPETUATE THE CO-
LONIAL STATUS OF PUERTO RICO."
     The Ministers noted with satisfaction the great successes of the period
since the Algiers Summit of 1973:

> NON-ALIGNED COUNTRIES HAVE BECOME THROUGH THEIR STRUGGLE
> AGAINST IMPERIALISM, COLONIALISM, NEO-COLONIALISM, RACISM, ZIONISM,

APARTHEID AND ANY OTHER FORM OF FOREIGN DOMINATION ONE OF THE
DECISIVE ELEMENTS IN THE SIGNIFICANT CHANGES THAT ARE TAKING PLACE
IN . . . INTERNATIONAL RELATIONS. . . .

Again and again the document returned to Israel and its connection
with the United States:

THIS MASSIVE SUPPORT TO THE ZIONIST REGIME ELIMINATES ALL DOUBTS
AS TO THE DELIBERATE INTENTION OF THE UNITED STATES AND OTHER IM-
PERIALIST POWERS TO MAKE ISRAEL A BASE OF COLONIALISM AND IMPERIAL-
ISM WITHIN THE THIRD WORLD, AND USE IT TO BREAK THE LIBERATION
MOVEMENTS, CONSOLIDATE RACIST REGIMES, THREATEN PEACE AND SECURITY
IN THE DEVELOPING COUNTRIES AND PLUNDER THEIR NATURAL RESOURCES.

There was no effort to conceal an implicit alliance with the Soviet Union.
The next summit meeting of heads of states or governments, the fifth,
would be held in Colombo in 1976. The Cubans had proposed that the
sixth be held in Havana. The Foreign Ministers urged this course. And
so it went.

Paragraph 66 of the political communiqué seemed unmistakably clear:

THE CONFERENCE CONSIDERS THAT THE UNITY OF THE NON-ALIGNED
COUNTRIES WITH OTHER PROGRESSIVE AND PEACE-LOVING NATIONS HAS RE-
SULTED IN A PROGRESSIVE AND POSITIVE CHANGE IN THE CORRELATION OF
FORCES WITHIN THE UNITED NATIONS ORGANISATION. IN THIS RESPECT, THE
NON-ALIGNED COUNTRIES AGREE TO PRESERVE AND EXTEND THAT UNITY AND
TO DEDICATE ALL OF THEIR EFFORTS FOR THE STRENGTHENING OF THE
STRUCTURES OF THE UNITED NATIONS. . . .

They wanted more power at the U.N.: they assumed the Soviets would
help them to get it.

And yet the Soviets were never going to help anyone strengthen the
structures of the United Nations, least of all of the General Assembly.
As for the Seventh Special Session (to which most of the Foreign Ministers would travel directly from Lima), the Soviets had made clear in a
long sequence of preparatory meetings that spring and summer that no
help should be expected from them. The Chinese had said the same. For
all their denunciation, the Non-Aligned had no choice but to look to
the United States as the one realistic source of aid. Thus: "MEMBERS
ATTENDING THE CONFERENCE RECALL THAT CONTRIBUTION TO THE RE-
CONSTRUCTION OF VIETNAM IS A COMMITMENT THAT WAS SOLEMNLY UNDER-
TAKEN BY THE UNITED STATES UNDER THE PARIS AGREEMENT."

For all the assertion of strength, there was the nagging fact of instability. The Lima conference had been scheduled to close Friday, August 29, but on that day the government of Peru was overthrown, and the conference was held over a day while its Chairman, General Miguel Ángel de la Flor Valle, Foreign Minister of Peru, to whom was entrusted the task of submitting to the Seventh Special Session the Lima Programme for Mutual Assistance and Solidarity, slipped away to find out whether he was still Foreign Minister. (He was.) For all the assertions of solidarity, there was the fact also of genuine and possibly growing internal divisions. In a wide-ranging press conference in the course of the summit meeting, Mandungu Bula Nyati, Minister of Foreign Affairs of Zaire, made what appeared to be the first break in ranks on the subject of OPEC. All member countries, he claimed, needed to review the cartel's "activities and decisions." He accused the Portuguese representative, Admiral Rosa Coutinho, of being "an active defender of Portuguese colonialism in Angola" — because he supplied the M.P.L.A. faction in Angola with arms and aid furnished by the Russians. The Lima Embassy's summary cable on the meeting indicated that Angola was becoming a more general center of controversy:

> IN SEPARATE PRESS CONFERENCES . . . ANGOLA'S MPLA AND FLNA REPRE-
> SENTATIVES EXCHANGED INSULTS AND ACCUSATIONS. THE MPLA'S JORGE LED
> OFF BY ACCUSING THE FLNA OF CANNIBALISM. HE SAID MPLA FORCES HAVE
> DISCOVERED IN FLNA STRONGHOLDS REFRIGERATORS CONTAINING CADAVERS
> OF CHILDREN WITH FRUIT STUFFED IN THEIR MOUTHS, READY FOR THE
> OVEN. THE FLNA'S . . . NOTE REJECTED THESE CHARGES AND SAID THEY
> IMPUGNED ALL ANGOLANS. [IT] SAID THE MPLA WAS "PRO SOVIET" AND RE-
> CEIVED SUPPORT FROM THE U.S.S.R.

In contrast to all this, the cable reported that the most enthusiastically received speech had been a measured and conciliatory address by the Algerian Foreign Minister, Abdelaziz Bouteflika, who was still President of the General Assembly, and would preside at the Special Session. In a *New York Times* dispatch from Lima, Kathleen Teltsch reported a softer stand, noting:

> Third-world members concede that they are disappointed — some use the word "distressed" — that during months of consultation the Soviet Union and China have offered them voting support but no practical help and seem intent on using the special session to accuse each other of propagandizing.

In fact, she observed, Europeans were privately voicing concern that Kissinger might go too far to meet the Non-Aligned.

———◆———

Reality had changed. Sensibilities had not quite caught up with the change, but the first adumbrations were to be seen in the speech of the Zairean minister, in the private comments of the Europeans. The great transfer of wealth from North to South had already taken place. But OPEC had got it all. And wasn't sharing it. The heart had gone out of the old rhetoric. For the losers it hurt too much to admit this, but it was nonetheless so.

———◆———

Kissinger was scheduled to speak on the opening day of the Special Session on Monday, September first. But by the weekend it was clear that he would not get back from the Middle East, where a Sinai agreement was being worked out and I was asked to give the speech for him. This could not have been an easy thing for him to pass up; but if our proposals came too late in a two-week conference, we would lose our impact, and he was determined to succeed. There were, in fact, quite narrow limits to his vanity where something was involved that he judged to be in the national interest.

The speech opened:

> We assemble here this week with an opportunity to improve the condition of mankind. We can let this opportunity slip away, or we can respond to it with vision and common sense.
>
> The United States has made its choice. . . .

There followed one hour and forty-five minutes of text. Nothing like it had ever been presented to an international forum. The proposals were concrete, grouped in five clusters, of which the first was "income maintenance," now termed "basic economic security":

> First, we must apply international cooperation to the problem of insuring basic economic security. The United States proposes steps to safeguard against the economic shocks to which developing countries are particularly vulnerable: sharp declines in their export earnings from the cycle of world supply and demand, food shortages, and natural disasters.
>
> Second, we must lay the foundations for accelerated growth. The United States proposes steps to improve developing countries' access to capital markets, to focus and adapt new technology to specific development needs, and to reach consensus on the conditions for foreign investment.
>
> Third, we must improve the basic opportunities of the developing

countries in the world trading system so they can make their way by earnings instead of aid.

Fourth, we must improve the conditions of trade and investment in key commodities on which the economies of many developing countries are dependent, and we must set an example in improving the production and availability of food.

Fifth, let us address the special needs of the poorest countries, who are the most devastated by current economic conditions, sharing the responsibility among old and newly wealthy donors.

The details took twelve thousand words. There would be a financing agency connected to the International Monetary Fund to lend developing countries up to $10 billion at the rate of $2.5 billion a year to sustain their development programs in the face of fluctuating earnings from exports. An international investment trust linked to the World Bank's International Finance Corporation would attract capital for developing countries. There would be an international energy institute. A thirty-million-ton world grain reserve. A major change in the tariff systems whereby industrial countries favored the import of raw materials over manufactured goods.

The closing passage was of equal note:

> I began today with the statement that we have, this week, an opportunity to improve the condition of mankind. This fact alone represents an extraordinary change in the human condition. Throughout history, man's imagination has been limited by his circumstances, which have now fundamentally changed. We are no longer confined to what Marx called the *realm of necessity*.
>
> The steps we take now are not limited by our technical possibilities, but only by our political will. If the advanced nations fail to respond to the winds of change, and if the developing countries choose rhetoric over reality, the great goal of economic development will be submerged in our common failure. . . .
>
> My government does not offer these proposals as an act of charity, nor should they be received as if due. We know that the world economy nourishes us all, we know that we live on a shrinking planet. Materially as well as morally, our destinies are intertwined.
>
> There remain enormous things for us to do. We can say once more to the new nations: We have heard your voices. We embrace your hopes. We will join your efforts. We commit ourselves to our common success.

At last it was over. I stepped down, wondering how the word "can" had got into the last paragraph. As the press reported, delegates had tended to drift out for coffee during the middle of the speech, but the hall was again crowded at the end and there was long applause. "Envoys from scores of nations," a press report went, "crowded around" to offer congratulations. Ivor Richard pronounced it "the most significant American speech on economic policy since the Marshall Plan."

The press reaction around the world was overwhelmingly favorable, and most curiously so in France. *Quotidien de Paris,* an intellectual-left publication, wrote on September 3 that "in the corridors of the U.N. no one hesitates to speak of a 'new deal' for the world. Most delegates admit that the proposals advanced by Mr. Kissinger . . . indicate a profound revision in the main directions of U.S. foreign economic policy." Jean Schwoebel, in *Le Monde,* noted that the U.S., Japan, and the European Community participated actively in the Special Session working groups, while "the socialist countries have been all but absent." He found that even the "hardliners" among the developing nations, and the most radical, such as Algeria, were saying that

> the Americans for the first time are using a language understandable to the countries on the road to development, even if they still refuse to talk about a "new world order" and substitute "stock regulators" for "indexation."

The *Frankfurter Allgemeine* judged that I was "leading a more self-confident America in the United Nations." The U.N. correspondent of the *Kölner Stadt-Anzeiger* reported that the rhetoric of some hotheads had cooled down: "Not a few developing countries now concede that they are dependent on know-how and capital from the once-despised multinational concerns."

The London *Times* of September 3 discerned "signs of an awakening similar to that which grew out of the industrial revolution when the power of the poor and the conscience of the rich began to alert the structure of society." The Swedish state radio commented that the new U.S. proposals "mark a turning point in U.S. policy" and had brought us much closer to the less developed countries. "Likened in some quarters to the Marshall Plan," the Swedes said, "the new plan puts the U.S. far ahead of the European community countries." The Japanese press, with a perhaps disconcerting realism, concentrated their reporting and comment on the International Monetary Fund meetings then taking place in Washington, but did append the notice that the U.S. had taken "a positive posture" in New York. The Indian press, not surprisingly, was sour. T. V. Parasuram, the Washington correspondent of the *Indian Express,* showed a typical Indian grasp of reality: "The Russians," he wrote, "are a little more helpful than the Americans in that they are

willing to give their votes to the developing countries." The Nairobi
Standard, by contrast, editorialized that the U.S. position, and Kenya's
call for a "new deal" at the Special Session, showed that the "world's
developing and industrialized nations are now on the brink of a work-
able compromise." It even criticized some of the Group of 77 as behaving
like the "ideological misfits they are." In Mexico City the middle-of-the-
road *Novedades* declared of the Secretary's speech, "It is the first time
that the U.S. has supported the recommendations of the U.N. Charter
of Economic Rights and Duties of States. . . ." Caracas was not so
pleased. The news magazine *Resumen* said: "Henry Kissinger in the
forum of the United Nations characterized the oil price rises of the
OPEC producers as 'arbitrary and monopolistic.' This is not the vocabulary of dialogue. . . ." But this was predictable from an OPEC country.
By far the majority of other commentators asserted that something large
was taking place.

———◆———

In the speech, Kissinger was at pains to point out that the "senior
economic officials of our government" had joined him in developing the
United States position, that Treasury Secretary William Simon had
worked closely on the program, that a large Congressional delegation
would attend the Special Session. The American delegation was indeed
huge. As was customary, two members of Congress were appointed as
members of the delegation — Donald M. Fraser, Democrat of Minnesota,
and J. Herbert Burke, Republican of Florida — along with Clarence
Mitchell as the public member. But with them for the Special Session
came twelve Senators and six Representatives. Each was assigned a subject — "industrialization," "restructuring," "international trade,"
"science and technology," "food," "resource transfer" — and commenced
attending the working group sessions that were established at the outset.
Senators Jacob K. Javits of New York and Charles H. Percy of Illinois
had a wide acquaintance among the thirty to forty foreign ministers who
were on hand and worked double time at their tasks. Kissinger had done
what they had asked. It was now their turn to tell others that this was
all the United States was going to concede, and, more important, that it
represented our honest judgment as to what would work. The speech
had defended the multinational corporations and attacked the oil cartel;
it had called for guidelines to protect foreign investment and asked an
end to the climate of retaliation and threat in which investment had so
fallen off. This was not the tone of the New International Economic
Order that the previous Special Session had called for, nor yet of the

Charter of Economic Rights and Duties, which had been adopted by the last General Assembly. But in what we did propose, we were dead earnest.

Following the speech, I gave a reception for our Congressional delegation and invited a host of ambassadors. Javits, as the senior member present from the Foreign Relations Committee, spoke and was at his most effective. The United States, he said, had come in good faith to do what had been asked of it. The Secretary's program could be enacted by Congress, but only if there was evidence of a good faith response. If the Special Session were to degenerate into vituperation and obstruction, an opportunity would have been lost which he could not guarantee would come again. This was the time for the developing nations to judge whether development was more important to them than ideology. The ambassadors heard him and agreed. Only Akhund of Pakistan raised the question as to whether the United States intended to deprive the developing nations of their ideology — and, if so, whether it would in truth be a fair exchange. A deeper thought than anyone was quite prepared for.

———◆———

The working sessions began; the foreign ministers continued to speak to the Assembly. James Callaghan of Britain gave a weak performance, immobilized as the British socialists were by memories of leadership and liberation, and by sudden, convulsive impulses to go over to the other side, to declare themselves bankrupt, to demand of the world's wealthy that something be done for the poor, including the poor British. By contrast, Hans-Dietrich Genscher of the Federal Republic of Germany gave a tough-minded speech; far more stern on the subject of economic realities than any American would have dared be, and from a government as impeccably socialist as any the British could field. The difference was that the Germans were earning their way, while the British at that moment were as much dependent on international assistance as any of the "Most Seriously Affected."

One by one the Western nations spoke; little was heard from the East. Gromyko did not appear; instead we got Gyorgy G. Shevel, Minister for Foreign Affairs of the Ukraine, a sure sign that the occasion was judged to be of no importance. China sent Li Chiang, Minister of Foreign Trade. From the first, the two large Communist powers went at one another, paying no attention and offering nothing to the developing countries in whose interests the Special Session had been called. On Thursday, September 4, I sent around the U.S. delegation a summary and comment on this, which, for what it may be worth (and at whatever cost to American diplomacy's reputation for realism) describes the American mood four days into the twelve-day meeting:

I

In the past three days, each of the three great powers has had its opportunity to present its case to the assembled countries. . . .

The Soviets responded to the needs of the poor countries by declaring with some satisfaction, "It is not the Soviet Union who for ages used to plunder the national wealth of former colonial possessions which nowadays have come to be sovereign states. It is not the Soviet Union who used to exploit their population for centuries. Therefore, the Soviet Union does not bear — I specifically underline it — does not bear any responsibility whatsoever for the economic backwardness of the developing countries. . . ." The Chinese had their own uplifting advice for the countries of the poor: self-reliance. "By self-reliance," Mr. Li patiently explained, "we mean that a country should mainly rely on the strength and wisdom of its own people, control its own economic life-lines, make full use of its own resources, work hard, increase production, practice economy and develop its national economy step by step by a planned way."

Indeed, the Chinese and the Soviets devoted most of their time to attacking one another. The Chinese judgment on Soviet socialism: "The other super-power which claims to be a 'socialist' country is energetically pushing its policy of plunder and exploitation on a global scale." And the Soviet riposte to the Chinese Delegate: "The state which he represents already long ago replaced socialism by great power chauvinism, ultra-nationalism and unbridled desire to world hegemony." . . .

We find ourselves in a situation which exposes with stunning clarity the practical difference between American and Soviet or Chinese standards of behavior in world affairs. . . .

II

But there is a danger in all of this. We must not let it be forgotten that what we have offered is not merely a superior set of proposals on specific issues; it is a sign of the more general claim we can fairly lay to the developing world's trust and respect.

We must draw this connection; we must make it frequently and forcefully. We cannot content ourselves with a single avoidance of defeat; we must use this opportunity to seek a deeper and more powerful influence over the ideas that govern men.

———◆———

Kissinger arrived on the fifth and gave us all of his day. Bouteflika was once again in the chair, and Kissinger showed him that particular deference that could be hugely flattering. They agreed that it was all, after all, mere words: words, words, words. Men of the world did not attach overmuch importance to words. With Emilio Rabasa of Mexico, Kissinger was just the opposite. Words were everything. For indeed they were to Mexico's President Echeverría, the author of the Charter of Economic Rights and Duties of States. And, in truth, by this point there was beginning to be trouble over words. The momentum from Monday was beginning to fade. Enders and Myerson were negotiating eighteen and twenty hours a day, but somehow nothing was happening. The U.S. and Mexican Foreign Ministers thereupon summoned their respective ambassadors, Alfonso García Robles and me. With the genuine style he reserved for such occasions, Kissinger let it be understood that the two of them had decided that the Special Session was going to be a success, and that we should work it out. Period.

On Saturday he met in Washington with S. S. Ramphal, Secretary-General of the Commonwealth, who reported that while the speech had been most favorably received (if not fully understood) by most Less Developed Country delegations, the Algerians "advocated digging in for a long siege." This was not good news. Bouteflika had quite dominated the Twenty-Ninth General Assembly, a master of symbolic defiance and protracted insult. On Wednesday, in the Soviet Union's speech, Malik began by thanking him, as presiding officer, for declaring, as presiding officer, that the Soviet bloc and the Third World were "natural allies." At this time the Western countries plus Japan, Australia, and New Zealand were providing more foreign aid in one year than the Soviets had provided in all of the postwar era (the Soviets had given less than $9.5 billion during this period). The Soviets' total share of world foreign trade at the time was 3.7 percent, a measure of the potential of their market. And yet Bouteflika was prepared to call them "natural allies."

The prime obstacle to agreement was the draft resolution that the Non-Aligned had brought with them from Lima, an interminable catalogue of accusation and demand assembled on the plebiscitary principle that the most extreme obtains the most support. It had been drafted without reference to the American proposals, and the working group simply could not fit the two documents together. Nor was there going to be much help from the chairman of the group, Jan Plonk, the Dutch Minister of Development and Cooperation. Plonk was far more a danger than Bouteflika, for he believed the things that Bouteflika merely said.

The moment was at hand for the unexpected. The reference to Marx in the closing lines of the Secretary's speech was calculated: my contention that we could quote scripture, had read the same books, had written some, were not only listening but *understood*. Understood more perhaps than some would wish, and could play the same game. It was time to demonstrate this.

The summer had been easy. Garment and I were both fresh. Over Saturday and Sunday, in a session that lasted some forty hours, we simply rewrote the Non-Aligned draft resolution, conforming to their format and using identical language, while changing the meaning of every sentence in ways we hoped that would take time and some wit to recognize. Thus, preambular paragraph five of the Non-Aligned draft contained the familiar threat: "Conscious that the accelerated development of the developing countries would best promote world peace and security. . . ." This was to be read as a threat: unless development accelerated, the poor in their frustration would rise and make war on the rich. The language we substituted was the same but different: "Conscious that the accelerated development of developing countries would best promote world harmony and well being." Between lines and in the margins we wrote in some forty-one distinct proposals that had been included in our speech. On Sunday we passed the word that a giant *new* American proposal was being prepared to break the deadlock of the conference. Monday was spent getting clearances from Washington, which was as alarmed by our new language as the conference was meant to be reassured by it. The American working paper was promised by afternoon . . . end of the day . . . early evening. At about eight-thirty I had to go across the street to tell some sixty waiting Ambassadors that our Xerox machine had broken down. Hoveyda offered the use of the Shah's. Finally the working paper was ready.

It worked. On Tuesday, September 9, in London, the *Financial Times* reported that the Special Session was on the verge of a breakthrough because of our working paper:

> The paper is considerably more radical than Dr. Henry Kissinger's speech to the session last week, which was itself seen as a major turning point in U.S. policy toward the third world. It is also more notably in tune with third world thinking than the working paper already submitted by the European community.

———◆———

This was tactics on our part, but not trickery. We were genuinely trying, and at mid-week almost produced a further American proposal of large proportion.

A focus of contention — it was just that, a specific point — between the developed countries and the West was the goal set in the 1960s that the developed countries should contribute 0.7 percent a year of their gross national product for development purposes. The United States had never committed itself to this goal. In money terms, we provided the most aid (although by no means the highest proportion of GNP) and we had done so the longest, but our levels had been declining and political support seemed to have vanished. It would have been out of the question to get commitment to the 0.7 percent goal included in the Secretary's speech. If the Department had agreed, which was unlikely, the Treasury would have blocked it; if Treasury had been careless, the Office of Management and Budget would have caught it. If the whole of the executive branch lost its senses, Congress would have stopped it somehow. But now, on Wednesday, I called Rumsfeld and said that we had to have the 0.7 percent if the Special Session was not to collapse. Garment got on the line too and said that this was what power was about, and he should use it: a nice combination of confirmation and challenge. Rumsfeld was, just then, the second or third most powerful man in the executive branch. If there were a dozen men in the government Rumsfeld genuinely trusted, Garment and I were among them, which gave us a kind of power also. A less likely trio would have been hard to find, but there we were and we knew it. Rumsfeld said yes.

Kissinger said no. We sent word to him of our coup, as we imagined it to be. He called back in two hours, not furious but implacable. No one under his command in the Department of State was to go over his head to the White House. The United States would *not* announce that it was committing itself to the 0.7 percent foreign assistance goal of the United Nations Development Decade.

———◆———

Negotiations now became continuous. Energy is the ultimate arbiter of government, and Enders was evidently capable of any exertion. He never noticed time, never tired. He was matched in this by Manuel Férez Guerrero, Minister of State for International Economic Affairs of the Government of Venezuela, who was near to twice his age, but who somehow suggested that if it came to something so coarse as a test of endurance he would prevail out of sheer disdain for such vulgarity. He had served in the League of Nations; one conference more or less was not going to transform his view of the world. By seven o'clock Sunday morning we had an agreement.

———◆———

At twenty minutes past noon, pancaked and wired, I was sitting next to Lawrence E. Spivak in the NBC television studios at Rockefeller Plaza awaiting the beginning of *Meet the Press,* when a message came from Garment. Bouteflika had rejected the agreement. Time had now run out. The regular General Assembly was to open Tuesday. And the United States had run out of concessions. The Seventh Special Session was about to collapse, much as the Sixth Special Session had done. Bill Monroe of NBC News, one of the panelists and a man who can tell when another man has been handed bad news, opened by asking what reaction we were getting now from the Less Developed Countries. I said the Special Session was about to collapse, and we did not much give a damn. My actual words were only slightly hedged; my meaning in the context was clear:

> To use a tired phrase of a tired negotiator, we are cautiously optimistic. We went to bed very early this morning thinking we had the substance of agreement. The other side has put in new language now, just a few moments ago, and I don't want to say an agreement is in jeopardy, but agreement has not been reached and the clock is running.

Robert Bartley of *The Wall Street Journal* then gave me the question I needed. Suppose we didn't get an agreement at the Special Session; "What difference will it really make?" My answer, with 138 delegations watching, was that it would no doubt disappoint us, but it wouldn't cost *us* anything at all. On the other hand, it might prove considerably costly to the representatives of the poor nations who had evidently decided to sell out their own people because the Communist powers wanted them to do so. Paul Hofmann of *The New York Times* asked the next question. At the Lima conference, he said, "they" had circulated copies of an edition of the *Daily News* of Tanzania that reprinted a supposed diplomatic note from the United States to the government of President Nyerere saying that if the Tanzanian representative to the U.N. voted against the United States on the issue of Puerto Rico, the United States would consider this a flagrant interference with our internal affairs and an unfriendly act. The *Daily News* of Tanzania, Hofmann further reported, had stated that this was a rude and intimidatory thing to do. The *Daily News* was correct, I answered; we had meant to be rude. I added that the Committee on Decolonization consisted of sixteen police states, four democracies, and four others: "We are not about to be lectured by police states on the processes of electoral democracy." If others wished to publish our diplomatic notes, they were free to do so. I returned to the Seventh Special Session:

> For an awful lot of these countries, while we are proposing to negotiate a substantive agreement, they want to negotiate a symbolic one. Indeed, for many of them you sometimes think they want a symbolic surrender from the United States, a symbolic admission of guilt. But we aren't

guilty any more than any other nation, any other people in the world, and we are not plea bargaining. . . .

What some of them want is the assertion that their present condition has been caused by the advanced nations, typically the Americans, as the largest and most industrialized, perhaps, and in consequence of which responsibilities flow, as from a plea of guilty.

And we tell them, "No, you can't get that." We keep saying, "Sorry. That is not going to happen."

Once they get that, everything else is plea bargaining in fact. That is what we are not doing. We don't feel our record is anything to be ashamed of. Have we been perfect as a society? Certainly not. . . .

The question is do the leaders of the present movement . . . really want that kind of consequence, or are they going to be stuck in that old Leninist proposition, "the worse, the better"? Don't kid yourselves, there are those who think "the worse, the better."

———◆———

The next day, Monday, I let it be known again that we assumed that Bouteflika had wrecked the Special Session, and that we were now busy getting ready for the regular General Assembly, which would open on Tuesday and would not have an Algerian president. Monday evening I gave a reception at the Mission for arriving delegates. Midway through, a messenger brought a copy of a resolution that had just been adopted by a special caucus of the Non-Aligned. I had formally been denounced by them.

In the Tuesday morning *Times*, Hofmann reported that the Special Session was closing, with the outcome much in doubt:

UNITED NATIONS, N.Y., Monday, Sept. 15—

The General Assembly's special session on the plight of the third world moved early today toward a weary and potentially grim end after delegates worked well into the night in search of a formula for narrowing the chasm between rich and poor lands.

But *The Times* was for once behind the news. At five o'clock that same morning, the Special Session had reached unanimous agreement on the broadest development program in the history of the United Nations and, for that matter, in the history of the world. Hours later I spoke in the General Assembly. "Mr. President," I said, turning to Bouteflika, now outgoing president, "This system works." We had called the Algerian bluff, and this time the genuinely poor nations would not be intimidated. We had bargained in good faith, had come forward with an extraordinary set of proposals, and the new nations had responded as I had argued they would do.

8

Amin

THE SPECIAL SESSION concluded toward noon on Tuesday, September 16,
and the Thirtieth General Assembly began at 3 o'clock the same afternoon. The auspices had rarely been better.

Gaston Thorn of Luxembourg succeeded Bouteflika — which is to
say that the European Community assumed presidency of the Assembly.
It is the theory of the Community that its members are equal and
sovereign; and in Community proceedings, which are numerous,
ministers and officials treat one another alike, such that the least of them
can acquire a considerable personal authority. To this arrangement
Thorn added the circumstance of being the senior Prime Minister in
Western Europe, and Senior Foreign Minister. (He was, moreover,
Luxembourg's Minister of Sport, a portfolio to which he manifestly
attached equal importance to that of Foreign Affairs when it came to
mustering electoral majorities.) French without resentment, and German without guilt, he was everything we could have hoped for. He was
never, I think, against us.

———◆———

The Foreign Ministers' fair commenced. In medieval France such
gatherings were called *piés poudreux,* which came over to English as

"piepowder," and there was indeed something of this in the rag-taggle of traders and brokers, jugglers and mendicants that gathered to visit the U.N. as they do each fall. Each gives a speech about disarmament, or world poverty; some of which are worse than others. After the current Indian spoke, a Norwegian remarked that one longed for Krishna Menon. This year also there was a mandatory but in truth quite genuine opening reference in most of the speeches to the success of the Special Session. Olaf V of Norway came, considerably more democratic than the potentates from the People's Republics to the east, and spoke for a general mood:

> The successful conclusion of the Seventh Special Session of the General Assembly has initiated a universal and co-operative process to effect changes in international economic relations which may have far-reaching impact on the daily life of millions around the globe.

Praise came from less expected quarters as well. Thus Kenya:

> The resolution unanimously adopted at the Seventh Special Session constitutes a truly historic and significant break-through in the right direction. Its provisions in the areas of trade, finance, industrialization and agriculture do, without a doubt, represent a concrete step toward the establishment of that new understanding and also that new system of international, economic relationship to which we all aspire.

And Algeria:

> The most recent Special Session meetings of the General Assembly appear . . . to favour a change. . . . The new economic order is no longer viewed as a piecemeal readjustment that was to be made to individual distortions of the world economic system. . . .

And even, grudgingly, the USSR:

> The Soviet Union is fully aware of the legitimate interests and demands of the developing countries, and it based itself precisely upon such positions in the course of the recently concluded Seventh Special Session of the General Assembly, the results of which we assess positively, although it is quite clear to everyone that much has still to be done before the relevant problems are actually solved.

Kissinger spoke on September 22, also opening with a discussion of the achievement of the Special Session which had "forged a sense of common purpose. . . ." He said that it was now the task to implement this "consensus": "Let us carry forward the spirit of conciliation into the deliberations of this Regular Session." He then went on to a general and familiar review of the state of the world, pausing to assert one new initiative. In a passage headed "Building For Peace" he set forth a series of goals, concluding: "We shall struggle for the realization of fundamental human rights." He spoke of the Helsinki agreements, asserted that "there is no longer any dispute that international human rights are on the agenda of international diplomacy," and specifically proposed that the General Assembly take action on the question of torture.

He ended well, speaking in a U.N. rhetoric that was no doubt debased by this time, but not for every government. We still believed such passages:

> My country's history, Mr. President, tells us that it is possible to fashion unity while cherishing diversity; that common action is possible despite the variety of races, interests and beliefs we see here in this Chamber. Progress and peace and justice are attainable.
>
> So we say to all peoples and governments: Let us fashion together a new world order. Let its arrangements be just. Let the new nations help shape it and feel it is theirs. Let the old nations use their strengths and skills for the benefit of all mankind. Let us all work together to enrich the spirit and to ennoble mankind.

------◆------

Three events now combined to foretell a different future for the Thirtieth General Assembly. First came Vietnam.

One by one, and two by two, new nations of the Third World were continuing to be admitted to the U.N., but fewer now with any pretense to nonalignment. Five decades of Portuguese misrule had given us overnight four Communist regimes in Africa, with Angola still to come. In September the Cape Verde Islands were admitted — with an audience in the Security Council gallery of Cape Verdeans recruited by Suzanne Weaver. (There are possibly more Cape Verdeans in the United States than in their homeland.) Also in September São Tomé and Príncipe, off the west coast of Africa, population 85,500, was welcomed, in this case by Bennett, who as Ambassador to Portugal had been to the place and was perhaps the only person in New York who could positively attest to its existence. Next Papua New Guinea, with about as many languages as São Tomé had people. Later the Comoros, off Africa's east coast, with the 18,000 Christians on Mayotte pleading to be left to take their chances with French colonialism.

But it was to the Vietnams that attention turned. The war was over: the Communists had won; we had lost, and in the end been utterly humiliated. The admission of the two new regimes would symbolize and confirm that, and also the end of the period in which the United States was *the* principal actor in world affairs, responsible for everything going on and for whatever changes were taking place; required to facilitate some and to prevent others; responsible for keeping order. Salvador de Madariaga had allowed that the world would miss the British when they were gone. Few were as yet prepared to miss the Americans. The issue came down to whether to accept the admission of the two Vietnams. (Hanoi had announced the eventual intent of the two governments to merge, but for the moment they insisted on a separate identity.) The subject was waiting when I got back from Geneva in July. The Mission staff was unanimous. In no circumstances must we block the entry of our former adversaries. To do so would outrage the General Assembly, jeopardize everything that was at stake in the Special Session, and bring on the expulsion of Israel. Bennett did not dissociate himself from the argument, while others made it with an intensity unusual in the Foreign Service. Only in time did I come to suspect that the intensity was from fear. Fear of what the foreigners would do, fear of what Americans would say Sundays at brunch in Scarsdale. The career officers were in truth in a hard position, for their own culture no longer approved what they were doing; and they were doing it in New York, not in someplace far away. It was the first major decision I had to make, and I took their advice. I had no disposition otherwise.

On August 6, the Security Council had met to receive new membership applications, the routine being for these to be referred to an Admissions Committee, which would thereafter report them back with recommendations. The applications of the Vietnams were routinely referred. But next, by a 7 to 7 vote, the Council decided not even to receive the application of South Korea. The South Korean application had been before the Security Council for twenty-six years. When South Korea first applied in 1949 and on three subsequent occasions, there had been a majority on the Security Council in favor of receiving the request, a procedural matter not subject to the veto. Only at the next stage, when admission had been recommended, were the Soviets able to veto the actual admission. But by 1975 we could not even get the application considered.

I stated explicitly to the Security Council that we would vote to admit both North and South Vietnam, and also North Korea, but that our condition was that South Korea come in too; South Korea, which was even then seeking membership in the Non-Aligned bloc. But the balance of forces was now with the Soviets, and they would give nothing.

In the August 6 Security Council meeting, I had invoked the authority of the Charter, under which it was a reasonably clear duty of a Security

Council member to agree to having the Admissions Committee consider an application and report back as to whether qualifications for membership were met. The Soviets were predictably unmoved, but so equally were the new nations, no one of which had any greater right to membership than did South Korea. Ivor Richard and I made the most of the matter procedurally until at one point the President of the Council, Shizuo Saito, unexpectedly (and probably unintentionally) ruled in our favor on a point of some importance. We seized on this. The Soviets, for their part, denied that the hapless Japanese had said what in our plain hearing he *had* said, and insisted that any resolution of the matter would have to await an official transcript. The British thereupon produced a tape recording made by a Reuters man in the gallery. We had been altogether correct in our claim, but the Russians insisted that the journalist was not an official, and could not affect official decisions. I was left to note for the record that "it is a long-standing tradition in my country to prefer the word of Reuters to the word of any government."

In the wake of this preliminary defeat, I was ready to confront the Soviets. They were in a position that could not win on the merits, regardless of how a vote might turn out. They were acting in a totalitarian mode, in the face of a Charter which quite unmistakably mandated democratic procedure. The Chinese were staying out of it. Let the Vietnamese enter, I reasoned, and never let anyone forget the exclusion of South Korea. I sent off my first long cable to Washington:

ONE

THE DECISION ON THE ADMISSION OF NORTH AND SOUTH VIETNAM . . . WILL BE A FATEFUL ONE. ACCORDINGLY AS WE ACT, THE WORLD SYSTEM THE UNITED STATES ESTABLISHED AFTER THE SECOND WORLD WAR COULD COMMENCE TO COME APART ALTOGETHER. OR BY ACTING WITH COURAGE AND CONVICTION ON THIS AS THE PRESIDENT PROPOSED IN HIS TULANE SPEECH, WE "CAN REGAIN THE SENSE OF PRIDE THAT EXISTED BEFORE VIETNAM. . . ."

TWO

THE UNITED STATES SHOULD STATE THE GRAVEST POSSIBLE DOUBTS THAT EITHER OF THESE REGIMES CAN BE JUDGED TO UPHOLD THE PRINCIPLES OF THE UNITED NATIONS CHARTER. A DETAILED, AND IF THE SECRETARY SO DESIRES, AN EXCORIATING ACCOUNT OF THEIR PAST AND PRESENT ACTIONS CAN BE STATED FOR ALL THE WORLD TO WATCH, IN A COUNCIL SESSION THAT WILL ATTRACT WORLD WIDE ATTENTION. WE CAN THEN SAY THAT WE ARE FORCED TO CHOOSE BETWEEN TWO PRINCIPLES. ON THE ONE HAND THE ADHERENCE BY PARTICULAR COUNTRIES TO THE UNITED NATIONS PRINCIPLES: ON THE OTHER HAND THE PRINCIPLE OF UNIVERSALITY OF MEMBERSHIP OF THE UNITED NATIONS ITSELF. THESE TWO PRINCIPLES CONFLICT IN THIS CASE. AND OF THE TWO THE UNITED STATES CONSIDERS THE PRINCIPLE OF UNIVERSALITY TO BE THE MORE IMPORTANT. ACCORDINGLY WE HAVE DECIDED TO

ABSTAIN ON THE RESOLUTION AND SO PERMIT THE ENTRY OF THESE TWO NATIONS.

THREE

ON THE SAME OCCASION THE UNITED STATES SHOULD REITERATE OUR WHOLE-HEARTED SUPPORT FOR THE ADMISSION OF SOUTH KOREA, EITHER SOLO OR TOGETHER WITH NORTH KOREA. . . . IF OUR WILLINGNESS TO SEE THE VIETNAMS ENTER IS KNOWN IN ADVANCE, WE OUGHT TO BE ABLE TO INSIST ON A VOTE ON KOREA.

FOUR

AT THE SAME TIME THE UNITED STATES REPRESENTATIVE SHOULD MAKE AN EXHAUSTIVE AND UNYIELDING STATEMENT IN DEFENSE OF THE OBVERSE OF THE PRINCIPLE OF UNIVERSALITY. . . . WE WILL HAVE THE OCCASION TO REMIND THE WORLD THAT THE UNITED NATIONS IS A SYSTEM BASED ON THE PRINCIPLE OF REPRESENTATION. THIS IS A WESTERN PRINCIPLE, NO DOUBT. MOST MEMBERS OF THE UNITED NATIONS DO NOT THEMSELVES HAVE REPRE-SENTATIVE GOVERNMENTS. BUT IF THEY WANT A UNITED NATIONS THEY WILL SIMPLY HAVE TO ACCEPT THAT PRINCIPLE IN THE WORLD BODY. . . .

FIVE

WE WILL NOT GET KOREA INTO THE UNITED NATIONS UNLESS NORTH KOREA ABOUT-FACES. BUT THIS AMERICAN REPRESENTATIVE WILL DEMAND DAILY TO KNOW WHY WE HAVE NOT, WHY THE COMMUNIST POWERS ONLY WANT OTHER COMMUNIST POWERS AS MEMBERS. FOR THE FIRST TIME IN A LONG WHILE THE INITIATIVE WILL BE WITH US, AND THE UNMISTAKABLY BEST ARGUMENT WILL BE WITH US. . . .

SIX

WE WILL HAMMER AT THIS THEME THROUGHOUT THE ASSEMBLY. THE UNITED NATIONS NEEDS SEOUL. AND WE WILL RELATE THIS ISSUE DAY AFTER DAY TO THE QUESTION OF ISRAELI MEMBERSHIP. THE NONALIGNED WILL END UP WISHING THEY HAD NEVER HEARD OF VIETNAM. . . .

SEVEN

THE ALTERNATIVE SCENARIO, OF COURSE, FOLLOWS FROM A VETO. I MUST REPORT THAT IT IS THE UNANIMOUS AND FIRM CONVICTION OF THE POLITICAL AND LEGAL OFFICERS OF THIS MISSION, AND IT IS MY OPINION, THAT FOR US TO VETO THE ADMISSION OF THE VIETNAMS WOULD BE A CALAMITY. WE WOULD BE SEEN TO ACT OUT OF BITTERNESS, BLINDNESS, WEAKNESS AND FEAR. WE WOULD BE SEEN NOT ONLY TO HAVE LOST THE HABIT OF VICTORY, BUT IN THE PROCESS TO HAVE ACQUIRED THE MOST PITIABLE STIGMATA OF DE-FEAT. BUT THERE WOULD BE LITTLE PITY. THE OVERWHELMING RESPONSE WOULD BE CONTEMPT.

EIGHT

. . . SOUTH AFRICA WOULD BE EXPELLED FROM THE GENERAL ASSEMBLY. CHILE PERHAPS. AND THEN ISRAEL. IT IS THE OPINION OF THE PROFESSIONAL OFFICERS OF THIS MISSION THAT THE NEGATIVE ATTITUDES WHICH A VIET-NAM VETO WOULD AROUSE COULD MAKE THE DIFFERENCE BETWEEN VICTORY AND DEFEAT ON THE QUESTION OF ISRAELI EXPULSION FROM THE GENERAL ASSEMBLY. . . .

NINE

AFTER THE EXPULSION OF ISRAEL FROM THE GENERAL ASSEMBLY, THAT BODY, INDIFFERENT TO ANY APPEAL WE MIGHT MAKE OR ANY THAT MIGHT BE MADE ON OUR BEHALF, WILL PROCEED TO DEMAND THE EXPULSION OF AMERICAN FORCES FROM SOUTH KOREA. . . .

TEN

. . . THE EXPULSION OF ISRAEL WILL BE DISASTER ENOUGH. THE UNITED STATES SENATE HAS ALREADY RESOLVED THAT IN SUCH AN EVENT WE MUST CONSIDER WITHDRAWING FROM THE UNITED NATIONS. WE COULD QUICKLY FIND OURSELF HAVING WITHDRAWN FROM THE VERY INTERNATIONAL SYSTEM WE OURSELVES CREATED, LEAVING IT TO OUR ENEMIES TO TREAT US AS AN OUTCAST, AN INCREASINGLY OUTLAWED NATION IN A WORLD SYSTEM THAT IS THEIRS, NOT OURS.

ELEVEN

BUT THIS NEED NOT HAPPEN. WE CAN ACCEPT THE VIETNAMS AND FROM THERE COMMENCE A SUSTAINED AND UNYIELDING INSISTENCE THAT THE UNITED NATIONS LIVE UP TO THE CHARTER AND TO THEIR OWN PROFESSIONS. WE WILL HAVE . . . RIGHT ON OUR SIDE, AND WHO KNOWS BUT THAT AFTER A POINT A FAIR NUMBER OF U.N. MEMBERS WILL NOTE THAT WE HAVE A VERY CONSIDERABLE AMOUNT OF POWER ALSO.

◆

Kissinger had been fair, or at least correct, as he could be in such matters. He had no intention of letting in the Vietnamese, a government that had betrayed him, outwitted him, beaten him. But if I wished, he would take the matter to the President. I did. The President backed him. Cheerfully enough, I set to writing the speech I would give on the occasion of our veto. It was the case, I began, that the U.S. was breaking with thirty years' practice by vetoing the admission of a new member. But,

> . . . What in the end changed our mind was the decision of the Council. . . . It became absolutely clear on that occasion that the Security Council, far from being prepared to support the principle of universal membership, was denying to one applicant even the right to have its case considered. . . .
>
> It may be recalled what I said. . . . The United States had made clear that we were prepared to vote for the admission of each and all of the three applicants then before us. . . .
>
> . . . The United States would be equally willing to vote for the admission of North Korea as well. We would have done so in plain pursuit of the Charter principle of universality. But . . . we would have and we will have nothing to do with selective universality, a principle which in practice admits only new members acceptable to the totalitarian states. . . .

Now what is the character of the seven nations which voted to consider the admission of this applicant, which were prepared to see it admitted along with the other applicants? Without exception these are nations which permit organized opposition to the government in power in their own countries. . . .

And what is the character of the six nations which voted not even to consider, let alone consider favorably, the application of this particular, noncommunist applicant? Without exception these are nations which do not permit organized opposition to the government in power. . . .

Two nations abstained. In a curiously symmetrical manner,. one is a state that permits opposition, one a state that does not. . . .

It would seem all the more important, then, to try to impress on the one-party states, especially the new nations among them, that *the United Nations is different.* There is no way to state it save bluntly thus. The United Nations Charter was drafted by men to whom the existence of opposition in a political system not only seemed normal, but also necessary. . . . They believed, and they were right, that a *world* organization could only function if it made possible the expression within it of all the various viewpoints and interests that actually existed in the world at large. The world organization had to *represent* the world. It could not be selective in its membership. . . .

Now obviously this is an idea that comes more easily to representatives of states where political opposition is normal and legal than to representatives of states where it is not. . . . Just as obviously, there are more states of this latter sort than otherwise, and this is especially true among newer members. But there is no cure for this, and because there is none, it is perhaps just as well that the time has come when the United States has taken the drastic action it has done today in order to press home the point.

To the nations, new and old, which are members of the United Nations, we say that however unprepared you yourselves may be to admit internal opposition, you must accept it as a fact of international life. That is to say, if you desire the United Nations to function. . . .

Ours is not a one-party world, and the United States has no intention of helping to bring about a one-party U.N. . . . The United Nations should be as near as possible to universal in its membership. As new nations are formed, they should be seen as having a presumed right to membership, given their fealty to the Charter.

I had in mind to use this occasion as a kind of opening shot: we would make the connection between the unwillingness to tolerate democracy at the U.N. and the refusal to allow it at home. But even as the Mission had no stomach for a row, neither, from the opposite perspective, had the Department. The common denominator, apart from an incapacity to deal with ideas, was a fear of making a scene, a form of good manners that is a kind of substitute for ideas. I had sent a strong draft: Back came a limp four pages, "sans teeth, sans eyes, sans taste, sans everything." I was to speak solely of "the principle of universality," which I did on August 11, taking the initiative on my own to "welcome the South Vietnamese to the Security Council Chamber." Hofmann in *The New York Times* nicely reported this as "a gesture of courtesy."

Now came the irony of it all, as used to be said. I had argued, at length and in the highest circles, in favor of admitting the totalitarian Communist regimes of North and South Vietnam into the United Nations. Across the country, in the press and on television I was now seen, face fixed, arm straight up, vetoing that admission. This turned out to be something people wanted to see. I commenced to be noticed.

Rowland Evans and Robert Novak picked up the story of the draft veto speech and reported that I had proposed to take the issue straight on, but that the "State Department bureaucracy," given its "congenital insistence on maintaining warm bilateral relations with individual countries no matter how roughly they treat this country in multilateral organizations," succeeded in "ash-canning" the draft. Even so, they reported, it was "a surprisingly close call." It must have been, for the story did not come from us, as would be normal in Washington accounts of unsuccessful battles within the bureaucracy. We had commenced a line of argument, and evidently had won adherents, though we were still as much a minority in Washington as we were in Turtle Bay.

———————◆———————

There was *no* reaction to our veto; no move to expel Israel; none of any consequence to remove American forces from Korea. Nothing I had forecast happened. If anything, the United Nations seemed to have been reminded of American power.

At the same time I had learned just how deep was our own impulse to "damage limitation." The President had other things on his mind. The Secretary of State was contemptuous of the place. The responsible Assistant Secretary was planning to retire there. Whatever, if any, trouble I caused, I would cause on my own. By the end of September I had learned this.

———————◆———————

I had learned another thing. In mid-September the government of Spain announced that five men convicted of murdering policemen would be executed. The rights and wrongs of the affair were not especially clear, although unquestionably policemen had been murdered. Suddenly the government of Mexico addressed an urgent appeal to the Security Council, asserting that the pending executions were a threat to the peace under the U.N. Charter, that the Security Council should be seized of the matter, and that Spain should be suspended from the United Nations.

The practice had developed of the Security Council holding informal "consultations" before taking up such questions in formal session. The meetings took place in a narrow room off the Council lounge. No records were kept, and no special rules were followed. There was usually an atmosphere of crisis, owing mostly to the crowding. The Mexican proposal was a classic Non-Aligned initiative. A government of the right was about to execute partisans presumably of the left. The United States supported this rightist government, providing huge subsidies in return for air base rights where evidently atomic weapons were poised to attack the "socialist" world. The government of the Soviet Union had taken part in the Spanish Civil War, against the Falangist government. The governments of Nazi Germany and Fascist Italy had supported the Falangists. The governments of Western Europe were still assailed by the guilt of their appeasement. The United States could be relied upon to disgrace itself by challenging the Mexican petition, and if necessary vetoing it in Council.

The consultation began in a mood of tension and impending triumph which I had encountered there before. I asked to speak. I praised the Mexican *démarche*. I praised the President of Mexico, Luis Echeverría, a world leader sprung from the indomitable Basque people who had fought fascist armor with rifle and bayonet as long as the Republic was alive and, when the fascists triumphed, had nonetheless fought on with bare hands and unconquerable hearts. I looked forward to the day when the Security Council would consider the candidacy of Luis Echeverría for Secretary-General of the United Nations. I recalled with praise the action of the Polish and Soviet governments, which in 1946 had blocked the admission of Spain to the United Nations on the altogether proper and legally unassailable grounds that Spain was not a democracy, which the United Nations required every member to be. The government of Poland had pointed out on that occasion that Spain did not have free elections, that Spain had only one party, that Spain had a government-controlled press. For myself, although I had no instructions from my government, I could state my horror at the pending executions. I fully agreed with the government of Mexico that the execution anywhere of any person accused of a political crime was potentially a threat to the peace everywhere and a matter to be considered by the Security Council. I recalled the tragedy of Spain in the 1930s, when the League of Nations had failed to act. Surely the United Nations would not now repeat that tragedy. The imprisonment and execution of any person for any political crime anywhere, I could not repeat too often, was a matter of international concern, and should be the subject of direct and on-the-spot investigation by agents of the Security Council, no matter where it took place. The room fell silent. At length the Mauritanian delegate, diminutive and taciturn, but whom one suspected of a first-rate intelligence, suggested that this was a complex matter on which all delegates would wish to have instructions.

The Council met next day, again in private consultations, but absent the buoyancy of the first meeting, prior to the American intervention. Had the Government of Spain no views? It did. First it recalled for us the role of Mr. Echeverría, then Mexico's Minister of the Interior, in the killing of some fifty students and the wounding of hundreds more during a protest prior to the Olympic Games in Mexico City in 1968. Next the Spanish Mission to the U.N. distributed, without comment, Xerox copies of a page of Philip Agee's book *Inside the Company*. Agee had been a CIA agent in Mexico City, and in his confessions he included a list of Mexican officials with whom the CIA had dealt. There was inscribed the name Luis Echeverría.

I spoke a second time. What, I asked the gathering, was the matter with being a CIA agent? It was well known that the world over there were CIA agents at the highest levels of government. In India a dear friend of mine, the Honorable Piloo Mody, a Member of Parliament and a great Indian patriot, since unfortunately imprisoned by the Gandhi government (a matter the Security Council might also wish to inquire into), had not three years previously appeared on the floor of the Lok Sabha wearing a button that announced, "I AM A C.I.A. AGENT." Mr. Mody, a man of liberal politics and engaging enterprise, had caused a number of these buttons to be manufactured, which he proceeded to sell to fellow parliamentarians at a profit that was considerable though not excessive. In time many members of the Indian parliament were proclaiming that they, too, were CIA agents. Was it not a most regrettable act of the government of Spain to attempt to discredit President Echeverría, and distract the attention of the Council from the matter before it, by bringing up the matter of the President's alleged affiliation with the intelligence services of the United States? The United States could not but be troubled by this. Salim of Tanzania asked for adjournment.

I was denounced next morning in a statement from the Indian mission. It happened that on that day, October 2, the Indian delegation was giving lunch for the Indian Foreign Minister, Y. B. Chavan. The lunch, as is de rigueur for the Indians, was at the Trianon Room of the

Carlyle. I had known Chavan well enough, and had liked him hugely. But here he was, the Foreign Minister of a semidictatorship. As I went through the receiving line I asked, "How is our friend Piloo?" The vast Rabelaisian Piloo; unmeasurable; irrepressible; irreplaceable; a sane man in a mad world, but who loved the madness withal. A Member of Parliament, no different from Chavan. "How is our friend Piloo?" Chavan, in his Congress cap and white *dhoti,* summoned an unctuousness no viceroy could have attained. "Piloo," he assured me, "is in a most comfortable jail."

The Security Council took no action on Spain. But the Indians denounced me for daring to state that *they* had political prisoners. They had to denounce me because they could not deny what I had said. In the meantime, the Mexicans had been caught taking American money to spy on themselves. The Non-Aligned seemed suddenly to sense a vulnerability that I suspect had not occurred to them. Echeverría's candidacy for Secretary-General was finished. I thereafter for several weeks spent a half hour or so every evening at the bar of the delegates' lounge, beckoning at random a moment to whichever Non-Aligned ambassador hove into view. I had been asked especially by my government, I would explain, to seek His Excellency's advice and counsel. We had learned there were governments which unaccountably were saying that, in light of the revelation that President Echeverría was or had been a CIA agent, President Echeverría should withdraw his candidacy for the Secretary-General's post. My government felt that this was not fair. Indeed, what we wanted was fair play for Echeverría. It might or might not be true that the allegations against him were factual. But surely the Ambassador, an experienced man of affairs, would know that it was common for persons in other governments to have connections with the Central Intelligence Agency. No doubt Echeverría had believed at the time of his involvement, and if by some chance those connections were still active still believed, that this was in the best interest of Mexico and the people of Mexico. Would the Ambassador have just one more scotch? Surely it was not to be held against President Echeverría that he had done what he had thought best. My government felt strongly about this, and felt that the Ambassador would surely recognize that the KGB was also active in world capitals and that no good could come of washing our dirty linen in public, as the British say.

There was a glut of dining, with Kissinger in and out of New York, staying when in town in the Presidential Suite at the Waldorf, confining his entourage to a third of a floor in a deference not so much to New York prices as to the local press. He gave a dinner for the Chinese. This was his domain, and he was superb, solemnly attending to the most idiot drivel, countenance placid and reassuring, mind fair to whirring with textual analysis: Were those precisely the terms they had used at Peking? At Shanghai? Like some invincibly psychotic teenager, Chinese Foreign Minister Chiao Kuan-hua sat at my left cheerfully forecasting the imminent outbreak of world war, an event that would be difficult in some aspects and costly in others but that could eventuate only in the final liberation of mankind from the insatiable imperialist ambitions of the Union of Soviet Socialist Republics, a deliverance that, it was implied though never quite stated, would be brought about by the co-operation of the United States of America and the People's Republic of China, and from which they would equally benefit. He thereupon knocked over a glass of *mao t'ai*, which reeked from the tablecloth the rest of the evening, seemingly sharpening his desire for more.

◆

His Excellency Field Marshal Al Hadji Idi Amin Dada, V.C., D.S.O., M.C., President of the Republic of Uganda and current Chairman of the Organization of African Unity, arrived on October 1 and the party was over. There was no notice. He landed early in the afternoon, accompanied by an array of aides and one of his wives, Sarah, described, possibly with justification, as a former member of the Uganda Armed Forces "Suicide Squad." He spoke to the General Assembly that afternoon. I listened on a radio hookup that the Mission owned, as I had chosen not to be present in person, albeit we did not expect anything special. For the longest while it was a plain enough speech. Before turning the task of reading the speech over to his ambassador, Amin spoke briefly in Luganda, a language of his country. He did not believe, he said, "in any colonial and imperialist language." This sort of thing bothered some, and probably it was intended to, but certainly it did not bother me. There was not a writer or friend I admired more than Sean O'Faolain, who was born John Whelan but who broke away from the — yes — "colonial and imperialist language" that the British had imposed on Ireland no less than Uganda. As a youth I had thought pathetic the old men in barrooms talking of "The Isle of Saints and Scholars," but I grew up to be a bit ashamed of my early contempt. They hadn't known much, the old men, but they'd known more than I did. For there had been such an Ireland. The Vikings destroyed the culture, which was bad enough, but the British destroyed its believability, which was worse.

Amin, like so many, began by praising the Seventh Special Session:

. . . recent international meetings have furthered a positive trend towards the attainment of a realistic and just international economic order fair to all parties to it. . . . For this progressive development, I wish to pay a special tribute to the United States authorities, especially the President and the Members of Congress who approved a change in the American attitude and policy towards the third world, and, consequently, directed the Secretary of State to communicate that position to the world during the seventh special session of this Assembly. . . .

He went on to demand that the U.S. leave Panama and to give the ritual accolades to the "Soviet Union and the People's Republic of China and other socialist countries for their generous assistance, both moral and material, to the peoples of Africa still fighting to free themselves from the bondage of imperialism, racism and *apartheid.*" These were passages turned out by the O.A.U. secretariat, and if no occasion for rejoicing were equally no cause for alarm. There was in truth little or nothing very much to object to in the speech until suddenly he turned on Israel and the United States in language of the purest hatred and rage. It could have been an episode from James Gregor's *The Fascist Persuasion in Radical Politics:*

. . . Israel, like South Africa, has absolutely ignored the United Nations resolutions commanding it to withdraw from the Occupied Territories of Egypt, Palestine, Jordan and Syria. It is disappointing to note that some major Powers, notably the United States of America, which are founder Members of this Organization which was established to bring about a world order based upon law, justice and peace, have not only continually supported Israel in flouting United Nations resolutions, but have also equipped it with powerful armaments to make it strong enough to defy, grab and plunder its neighbour's territory. Today, without the United States of America, there would be no Israel.

The United States' persistent support for Israel stems from the sad history of colonization. The United States of America has been colonized by the Zionists who hold all the tools of development and power. They own virtually all the banking institutions, the major manufacturing and processing industries and the major means of communication; and have so much infiltrated the CIA that they are posing a great threat to nations and peoples which may be opposed to the atrocious Zionist movement. They have turned the CIA into a murder squad to eliminate any form of just resistance anywhere in the world. . . . How can we expect freedom, peace and justice in the world when such a powerful nation as the United States of America is in the hands of the Zionists? I call upon the people of the United States of America whose forefathers founded this State "conceived in liberty and dedicated to the proposition that all men are born equal" to rid their society of the Zionists in order that the true citizens of this nation may control their own destiny and exploit the natural resources of their country to their own benefit. I call for the expulsion of Israel from the United Nations and the extinction of Israel as a State, so that the territorial integrity of Palestine may be ensured and upheld.

It would later be argued that this passage came in that section of the speech in which he spoke only as the chief of state of Uganda, and this was true enough. But, in another section, speaking as Chairman of the O.A.U., he had already introduced the theme: "We do not only want a world free of colonialism, neo-colonialism, imperialism and Zionism. . . ." His purpose was to equate Israel with everything the world community deplored and Africa detested, and to equate the United States with Israel. He received a standing ovation from the General Assembly when he arrived, was applauded throughout, and departed to yet another ovation. He spoke for forty-six African nations; but in truth in that moment he spoke for the authoritarian majority in the General Assembly itself. Some representatives would later contend otherwise and explain that they hadn't really clapped at this passage or that passage. But they had.

There was little likelihood of serious objection to what Amin had said coming from anywhere. Nothing would come from Washington; or if something did, it would touch some point of procedure or nicety of language. Our diplomats had no ideas left. Communism was near to nothing to them: fascism was only a word Communists used. They would have no sense that, if Amin, chairman of the O.A.U., could say such things, it signified a further advance of a profoundly dangerous totalitarian lie. They had little or no sense of how world politics was coming to be influenced by the capacity of totalitarian regimes to "obliterate facts" about themselves, and, in Jacques Ellul's term, to exploit the openness of democracies. In *The Political Illusion*, Ellul argued:

Under Stalin's rule, Communist peace propaganda in no way corresponded objectively to Soviet policies. Between 1948 and 1952 Stalin did not take a single concrete step in favor of peace or an international *détente*. During the same period, it increased its army and stepped up its military preparations. Yet, despite an utter absence of facts, the propaganda issued by the peace fighters, by defining the problem of peace in Communist terms . . . monopolized the word "peace" for the Soviet Union and communism and made it symbolic of Communist language and attitudes.

———◆———

> When information is obliterated in a country, political problems no
> longer arouse public opinion — they have reality only for the enemies
> of the regime, and are promulgated by unorganized individuals.

If anyone in the Department of State ever bothered to wonder why we
were defeated in Vietnam, it was not likely he would think back to
Picasso's dove and wonder whether the world had not been carefully
prepared for our defeat, made to want it so much that we ought never
to have gone near the place. Such thoughts were none of the business
of American diplomacy. Israel would protest Amin, but Israel always protested. Americans who might protest would fear appearing to be antiblack. (This was nine months before the Entebbe raid.) In any event,
there were now so few American journalists covering the U.N., Americans generally would hear little of what happened.

As expected, no reaction came from Washington. But then there had
been no reaction to the resolution adopted by the Assembly of Heads of
State and Government of the Organization of African Unity held in
Kampala July 28 to August 1, asserting that

> the racist regime in occupied Palestine and racist regimes in Zimbabwe
> and South Africa have a common imperialist origin, forming a whole
> and having the same racist structure and being organically linked in
> their policy aimed at repression of the dignity and integrity of the
> human being.

The next day, October 2, Amin stated at a press conference that New
York City was bankrupt "because the United States must send arms to
Israel to murder the Arabs." Still Washington was silent. Clarence
Mitchell of the New York Mission, acting on his own, characterized the
call for the extinction of Israel as "ridiculous" and rejected "unsolicited
advice on how black Americans should conduct their affairs." I was
reduced to the small gesture of not attending the reception and dinner
given in honor of the Field Marshal by the Secretary-General and the
President of the General Assembly. The press asked why I was absent and
reported that I would not explain, adding: " 'However,' he said: 'I made
the decision. I did not want to go to Washington with this question, but
I would have got the same decision.' " Which was precisely what I did
not believe. I believed that had I asked Washington I would have been
instructed to attend the dinner as being in honor of the President of the
Organization of African Unity. Instead, that evening I went to dinner at
Theodore H. White's, where I got into an argument with Stephen Smith
over the merits of the A.F.L.-C.I.O., which I was to address the next day

in San Francisco. I did not mind that Smith was so bitter about the labor movement. What I minded was that John F. Kennedy's brother-in-law, the man whom Kennedy had once appointed to head the "crisis center" in the State Department, could not decide whether he despised labor because it was too radical or because it was not radical enough. I was surfeited with people who could not recognize their own interests or even describe their inclinations. It was time to create a crisis.

◆

I wrote my speech on the plane to California the following morning and gave it in the afternoon. By chance *The Times* that day carried an editorial supporting the Security Council's decision to sidetrack Mexico's demand for the suspension of Spain. It was all very well for Echeverría to pursue his campaign for Secretary-General, the editorial observed, but it would be "monumental hypocrisy" to suspend Spain for a practice indulged in to a far greater extent by other U.N. members: Ethiopia, for example, or Burundi, or Uganda, whose president, a "racist murderer," had just received an ovation from the General Assembly. This gave me one theme. Garment had given me another. A resolution had been introduced into the Third Committee that declared that "Zionism is a form of racism and racial discrimination."

Weeks later, on November 12, two days after the adoption of that resolution, Tass would carry a long and approving commentary describing how well the way had been prepared:

> The 30th session of the U.N. General Assembly has carried by an overwhelming majority of votes a resolution condemning Zionism as a "form of racism and racial discrimination." Some quarters in the West would have us believe that this resolution is "unexpected" and "sensational." However, there is nothing unexpected in the stand taken by the United Nations. This year alone, Zionism has been condemned by the OAU summit in Kampala, by the non-aligned countries' foreign ministers' conference in Lima, the U.N. world conference to mark the International Women's Year held in Mexico City, and other international forums. All this goes to show that the problem has long been crying for solution. The General Assembly of the U.N. has just summed up the conclusions which have long been drawn by the broad circles of world public opinion.

Something was going to happen. The Non-Aligned and the Soviet blocs were reinforcing one another in a generalized assault on the democracies and a specific attack on Israel. Just how planned and coordinated this was I certainly didn't know; and the American government, as usual, had no intelligence. But it had been clear something was going to happen, and in the course of the third week of the General Assembly it became clear what it would be.

Instead of rejecting the credentials of the Israeli government, the two blocs would move to deny the legitimacy of the Israeli national movement itself. Israel would thus be declared an illegitimate state. I believe I somehow sensed this from the day in Geneva when the reporting cable arrived on the International Women's Year. But now a resolution was actually being circulated, sponsored by Somalia with Cuba and Libya as cosponsors. *Somalia, Cuba, Libya:* Third World nations, Soviet agents. If that seems too simple, it was hardly a time for qualification.

A pattern had by now emerged in Soviet tactics with the Non-Aligned. A symbolic issue would come along: they might think it up; just as often it would emerge on its own. But they would seize on it, and either directly, or, more often, through others, bring it to the General Assembly where it would command general assent as a matter more or less beyond disputing. All nations, or most, are for peace, and against exploitation, and much in favor of sufficient food supplies. As the matter progressed, however, more and more specific attacks on the West would be added to or associated with the general issue. In this manner the specific issue of Zionism was gradually associated with the general issue of racism. At the Thirtieth General Assembly a specific linkage was to be forged.

Some years earlier the General Assembly had decreed a "Decade for Action to Combat Racism and Racial Discrimination." The United States had fully supported the idea, and was now supporting the specific programs which were to implement it. The ECOSOC meeting in July had developed a number of such programs. These now came to the Third Committee, where they would be passed on to the General Assembly. This was an enterprise of great interest to African nations; the obvious targets were South Africa and Rhodesia. Suddenly, beginning with the Women's Conference, the charge was made that Zionism was a form of racism, from which it would follow that Israel, too, would be an illegitimate, proscribed state, subject to censure, expulsion, and ultimately to extinction. That an honorable cause was being put to the service of a dishonorable one, few seemed to understand or care.

At the airport in San Francisco I telephoned Garment, who was about to speak in the Third Committee, where he proposed to make clear the enormity of the untruth about to be sanctioned, and the consequences that would follow. His speech was not threatening, but his meaning was unmistakable:

> The content of these amendments is not only unjust but ominous. It is ominous because it treats the word racism as if it were not the name

of a very real and concrete set of injustices, but merely an epithet to be flung at whoever happens to be one's adversary. It turns an idea with a vivid and obnoxious meaning into nothing more than an ideological tool; it deprives us of our ability to see reality together and to deal with it together. And that, for an organization so dedicated to and so dependent upon the possibilities of reason and persuasion, can be nothing short of a tragedy. . . .

However one views the particular issues in the Middle East conflict, to equate Zionism with racism is to distort completely the history of that movement, born of the centuries of oppression suffered by the Jewish people in the western world and designed to liberate an oppressed people by returning them to the land of their fathers.

It is no service to the great goals of the United Nations and its Commissions, Committees and Agencies to ignore and to distort history in this fashion. The tragedy in the Middle East today stems from our failure, thus far, to find ways of protecting and accommodating the rights of all the groups in the area — those of the Jews and those of the Arabs — both with a long, proud history in the region.

Accordingly, if put to a vote, my delegation will vote no on the amendments. . . . The adoption of any of those amendments will cause the United States to cast a negative vote on the entire resolution.

This was Garment at the top of his form. Reasoning. Hopeful. Seeking to understand. A counselor. At times almost devoid of a sense of himself, yet equally, at times, capable of deciding quite on his own what ought to be the position of the United States of America on a moral and political issue of the highest order. He concluded:

The agenda of this Committee is filled with history and passion. It is an easy indulgence for individuals to use words which distort and divide, which inflict wounds and draw attention.

It is our collective responsibility to use language enlightened by history, to use it precisely, to use it carefully, mindful of our differences but determined to overcome, not enlarge them.

I went straight from hearing of his speech to make my own to the A.F.L.-C.I.O. convention, interpolating a passage on the Zionism resolution:

In his statement yesterday George Meany said that . . . "Democracy has come under increasing attack. . . ."

I see it every day at the United Nations. Every day, on every side, we are assailed. There are those in this country whose pleasure, or profit, it is to believe that our assailants are motivated by what is wrong about us. *They* are wrong. We are assailed because of what is right about us. We are assailed because we are a democracy. . . .

In the United Nations today there are in the range of two dozen democracies left. Totalitarian Communist regimes and assorted ancient and modern despotisms make up all the rest. And nothing so unites these nations as the conviction that their success ultimately depends on our failure.

It is no accident that on Wednesday, "His Excellency Field Marshal Al Hadji Amin Dada, President of the Republic of Uganda" — to give him his U.N. title — called for "the extinction of Israel as a state." And it is no accident, I fear, that this "racist murderer" — as one of our leading newspapers called him this morning — is head of the Organization of African Unity. For Israel is a democracy and it is simply the fact that despotisms will seek whatever opportunities come to hand to destroy that which threatens them most, which is democracy. At this very moment in New York, for example, Mr. Leonard Garment, Counsel to the U.S. Delegation, is fighting back the latest such move, a resolution now before the Third Committee which equates "Zionism" with "racism," calling for the eradication of both. I put it to you that this outrage is likely as not to be voted for by a majority of the membership of the United Nations. . . .

There will be more campaigns. They will not abate, for it is sensed in the world that democracy is in trouble. There is blood in the water and the sharks grow frenzied. They commence, of course, to consume one another and the chaos mounts. Let me offer you a statistic. There are 142 members of the U.N. We calculated last evening for the benefit of this occasion just what was the length of time in which the typical U.N. member had enjoyed a relatively stable government without violent overthrow or usurpation, including revolution. We put ourselves down for 199 years, Belgium for 144, France for 127, Australia for 74. And what did the median come out to be? 11 years since the last overthrow of government in the median member of the U.N. In a world where technologists in the field of nuclear energy measure the length of storage of reactor wastes in what they have come to term "geological time": five thousand years, 30,000 years. Such are the issues we are handling with governments which cannot survive even eleven years.

A year ago I was far more optimistic about all this than I am today. It seemed to me then that many of the new countries of the world had inherited, mostly from Western Europe, a decent and honorable tradition of democratic socialism which if it had a certain anti-American bias was nonetheless a tradition we could work with and respect. A year later I am not at all sure about that. Such has been the success of Communist arms, Communist intrigue, Communist treachery in Asia and Africa that the reputation of democracy in those regions has all but collapsed.

Certainly it has done so where I work. There is much that the United

Nations has done in its 30 years that is honorable and good. But it has done damn little for democracy. . . .

What is going on is a systematic effort to create an international society in which government is the one and only legitimate institution. The old dream of an international economic order in which one single nation dominated is being replaced by a not different vision of the domination of a single idea, the idea of the all-encompassing state, a state which has no provision for the liberties of individuals, much less for the liberties of collections of individuals, such as trade unions.

I think we are in a position to respond to this. Everyone has been talking about the new international order, and as the United States has already indicated in Secretary Kissinger's address on September 1, we stand ready to participate in the creation of a world from which starvation would be eliminated and in which everyone would be assured a basic minimum of economic sustenance. It must be clear, however, that the United States doesn't wish to do this because we accept responsibility for the economic condition of the Third and Fourth Worlds. We repudiate the charge that we have exploited or plundered other countries. . . .

What we acknowledge is a common humanity and a common concern arising out of our own sense of what we can and ought to do. . . .

But it is important to stress — as important, it seems to me, as any thing can be — that this willingness of ours has as its object the fate of *individuals*. Ours is a culture based on the primacy of the individual — the rights of the individual, the welfare of the individual, the claims of the individual against those of the state. We have no wish, therefore, to participate in any new economic arrangements whose beneficiaries will be the state rather than the individual, leaders rather than the individual, politicians and bureaucrats rather than the individual. If there is to be an increased flow of wealth to the countries of the South, the United States will insist that it be channeled into the pockets of individuals and not into Swiss bank accounts, and we will insist that necessary precautions be taken to that effect. . . .

. . . If there is to be a new international order, the United States will insist that the right to a minimum standard of political and civil liberty is no less fundamental than the right to a minimum standard of material welfare. President Ford affirmed our commitment to universal human rights at Helsinki, and we reaffirm it here.

The new nations when we say things like that respond, and understandably in some cases, that we talk about individual rights but they care about economic rights. There is, or so it seems to me, one indisputably valid response to this point. It is for the United States Government to put the utmost emphasis, in multilateral relations and in bilateral relations, on the single most important area where individual rights and economic rights can be seen to merge, to complement one another, and that is the area of trade union rights, and trade union responsibilities. . . . For one of the lessons of the 20th century is that democratic trade unions can be a lot tougher than democratic governments.

They survive when almost everything else disappears. . . .

The American labor movement has done its share of upholding this standard. The American government can do no less. There is, it seems to me, no question of the way we have to go.

This will involve different individuals at different times. A trouble with your U.N. representatives, indeed, is the rate at which we come and go. Since 1945 there have been thirteen U.S. Representatives to the United Nations. By comparison, since 1886, there have been three heads of the AFL and now AFL-CIO. . . .

The very stability of this movement, its strength, its confidence, its understanding of what has gone on — not for the past 11 years but for the past 111 years — is a fundamental resource of the American democracy at a moment when it needs all the help and resources it can get. . . .

. . . In Paris, in 1919, where he headed the Commission of the Peace Conference and drew up the Charter of the International Labor Organization, Samuel Gompers spoke one evening to a group of officials and dignitaries outlining the plans for the new organization. He could sense the fear he was arousing: new ideas; new men; new methods. Above all, new freedoms. Suddenly he interrupted his talk. He paused a moment; he looked at his audience and he pronounced one of the purest, most moving sentences in the literature of American democracy. "You do not know," he said, "how safe a thing Freedom is."

————◆————

The crisis came, but not wholly as I would have wished. I had blundered in asserting that it was "no accident" that Idi Amin was head of the Organization of African Unity. It was "no accident" in the sense I mean it, which is to say as a mock-Marxist assertion that history, howsoever adventitious in its surface appearance, was evolving according to identifiable principles. But the fact was that Amin had not been specifically chosen as head of the O.A.U. Uganda's turn had simply come around in a more or less fixed succession. This *was* an accident, and I had said otherwise. I could thus be accused of being opposed not to Amin, but to Africa; and the accusations came in short order.

The story appeared on the front page of *The New York Times*: "Moynihan Assails Uganda President — Delegate to U.N. Endorses Description of Amin as 'Racist Murderer.'" The third paragraph began: "It is no accident, I fear. . . ." The story, written in San Francisco by Damon Stetson, was straightforward and professional. By any standard, the "no accident" remark belonged "up front." But the desk in New York was aroused to elaboration. In the final editions the story contained passages reporting that Tanzania had boycotted the O.A.U. meeting in Kampala that summer on " 'moral and political' " grounds (for which read that Amin *was* an accident, not representative of O.A.U. members' attitudes towards human rights), and further that in 1970, "angered by black discontentment over the progress of civil rights," I had proposed "benign neglect" to President Nixon. Stetson also reported that I had not cleared my address "with anyone in Washington."

◆

There are morals to be drawn from this. The first is to avoid writing speeches in airplanes. Another, translated from the Gaelic, is that if you want an audience, start a fight. The next day's headline ran: "Moynihan Criticism of Amin Has U.N. People Buzzing." Africans and members of other delegations told Paul Hofmann they were "stunned" that I had approvingly quoted *The Times*. Hofmann and Kathleen Teltsch were both increasingly troubled by what they were seeing at the U.N. He was Middle European, and clearly affected by the horror of his early years. His story recalled the *Commentary* article and the proposal I had made there to talk back. " 'Such a reversal of roles would be painful to American spokesmen,' Mr. Moynihan wrote, 'but it could be liberating also.' " He cited a 1974 report of the International Commission of Jurists that 25,000 to 250,000 Ugandans had been murdered since Amin seized power in 1971. He reported that my San Francisco remarks were now the main topic of conversation at U.N. headquarters and in telephone conversations between delegations. Although none would comment for the record, "several black African and Arab delegates said that President Amin had forcefully expressed a strong current of feeling of the third world in his remarks about Israel and other matters." Then in the concluding paragraph of his story came the first countermove. Several persons conceded that I may have struck a note that appealed to many Americans: "One American said, 'What is Pat Moynihan running for?' implying that by his public criticisms of the third world and other attitudes, he was building a personal constituency that could become the basis for some future quest of elective office."

Whether or not this came directly from the U.S. Mission, it may as well have done. From this moment, with only a few exceptions, the career officers gave little or no support. I had offended Africa. On Monday morning, October 6, the staff had an explanatory press release ready. I was to explain that "some of Amin's statements before the General Assembly earned wide approval: others were morally offensive." I was to make clear that I dissented only from the latter. I let it be known that not one goddamn thing Amin had said had won my "wide approval."

In Washington a not dissimilar distancing began. That morning a "press guidance" sheet was prepared for the noon briefing at the Department of State. "Our positions on certain policies and actions of Amin are well known. Ambassador Moynihan's words were his own." By noon, however, this had been changed at the request of the State Department's African Bureau:

> Q. Would you please elaborate on the remarks Ambassador Moynihan made recently about President Amin of Uganda?
> A. According to news accounts, Ambassador Moynihan said that his remarks had not been cleared by the Department of State. I would suggest you address the question to Ambassador Moynihan, as the remarks were his.

Nothing unkind was even to be implied about Amin, if the African Bureau had any say.

In the course of Monday's plenary session, the representative of Dahomey, Tiamiou Adjibade, speaking on behalf of the O.A.U., said that my discourteous attack on the person of Marshal Amin Dada "not only constitutes a deliberate provocative act, vis-à-vis President Amin, and an unfriendly act towards the Organization of African Unity, but also it is verging on irresponsibility and indicates a grave unawareness which is liable to vitiate dangerously relations between the United States and members of the O.A.U." Mitchell interrupted on a point of order. Adjibade continued even so: I was seeking "to camouflage the acts against human rights taking place in Spain, Israel and South Africa." I should ask whether I represented the United States or if I represented Zionism. If the latter, I would "do better to go to Israel." The Libyan representative, Mansur R. Kikhia, declared that Amin had expressed the views of Uganda and the O.A.U. "in the best possible way." He noted that the "intellectual elite" from the universities, including myself and the Secretary of State, were of the view that strong language was the only language the Third World understood, but the people of the United States would know the truth, especially about Zionism, and would reject this view. He read excerpts from a *New York Times* article of August 8 on the Israeli lobby and its influence on Congress. Mitchell finally replied in the evening, asking why no one that day had mentioned a recent report of the International Commission of Jurists on Amin's heinous policies: "This report, and the findings of the report, are the reality of the controversy. I might say a man is just as dead if he is killed by a black person as he is if he is killed by a white person."

I remained intransigent. The press quoted me: "I have said what had to be said." The same evening, Monday, that Mitchell spoke, the United Nations Association of the U.S.A. held a round table for U.S. editors. I spoke about things in general, but added that Amin had "slandered" all of us by saying the United States was "run by Zionists." I was quoted: "We are not here to hear totalitarian dictators lecture to us on how to run a democracy."

On Wednesday, October 8, the Cabinet met. The President brought up the subject and allowed that in his view what I had said and Clarence Mitchell had said needed to be said, and that he agreed. (Ron Nessen, the President's Press Secretary, later gave this to the White House press in just those words.) The President thereupon looked down to my end of the table and said: "You seem to be surviving." I answered, "If you say so, then I am."

Which I was. The President was with me. There was a sense in which I knew this anyway. Call it subliminal, a capacity of his for conveying his thoughts, or call it something more exotic, such as honesty. But through all this period it was clear to me — and was made clear to me — that Gerald Ford fundamentally agreed with what we were doing.

———◆———

So, in some measure, did some parts of *The Times*. I had been on the front page again Tuesday: "Africans and Arabs Denounce Moynihan in the U.N.," with a photograph of Mitchell seeking recognition to respond to Adjibade. Teltsch's story emphasized that I had called on the O.A.U. to disavow Amin, but instead had "caused them to close ranks." On the other hand, she depicted their doing so on the ground that the O.A.U. held the same view on Israel that Amin had stated in the Ugandan section of his address. She quoted the Dahomey representative:

> He said it was not surprising that journalists tried to defame the Ugandan, given what he described as the influence of Zionism on the mass media, especially in New York. Mr. Adjibade said that Mr. Moynihan's remarks served only to confirm President Amin's charge about the Zionists' control in the United States.

This was a repeated theme at the U.N. — that the U.S. media were Zionist-controlled, especially that *The New York Times* was a Zionist newspaper. It was a charge which had to stir *Times* writers, and certainly it did those whose role it was to convey opinion. On Thursday the Op-Ed page carried columns by William Safire and Anthony Lewis, in rare agreement, suggesting that I may not have been wrong. Safire, the conservative, was altogether supportive. I had talked to him after the Cabinet meeting, and his column pretty much stated the case as I put it to him, albeit the passage on the Munchkins in the State Department was his own:

> . . . "For too long," Ambassador Moynihan says, "we have been given private assurances that public obscenities were not meant. That currency is no longer acceptable."
>
> However, we can soon expect the handwriting of our own diplomatic Munchkins. Here it comes: We know other Africans privately despise General Amin: why do we drive them together? The dictator serves as head of the Organization of African Unity by rotation only; why should we take his speech to heart?
>
> The answer is that when a dictator with the blood of tens of thousands of his countrymen on his hands talks "extinction," he must be taken seriously. And when U.N. diplomats rise to their feet and clap their hands at a call to genocide by a man with such impressive credentials, they must understand that their public display of support cannot be ameliorated by murmurings of "we don't really mean it" in private.
>
> A new world order of rhetoric has arrived, which affirms that diplomats are to be held responsible for what they say in public. . . . If a nation wishes to act publicly as an enemy of democracy, or a supporter of racist murder, that will cost it something. Diplomacy is becoming a two-way street. The price of a delicious diatribe against the United States is the aid and friendship of the United States.

Lewis's column was about American guilt, much of which, he said, was deserved:

> Last summer Fidel Castro was asked by James Reston . . . about efforts to export his revolution to the rest of Latin America. He answered that he was doing no exporting — it was the United States that was exporting counterrevolution.

Most Americans resisted that thought, Lewis continued, but had not the CIA planned and perhaps attempted assassinations of foreign political leaders? Was not "the Phoenix program, our campaign of political terrorism in Vietnam" responsible for over twenty thousand deaths? Even so, he agreed. "When Ambassador Moynihan referred to President Amin of Uganda the other day as a racist murderer, it was inspiriting: An American official had spoken the truth out loud about a situation that shames mankind."

Much will be written about these commentators, for they helped shape the American political sensibility of this time. The great hours of Lewis's life had come in the administration of John F. Kennedy and the tenure of Attorney General Robert F. Kennedy. These two continued as his ideal of political leaders. Yet it was precisely during their brief authority that so many of the evils that so obsessed Lewis either commenced or were greatly intensified. He had not come to terms with this, and it had blocked the best part of him as a writer.

By contrast, Safire, a coarser talent but a larger one, had the advantage over Lewis that *his* President had been disgraced and deposed. There was nothing left to conceal, little to protect. Free of the past, he wrote far more insightfully of the future.

———◆———

There were many such personal histories around, Kissinger's included. He could not welcome these newest developments. I was *his* ambassador: What was I doing on the front page of *The Times?* And with Safire's approval. Safire had been convinced that Kissinger had had his telephone tapped in the Nixon White House, and he was not letting Kissinger forget this. On the other hand, if I was causing trouble, I was only doing what the Secretary of State had taken me on board to do. I had not been looking for trouble. Kissinger knew well enough that I had tried to avoid a confrontation over the admission of Vietnam, and to bring off a success at the Special Session. We were into October now and there had not been an angry word of mine in print since the *Times* interview the previous February. But I had said that if attacked we would defend ourselves.

The real problem was that the issue now was Israel. I knew little of the place, and now would come to its defense for reasons that had almost nothing to do with it. Kissinger, by contrast, knew almost too much. By this time, Glazer observed, Israel had become the religion of the Jews, and I believe it was Kissinger's as well. On the day in December, 1968, when Nixon, as President-elect, assembled his prospective Cabinet and White House aides for a day in Washington, Kissinger and I, the two professors and the two strangers, were perhaps equally uncomfortable and telling each other so, or, more precisely, he was telling me and I was agreeing. But I had my reasons for coming to Washington. We were each asked to present our thoughts. He spoke almost exclusively of Israel and the cost of the "War of Attrition" then going on with Egypt, translating Israeli casualties into what would be their equivalent in a population of America's size. For a thousand wounded, read one hundred thousand. I had an immediate sense of where his heart was. Something that took much longer with Garment, although with him it was more than attachment; it was passion. It was the reason he had gone to the White House, and the reason that, for so long, he stayed.

The problem for Kissinger was that as time passed *he* stayed for any number of new reasons as well. His interests had not changed: Vietnam never absorbed him. His phrase, "a decent interval," told everything anyone needed to know. He fully expected and at moments probably half desired that the Communists should win — he grew contemptuous of the South Vietnamese — but wished to have it appear that the American departure was not the reason for the South Vietnamese defeat. By contrast, Israel was never far from his thoughts. And yet *because this was so*, events led him to a role in the Middle East that complicated his commitment almost to the point of confounding it. He became the honest broker between Israel and its enemies, and, in the manner of Beerbohm's *Happy Hypocrite,* his true person slowly adapted to the mask he had put on for purposes of duplicity. He *became* neutral. At one point, evidently, he even turned to the Saudi Arabians in hopes of getting money Congress had refused for sustaining his "decent interval" in Vietnam. He gave in to his tendency to despise those who opposed him. Increasingly he would depict the Israelis he dealt with in the voice of someone who had put a good deal of emotional distance between himself and the tiny nation he had spoken about with such feeling in December, 1968.

Israel was not *my* religion. I had never even been there. For not inexplicable reasons I was one of the few Ivy League professors never to have been invited. Nor had I tried to get there on my own, apart from a brief proposal to the State Department that I be allowed to stop over on a trip back to India, which the Department refused. I both liked what I had heard of the new nation and was prepared to believe the criticisms made of it.

Ruhl Bartlett of the Fletcher School had been much concerned in 1947 and 1948 with what he saw as a violation of Arab rights and American involvement on the side of Israel that would result in great eventual costs to the United States. His student, I had been insouciant. The Jews would win, I had told him, because they were smarter and tougher than Arabs. This was a bit of a presumption, for I had never met an Arab, save one professor at City College. I knew the Jews of New York, and assumed the Israelis were much the same. But this was little more than an extended ethnocentricity. As for Zionism, I took it to be a kind of Jewish *risorgimento.* The Jews of the nineteenth century had lost the use of spoken Hebrew and much else that united them. As the Irish had lost Gaelic. As the Bretons had lost Brittany. And so down the list of overmastered or dispersed peoples. By the time Glazer and I began writing of ethnicity, in the 1960s, I had developed a combativeness of sorts about the Marxist-Leninist decree that ethnicity should vanish. I came to suspect that ethnic-based regimes were likely to be at least marginally more tolerant and somewhat less brutal than the competing Marxist state, especially where they could accept that, whatever the hopes of the

founders may have been, ethnic pluralism was an unavoidable condition
of twentieth-century statehood. There was of course Freud's dictum:

> *Homo homini lupus.* Who, in the face of all his experience of life and
> of history, will have the courage to dispute this assertion? . . . It is al-
> ways possible to bind together a considerable number of people in
> love, so long as there are other people left over to receive the mani-
> festations of their aggressiveness.

But it seemed to me that experience had proved rather more gentle than
theory. Most of the new nationalism arose from an extended period of
subservience or incapacity, and retained its memory, such that there
was often a less than the normal disposition to replace one subjugation
with another. Certainly Zionism had begun as nothing more than the
assertion that Jews were a people and had the same rights to nationhood
that other such peoples were then asserting.

But it was not the Jews that were in my mind as the crisis of the Thirtieth General Assembly took form, nor yet Israel. Not the accused at all,
but the accusers. For it came to me early in the proceedings — and for
once, what I knew early turned out to be true — that the charge against
Zionism somehow emanated from Moscow. It reeked of the totalitarian
mind, stank of the totalitarian state. So it was not at all from a concern
for Israel as such that I came to be occupied above all with its survival.
It was from a rather personal history of my own, a history marked for
me by Kennedy's promise to pay any price in the defense of liberty, a
history now mocked by Vietnam. Thus I entered into the Zionism debate. Not least of the ironies to come was that Kissinger, who must be
thought to have cared more, would see himself attacked for aloofness,
and would see me praised for commitment.

———◆———

9

"Zionism Is a Form of Racism and Racial Discrimination"

AS WITH MANY THINGS instantly known, the proposition that the Soviets were behind the Zionism resolution turned out to be difficult to prove. (It would, to be sure, have been equally difficult to *dis*prove.) At the rudimentary level, the Soviets sponsored the resolution; the only developed country to do so. Of the other twenty-five sponsors, twenty-one were Moslem countries, all Arab save Afghanistan and Somalia. Two, Cuba and Guinea, were client states of the Soviets, while Mali, another sponsor, has a large Moslem population. Of all the sponsors, only Dahomey fit none of these patterns.

More fundamental, Soviet propaganda had for some years, by this point, been asserting that Zionism was indeed racist, and more especially that Zionism was virtually indistinguishable from Nazism. For a congeries of reasons, neither the United States government nor the American Jewish community had paid much attention to this, with some prescient exceptions. But the fact was known, and in particular was known to us — Garment, Weaver, myself — at the Mission. Bernard Lewis of Princeton seemed to know most about the history of the subject, which he later recounted in *Foreign Affairs*. Following the Second World War, Soviet propaganda began to link internal pan-Turkish and pan-Iranian movements to Nazism (there may indeed have been German links there) and to apply the term *racist* to nationalist movements that tried to connect non-Slavic peoples of the Soviet Union with their kin elsewhere. Other nationalisms within the USSR could be dismissed as feudal, bourgeois, reactionary, or clericalist, but the term *racist* was reserved for these particularly threatening nationalist tendencies. Condemnation of these movements, and of pan-Islamism as well, was, in Lewis's words, "fierce and unremitting." Then, following the 1967 war, there was a great stirring among Soviet Jews, a people so labeled on their identity cards and even, technically, endowed with a Soviet homeland in Birobidjan. (Malik was fond of the tale of the Soviet Minister of Commerce who, visiting the Jewish Soviet Republic, remarked on the poverty of the people. It was explained to him that, since the place had been reserved for Jews, there were no Russians to cheat.) Outside of the USSR, efforts on behalf of Soviet Jewry increased after 1967. In response, Soviet propaganda began to describe Zionism as anti-Soviet and as racist.

In February, 1971, *Pravda* carried a two-part series called "Anti-Sovietism Is the Profession of Zionists." It was charged in the aftermath of the 1967 war, when all Communist countries but Rumania broke relations with Israel, that Zionist subversive activity had increased. "The first practical test of this theory and policy were the events in Czechoslovakia in 1968," stated Vladimir Bolshakov, the author. A number of the Czech "liberals" having been Jews, it followed that Dubček was part of a Zionist plot. Shortly after the *Pravda* article appeared, Bernard Gwertzman described these events in *The Times:*

> Zionist leaders are accused of having collaborated with the Nazis during the war and are charged with practicing a racism of their own.
> Soviet television recently showed a 50-minute documentary film largely devoted to the history of Zionism. The Nazi-Zionist theme was emphasized. On several occasions, David Ben-Gurion's face was superimposed on that of Hitler.
> Newsreel footage of Israeli forces on parade was followed by similar footage of Nazi storm troopers parading past Hitler. Pictures of inmates of Nazi concentration camps were shown immediately before victims of Israeli air raids in Egypt.*

---

* It appears that the publication of anti-Semitic literature in the Soviet Union considerably increased after 1975. Professor John Armstrong of the University of Wisconsin reports that books belonging to the genre, published in editions of 100,000 and 200,000, do not distinguish between Zionist and Jew, and blend "the main features of traditional anti-Semitic propaganda, as developed from the Middle Ages through the Nazi press, and including Soviet Cold War cliches in which Jews, Zionists, and Israel replace the Western powers as archvillains." A preferred theme is that Jews collaborated with Nazis during World War II.

Now all this was familiar as a pattern, and unmistakably Soviet: the enormous lie, the mind-numbing accusation. Enough to settle the origins of the Zionism resolution. Yet it is to be insisted that others were also involved, and probably independently involved.

Evidently the Arabs — the other natural source of anti-Israel propaganda — had shown but little interest in the Zionist movement as such. When Arabs attacked Zionism on ideological grounds, it was mainly for being pro-Bolshevik or socialistic. Such was the position, for example, of the Saudis and of King Faisal. Still, even for the Arabs things at length began to change, as the uses of ideology were perceived. From the 1960s onward, Bernard Lewis writes,

> . . . Arab attacks on the Zionist enterprise and on Zionist theory began to make extensive use of such terms as *racist,* and to seek resemblances between Israel and South Africa, and, even more remarkably, between Zionists and Nazis.

Thus in the Palestine National Covenant of 1964, *racist* is added to the list of pejorative adjectives applied to Zionism, while a 1965 Arab tract, which Lewis notes was, "significantly," published in English, classifies Zionism as a form of racism.

There the matter must rest. Arab propagandists can lay as good a claim to the 1975 Zionism resolution as can the Soviets, though it was the Soviet connection that preoccupied me at the time. (As usual, the question seemingly never occurred to anyone in Washington. What did it *matter* whose idea it was?) It was in any event clear that the Soviets were using the Zionism resolution as a fallback position from which to attack Israel — and to intimidate Egypt — after the momentum went out of the movement to expel Israel from the U.N. The plain fact of the time was that Israel and Egypt, with American sponsorship, were moving toward something like peace. The Soviets, especially after having been expelled from Egypt, would not have it.

On July 14, in his Milwaukee address, Kissinger made clear that the United States would do many things, possibly drastic things, if Israel were even so much as *suspended* from the coming General Assembly. On July 16, a conference of foreign ministers of forty Islamic countries called even so for the *expulsion* of Israel from the U.N. and from all international bodies. On July 17, the European Nine expressed their intention to "defend and promote respect for the Charter, for the rights of member states and for the existing rules of procedure," meaning that Israel's rights were not to be interfered with. On July 18, the U.S. Senate adopted a resolution saying that if Israel were expelled from the U.N. the United States would consider seriously the implication of continued

American membership in that body. On July 23, Israeli Foreign Minister Yigal Allon appealed to "enlightened" members of the U.N. to try to head off any move to suspend Israel from the Thirtieth Session by serving notice that they themselves would walk out if Israel was suspended. Nothing daunted, on July 25, the foreign ministers of the Organization of African Unity directed that their drafting committee prepare a resolution seeking the suspension of Israel. *Then,* on the same day, July 25, Anwar Sadat, President of Egypt, stated that "Israel must be present at the United Nations if it is expected to comply with its resolutions." He continued that if Israel did not comply, then it should be expelled. But the essential Egyptian statement was that for the moment Israel must remain if the movement toward peace between the two countries was to continue. On July 29, Allon stated that if Israel were ousted from the U.N., the U.N. would be ousted from Israel, and there would be no Geneva peace conference. Events turned. On August 1, the O.A.U. assembly of heads of state approved a resolution which spoke merely of "the possibility of eventually depriving Israel . . . of its membership." On August 30, the ministerial conference of Non-Aligned in Lima adopted a thirty-two-page declaration, which omitted a call for Israel's suspension or expulsion, calling merely for Israel to abide by the Charter and implement all United Nations resolutions concerning the Palestinian and Middle East questions.

The United States had won. Kissinger had won. The Egyptians, having broken with the Russians, succeeded in upholding their new relationship with the United States, and the step-by-step movement toward peace with Israel that rested fundamentally on U.N. resolutions.

The object of the Zionism resolution that followed was to spoil these relations and disrupt such progress, to force Egypt, as Lewis later wrote, "to join in this exercise and to sabotage independent Egyptian moves toward peace." The irony is that this second-best, fallback alternative for the Soviets was potentially far more devastating than expulsion. Instead of merely challenging the right of Israel to participate in the General Assembly, the Zionism resolution challenged the right of Israel to exist. The legitimacy of the Israeli state was denied. The official doctrine of the state, the ideology of the movement to create a Jewish homeland, was declared to be suffused with racism, the one doctrine that the existing world political community had outlawed. The United Nations system, in thirty years, had granted legitimacy to all manner of economic, social, and political arrangements: democratic and totalitarian; capitalist and socialist; pluralist and centralist. All were equally accepted as equally legitimate. *Only regimes based on racism and racial discrimination were held to be unacceptable.* This is not to say that anything that might be accorded the standing of international law held that a state determined to be racist had no right to exist, but this *was* very close to political reality, especially at the United Nations.

There were now but three states left in all of Africa or Asia still dominated by European whites: South Africa, Rhodesia — and Israel. To Israelis, and no doubt to great numbers of Americans and Europeans, it will seem absurd to put them in such company. Israel is, after all, the homeland of the Jews. But Africans and Asians so disposed reply to this that Israel is the homeland only of those Jews who have always lived there. The rest are Russian and Polish and Hungarian colonizers. Colonizers have no rights. None, certainly, at the United Nations. This was the devastating aspect of the Zionism resolution: it declared Israel to be a regime of the past.

If I knew little of Israel, I knew a fair amount about the Versailles Peace Conference, and was not impressed by the historical case the Arabs would make. The treaty of Sèvres clearly anticipated that there would be an Arab state in Syria and a Jewish state in Palestine. The Mandate granted at San Remo in 1920 only strengthened this presumption, while already, in 1919, the Emir Feisal and Chaim Weizmann had agreed to a Jewish settlement in Palestine. If the Jews at the time were in some sense stateless, so also were the Arabs. None had states. All would have. This was the age of Wilson.

This is what I knew. I think I also knew that it was quite possible for Asians, and others, to see things quite differently, to see the Israelis as a remaining remnant of white, European colonialists. I also knew that American Jews, and I assumed Israelis, had very great difficulty imagining that anyone could see Israel in such a perspective. Hence this attack was deadly dangerous. The Israelis and their supporters thought of themselves as the very model of the modern anti-imperialist, collectivist society. And of all the things they could never be accused of was racism: certainly not after the Holocaust. And so the jets came screaming in under their radar screen; undetected, utterly unexpected.

———◆———

A careful history may one day be written of the emergence of this issue. What I recount is what we knew at the U.S. Mission in October and November of 1975, where, thanks to a superb legal officer, Herbert Reis, we at least knew the U.N. background. The large causal events, of course, were cultural and political: the process by which it came to pass that, in Bernard Lewis's words, "the fashionable enemy in the West in our day is the racist, just as a few years back he was the communist." But the United Nations was an ideal institutional structure for facilitating this transition and for giving an institutional structure to the new attitude.

The transition was rapid. In 1965, on the basis of a draft prepared by the Human Rights Commission, the General Assembly took up and adopted the International Convention on the Elimination of Racial Discrimination. Article I defined the term:

> In this Convention, the term "racial discrimination" shall mean any distinction, exclusion, restriction or preference based on race, colour, descent or national or ethnic origin which has the purpose or effect of nullifying or impairing the recognition, employment or exercise, on an equal footing, of human rights and fundamental freedoms in the political, economic, social, cultural or any other field of public life.

In the expansive spirit of the proceedings (there was virtually no debate) the United States, with Brazil, proposed adding an additional article:

> States Parties condemn anti-Semitism and shall take action as appropriate for its speedy eradication in the territories subject to their jurisdiction.

The United States delegate, William P. Rogers, former Attorney General and future Secretary of State, explained:

> Article I makes it quite clear that this Convention is intended to protect ethnic as well as racial groups. Although all members of this Committee who have spoken have argued that the present language of the Convention is broad enough to cover anti-Semitism . . . [the] article proposed by Brazil and the United States would appropriately highlight the application of the Convention to anti-Semitism.

It was understandable that Rogers, with an American sensitivity to the racial language in which the Nazis had expressed their anti-Semitism, should want the U.N. to proclaim its abhorrence of the latter. But in the end the association proved to be a weapon accessible to enemies as well as friends, for it held within it support for the idea of Jews as a race, a complicated idea to begin with, but by 1975 especially dangerous, as enemies of Israel were beginning to claim that Jews justified their nationhood on racial grounds, and accordingly, somehow, did not deserve to have a nation. In 1965 the Soviets proposed an amendment to the Convention on the Elimination of Racial Discrimination, which suggests they were onto the idea:

> States Parties condemn anti-Semitism, Zionism, Nazism, neo-Nazism and all other forms of the policy and ideology of colonialism, national and race hatred and exclusiveness and shall take action as appropriate

for the speedy eradication of those inhuman ideas and practices in the territories subject to their jurisdiction.

Brilliant: to oppose *both* anti-Semitism and *Zionism!* To link "exclusiveness" with racial discrimination! The amendment was put off by a decision not to give priority to "any . . . specific forms of racial discrimination," but the idea remained.

This decision also put aside consideration of a Bolivian amendment that referred not only to "racial discrimination," the going term of the day, but to "racism" as such. Just what prompted the Bolivian delegation to invoke the term *racism* was not clear, but this was the first appearance of the word in the U.N. system that we could discover. It appeared also in 1965 in a Security Council resolution that asserted that the declaration of independence by Rhodesian white settlers had no legal validity. But for the longest while, the term scarcely existed in the U.N. vocabulary; speeches, resolutions, and conventions were directed against "racial discrimination." A very different matter, as Paul Weaver of *Fortune* was later to point out: racial discrimination is a practice, racism a doctrine. The implications differ considerably.

As a term, *racism* came into its own at the U.N. with the Tehran International Convention on Human Rights, convened in April, 1968, to observe the twentieth anniversary of the proclamation of the Universal Declaration. Just weeks before the Tehran conference, the Kerner Commission report had been released in the United States, and the term *racism*, especially *white racism,* achieved a huge vogue. The idea dominated the years that followed, and produced by analogy such variants as *sexism* and *ageism.* It was a clear enough idea to begin with, but now too fashionable for an exact meaning to survive. The American delegation to the Tehran conference included a member of the Kerner Commission, Roy Wilkins, and Morris Abram, a man active in both Jewish and racial affairs. For whatever reason, apart from this new word, the delegation brought little along with it, conceding almost the whole initiative on human rights to the dictatorships, avowing American failings at every opportunity. Language depreciated rapidly. "All recognized," the Afghan *rapporteur* of the conference noted, "that the tragic situation in southern Africa constitutes the vilest and most flagrant violation of human rights ever recorded in history." Worse than the age of Hitler, presumably, or of Stalin, or of Idi Amin. No American asked for precision. No American took exception as Israeli occupation of Arab territories, now a huge fact of Middle East life, was continuously associated with the situation of southern Africa. The initiative on specific human rights issues was almost wholly taken over by the Soviets. There had recently taken place in West Germany (where a thoroughly democratic government permitted such opposition) an outbreak of small neo-Nazi demonstrations. The governments of the USSR, Poland, and Czechoslovakia obtained from the conference the sternest condemnation of this "Nazism" and "neo-Nazism." Nigeria proposed adding the words *and racism* after "neo-Nazism," and the sponsors agreed. The resolution was thereafter modified only in that the conference rejected the Soviet contention that these outbreaks "constitute a threat to the peace and security of peoples." The Soviets similarly introduced the resolution calling on the General Assembly to declare 1969 "the International Year for Action to Combat Racism and Racial Discrimination." In time, the General Assembly expanded the period from a year into a decade, which technically began in 1973. It will be recalled that the resolution to declare Zionism a form of racism and racial discrimination was one of several amendments to the basic charter of the "Decade," and as such had now come before the Thirtieth General Assembly.

In the interval, a more specific attack on Israel had also proceeded. The first direct move against Israel's part in the U.N. system had come in the United Nations Educational, Scientific, and Cultural Organization, which will seem appropriate to those who believe that the largest political phenomena appear first in the culture. On November 20, 1974, by a vote of 64 in favor to 27 (including the United States) against, with 26 abstentions, the UNESCO General Conference condemned Israel for altering the historical features of Jerusalem and undertaking excavations that constituted a danger to its monuments. (The vote, in percentage terms, was almost precisely that on the Zionism resolution a year later. Fifty-five percent for, 23 percent against, 22 percent abstaining in UNESCO. Fifty-two percent for, 25 percent against, 23 percent abstaining in the General Assembly.) The UNESCO General Conference next rejected a motion to include Israel in UNESCO's European regional group, leaving it the only member state not included in any such grouping. Finally the conference called on the Director-General to supervise the educational and cultural institutions in the occupied Arab territories, in cooperation with the Arab States and the Palestine Liberation Organization, so that these populations might have access to education and culture to preserve their national identity. Much work had been done by the time the Third Committee of the Thirtieth General Assembly convened.

———◆———

Chaim Herzog, the Israeli Ambassador to the U.N., later recalled that the issue took the Israelis by complete surprise. This suggests the extraordinary vulnerability of that nation, and of Jews generally, to the kind of attack now being made upon them. Here was Israel, born in bloody struggle and surviving by virtue of intense, unceasing vigilance of the highest intellectual as well as spiritual order. The nation lived like an aircraft carrier in a hostile sea, ready to fight on six or seven minutes' notice. Off would go the sirens, the fighter bombers would be in the air in seconds, minutes later taking out air bases on another continent. It was such a matter of minutes that saved the nation in the Six Day War. Yet now there was taking place an attack on Israel's national movement as such — indeed, the first attack of this kind in the history of the United Nations. Before six weeks had passed, dimwitted Tass, the Soviet news agency, would state that surely the event came as no surprise to anyone, surely everyone saw it coming. But no, it came as a complete surprise to those who had the greatest need to see it coming.

The State of Israel was surrounded by nations formally committed to its destruction. Huge majorities for this proposition could be summoned in the United Nations. The world's second greatest power, the Soviet Union, was openly anti-Semitic. The world's greatest power, the West generally, and Japan particularly, had entered a time of prolonged economic difficulty consequent upon the decision of the Arab nations, which were also Israel's enemies, to quintuple the price of energy. It could be predicted that the Europeans would somehow begin to blame the Israelis for this, while for certain the Japanese would want to stay aloof. Our support had been effective in the 1967 war because we still had available to us the air bases of prerevolutionary Portugal. (A complex world.) Whatever would follow, that regime in Portugal had gone. In the meantime, with the outcome of that war and the quintupling of oil prices, the West had entered what was likely to be a protracted period of inflation and unemployment, with the normal difficulties of parliamentary governments considerably worsened. Whether Israel was responsible, Israel surely would be blamed: openly by some, privately by most. Israel would be *regretted*.

Somehow this reality was not making its way through, perhaps especially to American Jews. Here a long history was proving no guide. Jewish history seemed to deny the possibility that the enemies of Jews could be on the left. Jewish history seemed especially to deny that Jews could be thought guilty of crimes committed by *governments*. The State of Israel was so new. It was hard to think that *Jewish* thought and behavior might display the same characteristics found in other nations. Jews imprisoning others? Jews occupying the territory of others? Jews desecrating the culture of others? Surely there was some mistake.

But of course there was no mistake at all, as far as what was being said and believed. By 1965 the State of Israel had been in existence longer than most members of the United Nations. A clear majority of the states that sponsored the Zionism resolution were created *after* the establishment of Israel. They found no difficulty conceiving of a *state* of Israel, which might act as other states — as their own — did. Nor, let it be recorded, did the U.S. Permanent Representative.

This helped me to respond. I had no resistance to the evidence of what was going on, no difficulty in believing it possible. Israel was a small democracy to whose survival the United States had made a strong commitment, but not a commitment of a different order from that made to other democracies. I was clear in my mind that anyone wishing to see that commitment sustained should in any event emphasize its general rather than its particular nature. The whole experience was, at one level, rather abstract for me.

But there was another level on which my concern was anything but abstract. The Zionism resolution was aimed not merely at the State of Israel, but at Zionists. Which meant most of the Jews of the United States. I did not represent the State of Israel, but I most assuredly did represent the United States. And the peoples thereof.

———◆———

Chaim Herzog, the man who did represent Israel, had been born in Ireland, son of the Chief Rabbi of Ireland. He had served in the Guards Armoured Division, and was knighted. He was a man to be in a tank battle with; yet there was the part of him that made him publisher of the *Encyclopaedia Judaica*. A man of courage and grace, and great heart. Settled in law practice, he had been persuaded that spring to come to New York to combat the expected move to expel his country from the General Assembly.

We had met only briefly, and not especially as allies. All summer (indeed through all this period) the Security Council was involved in one negotiation or another having to do with renewing the mandates of various United Nations peacekeeping forces on the Israeli borders, and with the role of the Palestine Liberation Organization in the peace negotiations. Endless discussions would take place as to whether in one instance, in return for Egyptian agreement to a three-month extension, the Council should express its "appreciation" to Cairo or merely its "satisfaction." In all such proceedings, from first to last, I had precise instructions. In the critical moments at the Security Council table I would read from the texts prepared in Washington, without having made the least change. This was the proper thing to do, but it did not make for the warmest relations with the Israelis. They now distrusted Kissinger with great intensity, and even when not dissatisfied with the outcome of this or that negotiation never showed any face to the world save defiance. Thus it was that Herzog and I had no special relationship when, on October 1 — two days before I was to go to San Francisco for the A.F.L.-C.I.O. convention — he telephoned about the Zionism resolution, which had been sprung out of the blue. He asked, "Do you realize the import of this resolution?" I said that I did; that we would back Israel; that I was afraid, however, that we would remain isolated with Israel on the issue. Ours had been the only two votes against the proposition when it had been included in the final declaration of the International Women's Year Conference just three months before.

Later, in the aftermath of the final vote, we were asked, in effect, on what grounds we had chosen to enhance the importance of an encounter we would surely lose. I can only tell what I thought at the time. First, I had been asked to do so by the representative of the government of Israel, which had a claim on any democratic nation and especially our own. Second, my own government had already opposed the measure at the Mexico City conference. Third, the United States had at the Special Session given full evidence of its bona fides. All we had asked was an end to the assaults represented by this resolution. Instead, the Non-Aligned were now allowing themselves to be made party to a moral outrage. Fourth, the American people would absolutely support the position I proposed to take. Anyone even partially familiar with survey data would have known this. Fifth, to attack Zionists was to attack Americans no less than Israelis, and I had said at the outset we would defend ourselves.

As we were certain to lose the vote, it was essential that we win the argument. Herzog and I agreed we would fight on three grounds. First, that the resolution was a lie. This we could prove. Second, that the small and weak nations that voted for it would be voting for a principle — that the United Nations could lie and would lie — which would one day be turned against *them*. This was a proposition no one could disprove. Third, that if the Zionism resolution passed, the Decade for Action Against Racism and Racial Discrimination would be dead.

We agreed that the critical move would be to obtain the support of the European Nine, who had not been on our side at Mexico City. This turned out not to be difficult. On October 3, the day Garment spoke in the Third Committee, Italy's Piero Vinci, speaking for the Community, stated that they would not go along with the resolution, and that if it were to pass, the Nine would not participate in the Decade. This was more than we had hoped, and suggests that one shouldn't exaggerate the Israeli or American role in the days that followed. We were not alone.

Our next object was to dissuade a respectable portion of Africans, whose own Decade was in some respects at stake, to oppose the resolution on grounds of principle or prudence, however they liked. Then, to stir opinion in the United States, to which, after all, both Europeans and Africans looked for support in more than a few matters.

To this end Herzog called Rabbi Israel Miller, the President of the Conference of Presidents of Major American Jewish Organizations, an umbrella group that had been set up at the request of Secretary of State John Foster Dulles. In the classic mode of reorganizations, the result of drawing a big box around all the other boxes had been merely to create yet another box. Still, Miller was the appropriate person for the Israelis to look to. Unfortunately, as far as we could tell, instead of in turn calling the organizations he was supposed to represent, Miller commenced to call *me*, a development I reported to Herzog with some testiness. Herzog then saw Miller and asked why we weren't hearing anything from the American Jewish community. There had not been a word. No statements. No advertisements. No petitions. (By contrast, the American Jewish Committee had at least sent a telegram to the President supporting the statements Mitchell and I had made about Amin.) Miller replied, sorrowfully as Herzog judged, that he had raised the matter with the Israeli Embassy in Washington and had been told: "Ignore it, it's nonsense."

This only aroused Herzog further. The Israeli Foreign Minister, Yigal Allon, came through New York on the weekend following my speech to the A.F.L.-C.I.O. and Garment's statement in the Third Committee. Herzog gave him dinner in a kosher Chinese restaurant in the garment district, pitch black and deserted on a Sunday evening, adding rather to the drama of the occasion. We both spoke of the urgency of the matter as we saw it. Allon took the point. His next stop was London, where he spoke to Harold Wilson. The British thereupon became much more active.

As October progressed we were still surrounded by silence, but making some impression within the U.N. itself. Our one bit of leverage — whatever the elegance of our arguments — was the Decade Against Racism, and this began to show effect. The technical situation was as follows: Somalia, acting on behalf of thirteen sponsoring countries, had submitted *seven* amendments. These identified "Zionism as a form of racial discrimination to be included in the Programme of the Decade," proposed to provide "moral and material support to the national liberation movements and victims of apartheid, Zionism, and racial discrimination," and requested a study of the "colonial roots" of Zionism. Faced with the sudden show of Western opposition, Somalia requested that the vote be postponed, which was agreed. Two weeks of lobbying and negotiation followed, with the Africans under pressure from many sides. On October 15, Somalia withdrew the seven amendments and presented as a substitute, this time on behalf of twenty-six cosponsors, a single resolution that declared, "Zionism is a form of racism and racial discrimination." Zionism was no longer cited in the resolution dealing with the operational programs of the Decade. Evidently this was intended as a conciliatory move toward African nations concerned about their Decade. But we put it about that in our view Somalia was merely acting for the Soviet Union and that the Zionism resolution and the Decade were, as Garment later said, "inseparably linked." Adopt one, lose the other. We had no thought of defeating the resolution outright, but it was at least possible that a majority might be persuaded to put it aside.

———◆———

The final debate in the Third Committee took place Thursday and Friday, October 16 and 17. I met with Kissinger for lunch in Washington on the Thursday. He supported us completely in a plan to try to table the resolution rather than to defeat it.

Who is to say whether and how debate ever affects the outcome of a vote? This one did, I think, at least somewhat. It was intense and at times vituperative. The Arabs were at their worst, or best, as they might think. Replete with charters and pacts and proclamations of long ago, leering with proofs of Jewish wickedness snipped from the editorials of Israeli newspapers or the pronouncements of anti-Zionist Jews. Bitter with near to thirty years of defeat on the battlefield. Quick to belittle, incapable of praise. They would invoke Saladin, but these descendants had quite lost his largeness, his munificence. If the representative of Haiti said that "no one until today thought to name [Zionism] a crime against humanity," Iraq would then recall that "Haiti was one of the few countries prevailed upon by U.S. pressure to change its vote in 1947 when the General Assembly voted for the partition of Palestine."

The nearest to a tactical success we had was using the leverage of the Decade with southern Africans. As one went southward on the continent, the number of countries with Moslem majorities or sizable Moslem populations decreased. Blyden of Sierra Leone understood our position completely and shared it completely. In the end he voted with us, and led an African effort to table. Yet as I pressed for this or that, he had had continually to remind me that the majority of his cabinet was Moslem. Our principal tactical mistake was not to understand the willingness of the Arabs simply to buy themselves a majority. There had been an anti-Israel majority in the General Assembly for at least a decade. But with the West now for the first time pressing the marginal members of that coalition, the Arabs responded with what the Barbados representative, Waldo E. Waldron Ramsey, in his speech to the Committee, deftly termed "blandishments." A second error, disastrous and definitive, was to suppose that the Latin American countries, with significant Jewish populations almost everywhere and no direct stake in the issue, would be with us. When the vote came, Brazil and Mexico were against us, and there were many more Latin American abstentions than votes with us. Japan also abstained.

On the morning of October 17, still in committee, Sierra Leone and Zambia moved to postpone consideration for a year. The motion lost with 68 against and only 45 in favor, with 16 abstentions. The Dutch and others were doing their best to find a way to put the whole thing off, but Smid of Czechoslovakia was in the chair. Smid the liberal had become Smid the *apparatchik;* every ruling went against us.

At length Garment spoke. It was clear we would lose; but we wished the majority to be clear what it was about to do.

> My delegation has read the new proposal before us. It is unusually straightforward. It asks us to determine "that Zionism is a form of racism and racial discrimination."
>
> As simple as this language is, we are concerned that what may not be fully understood is that this resolution asks us to commit one of the most grievous errors in the thirty-year life of this organization.
>
> This committee is preparing itself, with deliberation and foreknowledge, to perform a supreme act of deceit, to make a massive attack on the moral realities of the world. Under the guise of a program to eliminate racism the United Nations is at the point of officially endorsing anti-Semitism, one of the oldest and most virulent forms of racism known to human history. This draft explicitly encourages the racism known as anti-Semitism even as it would have us believe that its words will lead to the elimination of racism.
>
> I choose my words carefully when I say that this is an obscene act. The United States protests this act. But protest alone is not enough. In fairness to ourselves we must also issue a warning. This resolution places the work of the United Nations in jeopardy. The language of this resolution distorts and perverts. It changes words with precise meanings into purveyors of confusion. It destroys the moral force of the concept of racism, making it nothing more than an epithet to be flung arbitrarily at one's adversary. It blinds us to areas of agreement and disagreement, and deprives us of the clarity of vision we desperately need to understand and resolve the differences among us. And we are here to overcome our differences, not to deepen them.
>
> Zionism is a movement which has as its contemporary thrust the preservation of the small remnant of the Jewish people that survived the horrors of a racial holocaust. By equating Zionism with racism, this resolution discredits the good faith of our joint efforts to fight actual

racism. It discredits these efforts morally and it cripples them politically.

The United Nations, throughout its thirty-year history, has not lived by the force of majorities; it has not lived by the force of arms. It has lived only — I repeat, only — because it has been thought that the nations of the world, assembled together, would give voice to the most decent and humane instincts of mankind. From this thought has come the moral authority of the United Nations, and from this thought its influence upon human affairs.

Actions like this do not go unnoticed. They do not succeed without consequences, many of which while only imperfectly perceived at the time soon become part of an ineradicable and regrettable reality. Let us make no mistake: at risk today is the moral authority which is the United Nations' only ultimate claim for the support of our peoples. This risk is as reckless as it is unnecessary. But it is still avoidable. . . .

Accordingly, the United States will support [the first two resolutions applying only to the Decade. . . .] We support, without reservation, the work of the United Nations to combat racism and racial discrimination. We have taken part in these vitally important activities in the past and want to be able to do so without obstruction in the future. We will vote against the third resolution. We call upon other delegations to do likewise. On its adoption the third resolution becomes inseparably linked to the first two. Therefore, if all three are sent to Plenary the United States will vote against all three at that time. . . . My government appreciates the fact that there were so many in this Committee who have shown that they wanted to consider this matter more carefully before committing the United Nations to so serious a step.

We then moved to adjourn without a vote; but this failed, 65 votes against, 40 in favor, and 21 abstentions. The Committee room grew crowded, hot, and excited. Something obscene was about to happen.

Garment sat in our chair. I sat behind him. There was to be no mistaking our presence. I had asked Podhoretz to be there; with him was the British critic Goronwy Rees, who had come to New York to say farewell to Lionel Trilling, but arrived just too late. Diana Trilling, as her husband would have expected, thought of their visitor first and called to ask if I would not find a moment to see him and perhaps to show him around. He had come for coffee that morning and I had suggested he come back for the vote that afternoon. Later, in *Encounter*, he described the moment:

> There were ghosts haunting the Third Committee that day; the ghosts of Hitler and Goebbels and Julius Streicher, grinning with delight to hear, not only Israel, but Jews as such denounced in language which would have provoked hysterical applause at any Nuremberg

rally. . . . And there were other ghosts also at the debate: the ghosts of the 6,000,000 dead in Dachau and Sachsenhausen and other extermination camps, listening to the same voices which had cheered and jeered and abused them as they made their way to the gas chambers. For the fundamental thesis advanced by the supporters of the resolution, and approved by the majority of the Third Committee, was that to be a Jew, and to be proud of it, and to be determined to preserve the right to be a Jew, is to be an enemy of the human race.

Finally, all moves to postpone having failed, Herzog spoke:

Mr. Chairman, we have listened to the most unbelievable nonsense on the subject of Zionism from countries who are the archetypes of racists. I ask you, does it not beg the question? Here is one small country, 3,000,000 in population — a free democratic country which can be visited by anybody in which all citizens, Jews and Arabs, are free and equal — being castigated hour in, hour out by countries whose regimes practice racism, incorporate racism in their laws and their daily practice. Does it not beg the question? Why not examine the racism practiced in so many countries who have been speaking so profusely? Why pick on a small Jewish state? I suspect because it is Jewish and small.

It doesn't surprise me, Sir, because we are a people who have lived with this form of discrimination — anti-Semitism — for centuries. How dare these people talk of racism to us — we, who have suffered more than any other nation in the world from racist theories and practices, a nation which has suffered the most terrifying holocaust in the history of mankind. For centuries we have suffered from racism. We suffer today from racism in a number of countries, including Arab racism as practiced in so many of the sponsor countries. The sponsors have the effrontery to talk of racism. It lies not in your mouths. You have degraded this world organization by introducing this anti-Semitic element into the world body and in so doing you may well destroy it ultimately. . . .

This . . . is a sad day for the United Nations. The Jewish people will not forget this scene nor this vote. We are a small people with a long and proud history. We have lived through much in our history. We have survived all our oppressors and enemies over the centuries. We shall survive this shameless exhibition. But we, the Jewish people, will not forget. We shall not forget those who spoke up for decency and civilization; and I thank the delegations who expressed themselves against this pernicious resolution. We shall not forget those who voted to attack our religion and our faith. We shall never forget.

These last words were shouted, and the room for a moment fell silent. Then, as if the others were rallying their ranks, the stirring commenced again, rising to a frenzy. The vote came, racing across the computer screen. 70 in favor, 29 against, with 27 abstentions.* They had picked up two votes over the Sierra Leone motion to postpone, five over ours. A long mocking applause broke out. The Israeli delegation, clearly on instructions, showed not the least emotion.

I rose and walked over to Herzog and embraced him. "Fuck 'em!" I said.

———◆———

As it happened, on the day of the vote I had accepted an invitation by Zbigniew Brzezinski to speak to a luncheon of the Trilateral Commission, the foreign policy study group of which, we were to learn, Jimmy Carter was a member. I arrived at the Louis XVI Room at the Waldorf full of news from the Third Committee. During lunch I remarked that I feared the pending vote would affect not only world politics, but American domestic politics as well. George W. Ball, former Under Secretary of State and former U.S. Permanent Representative to the U.N., replied, "Nonsense. The campaign finance act has broken the political power of the American Jews."

This was endemic at the Department of State: to suppose that we supported Israel because of Harry Truman's partner in that haberdashery. Because Abraham Feinberg stayed at the White House when Lyndon

———

* The Third Committee vote was:

In Favor: 70
Afghanistan, Albania, Algeria, Bahrain, Bangladesh, Brazil, Bulgaria, Burma, Byelorussia, Cameroon, Cambodia, Cape Verde, Chad, Chile, China, Congo, Cuba, Cyprus, Czechoslovakia, Dahomey, East Germany, Egypt, Gabon, Guinea, Guinea-Bissau, Guyana, Hungary, India, Indonesia, Iran, Iraq, Jordan, Kuwait, Laos, Lebanon, Libya, Madagascar, Malaysia, Mali, Malta, Mauritania, Mauritius, Mexico, Mongolia, Morocco, Mozambique, Niger, Nigeria, Oman, Pakistan, Poland, Portugal, Qatar, Saudi Arabia, Senegal, Somalia, Soviet Union, Spain, Sri Lanka, Sudan, Syria, Tanzania, Tunisia, Turkey, Uganda, Ukraine, United Arab Emirates, Yemen, Southern Yemen, and Yugoslavia.

Opposed: 29
Australia, Austria, Bahamas, Barbados, Belgium, Canada, Costa Rica, Denmark, Dominican Republic, Ecuador, Finland, France, Haiti, Iceland, Ireland, Israel, Italy, Ivory Coast, Liberia, Luxembourg, the Netherlands, New Zealand, Nicaragua, Norway, Sweden, United Kingdom, United States, Uruguay, and West Germany.

Abstaining: 27
Botswana, Colombia, Ethiopia, Fiji, Gambia, Ghana, Grenada, Honduras, Jamaica, Japan, Kenya, Lesotho, Malawi, Nepal, Papua-New Guinea, Peru, Philippines, Rumania, Rwanda, Sierra Leone, Singapore, Swaziland, Togo, Upper Volta, Venezuela, Zaire, and Zambia.

Absent: 16
Argentina, Bhutan, Bolivia, Burundi, Central African Republic, El Salvador, Equatorial Guinea, Greece, Guatemala, Maldives, Panama, Paraguay, São Tomé and Príncipe, South Africa, Thailand, and Trinidad-Tobago.

Johnson was there. Because Max Fisher was there under Nixon and Ford, and God knows who would be there if Jackson got in. In a word, that the Jews bought their influence in American foreign policy; that we did not support Israel primarily because it was in the United States' interest to do so.

Podhoretz, while I was in India, had written to tell me that the object of the movement for campaign finance reform then under way was to break the political power of the Jews. I had written back to tell him that he knew nothing of politics.

———◆———

The Zionism resolution was voted at about 6:30 in the evening. Most delegates went straight home to change for the United Nations Ball sponsored by the United Nations Association at the Waldorf. The Secretary-General waltzed with imperial *éclat*.

———◆———

I saw Kissinger a week later, at the annual United Nations Concert at the Kennedy Center in Washington. I told him what Ball had said, and he agreed. He added that one of the country's better known politicians had recently told him that his advice to any young man starting out in politics would be to "Be an anti-Semite."

The story goes that at the Congress of Vienna Metternich was awakened one night to be told the Russian ambassador had just dropped dead. He rubbed his eyes and asked, "What can have been his motive?" It was ever thus with Kissinger. What did he mean by that? To arouse me to greater effort?

That was not likely. To account for our failure to head off the Zionism resolution, a failure which would have to be in part his own for he was Secretary of State? Yes, surely, a little bit that. To be spiteful about Ball, who conceivably wanted his job? Probably. But then there was the other Kissinger, who truly thought that the lights were going out again. That somehow he might find a way to postpone the inevitable, to put it off a bit, even for a bit to confound it. But in the end the inevitable would come; and what a waste it would be.

———◆———

There was no hope now of defeating the resolution in the General Assembly. Technically there had not been a majority against either the Sierra Leone–Zambia motion to table, nor ours; but given the number of abstentions the actual vote was nearly two-to-one against us. I decided instead to try to shame the countries that voted for the resolution. I wished in particular to make the case that the democracies had been on one side and the dictatorships on the other. (By the Freedom House rating, 76 percent of those who voted for the Zionism resolution were Not Free. Only 7 percent of the favorable vote came from nations listed as Free. Just the reverse was true of those who voted against: only 7 percent were Not Free; 61 percent were Free.)

The Chileans gave me an opening. The previous week a U.N. working group had reported on the human rights situation in that country, this being a matter of special concern to the Soviets. The working group denounced the existence of torture centers in Chile, and reported much political repression. The matter would soon be before the Third Committee, and the Chileans began canvassing delegates, to see if they could not get it put off, much as we were trying to put off the Zionism resolution. On October 17, the Chileans voted in favor of the Zionism resolution. The next morning I called in Paul Hofmann of *The Times* and told him for "background" that the Chileans had been bought. The story made as much or more news than the Committee vote itself. "U.S. Aide Charges Chile Sold U.N. Vote to Arabs" ran on the front page. A "United States official" was quoted saying "The fascists in Chile and some like-minded military regimes are lining up with the anti-Semites." Many other Latins, the official was quoted, "deserted us." On the record I said that "the decent countries" had been with us, adding, "If you had to pick your company in the world, you couldn't pick better." Once again off the record, I pointed to the large number of black African states that had voted against the resolution: "The Africans are standing up for their own interests," I concluded.

This appeared on the *Times* front page Monday, October 20. On Tuesday evening I was scheduled to address the Appeal of Conscience Foundation dinner in New York. This group, while headed by Rabbi Arthur Schneier, was supported by Roman Catholic, Protestant, and Greek Orthodox, as well as by Jewish, religious leaders. (The Jesuits at *America* had, months earlier, asked me to give the speech.) I now found a theme. That the issue was not Israel but democracy. The action of the Third Committee had awakened us, none too soon:

> Joyce hit upon the term epiphany for such moments of showing through. "Its soul," he wrote, "its whatness leaps to us from the vestment of its appearance . . . the object achieves its epiphany." This happened Friday last in the Third Committee of the General Assembly of the United Nations.
>
> Self-destruction is what first showed through. For some time now the United Nations has been showing a seemingly compulsive urge so to

outrage those very principles on which it was founded as to suggest that a sinister transmutation has occurred in an organism that yet enough remembers its own beginnings as to be revulsed by what it has become and somehow to seek expiation in bringing on its own doom. Things like that happen. How else to explain the incessant quest for yet new devices for scandalizing the good opinion on which the survival of the institution depends? I do not refer to the occasional onset of role reversal in which some of the newer nations in the world display a certain disrespect for some of the older ones. Some of the older ones, our own nation included, have a certain amount of disrespect coming, and occasional irreverence will do no one harm. Nor do I refer to the debates over the distribution of wealth among the nations of the world which have much occupied the United Nations in recent years. Sufficiently long ago to suggest that it comes naturally, Aristotle noted that the founding of any truly political forum is the signal for a struggle between rich and poor to commence. It is one of the redeeming qualities of the institution that it has indeed begun at the United Nations.

The real problem is very different, and vastly ominous. It is that the United Nations has become a locus of a general assault by the majority of the nations in the world on the principles of liberal democracy which are now found only in a minority of nations, and for that matter a dwindling minority. It was not Zionism that was condemned at the United Nations on Friday, it was Israel; and not the State of Israel nearly so much as the significance of Israel as one of the very few places, outside of Western Europe and North America and a few offshore islands, where western democratic principles survive, and of all such places, currently the most exposed.

This may not be the view of others, but it is and was the view of the United States Mission to the United Nations, and that view was stated with as much clarity as we could command in the Third Committee debate. . . .

The Committee thereupon voted, and this obscene act, this reckless act was adopted by 70 votes to 29, with 27 abstentions. The epiphany occurred, and nothing more epiphanic than the wholesale decision of the despotisms of the right in the world to side with the despotisms of the left, in common concert against the liberal democracies of the center. It was an awful occasion, but it had about it, most of all, the awfulness of truth. . . .

The question now arises: What are we to do? About this resolution, which has now passed the Third Committee of the United Nations.

The answer is unavoidable. It must not pass the General Assembly. It must not receive that final — and admittedly in most instances automatic — sanction as the judgment of the world community. There can be no community of belief about such a judgment.

One could hope, however, for some common understanding about the kinds of encounter we are having with one another. The United Nations is now much preoccupied with economic issues of a distributive nature, having to do with the relative condition of various classes of nations, much as the internal politics of many societies are preoccupied with similar issues having to do with classes of citizens. This ought not surprise us, for by all the doctrinal lights of the 20th century, this is what we are *supposed* to be preoccupied with. And yet, as a number of academicians have been arguing with perhaps increasing force, this is not in fact what the Twentieth Century is turning out to be about. To the contrary, it is the ancient and supposedly recessive bonds of race and creed which increasingly occupy the political forums of the world.

Given this, is it not possible for nations caught up in the latest aftermath of the latest world movement to see at very least that the condition is not peculiar to one region or another, or one era or another, but rather is very much the stuff of history, and the experience of almost the whole of mankind? Is it not at very least possible for some of us to see that no matter who prevails in the disputes that so very much absorb us in the world, the ultimate victor in every instance seems to be the state, and the state system, and the increasing forced identity of the individual with the state and the fortunes of the state?

By now Congress was reacting. In the Senate, Javits of New York and Richard Stone of Florida, along with a number of colleagues, introduced a resolution condemning the Third Committee vote. Javits spoke with force: "It is time to speak out and call a halt to this vicious brand of name-calling, which brings echoes of the propaganda machine of Goebbels and his Nazi party colleagues in the nineteen-thirties." In the House of Representatives the Majority Leader, Thomas P. O'Neill, Jr., introduced a similar resolution with nearly a hundred cosponsors. On Friday, October 24, the President issued a statement deploring the Committee vote "in the strongest terms," adding: "The spokesmen for the United States in the United Nations have expressed well and forcefully the views of this Administration and the American people on this issue." On Sunday I appeared on television on *Face the Nation*. I tried to be confident with respect to issues that votes as such could not decide. Whatever the outcome, the vote would tell us who we were and who they were:

> The President, the Secretary of State, the Congress made it very clear. . . . We will stand with the rights of a liberal democracy. We will stand with racial tolerance, with ethnic tolerance. We will stand against that hideous thing.

That evening J. H. Plumb arrived from England. I knew no one whose judgment of Europe was better. He had been in his own way a man of the left, but absolutely a democrat and as fearless of Communists as, during the war, he had been fearless of the Nazis. Plumb, who had advised caution more than once in the past, now urged audacity. He felt that the European governments were terrified of the combination of the Soviets and the Persian Gulf Arabs, and would abandon the Jews as they had done in 1938 and 1939. But the European *public,* he said, would not have it; already they were beginning to hear what we were saying in New York and they approved.

Next came support from the least expected British source. *The New Statesman* of that week carried a long article, "The Resources of Civilization," by its former editor, Paul Johnson. He began with Gladstone's speech on terrorism, given in 1881: "If it shall appear that there is still to be fought a final conflict in Ireland between law on the one side and sheer lawlessness on the other, if the law purged from defect and any taint of injustice is still to be repelled and refused, and the first conditions of political society to remain unfulfilled then I say, gentlemen, without hesitation, the resources of civilisation against its enemies are not yet exhausted." What an age! thought Johnson. He then went on to events in the Third Committee:

> A fortnight ago the U.N. Social, Humanitarian and Cultural Committee — a nomenclature so rich in savage irony as to eclipse even a Swift — passed by 70 votes to 29 a resolution condemning Israel as a "threat to world peace" and Zionism as a "racialist and imperialist ideology." In fact, as all educated people know, Israel, far from being a threat to anyone, stands in perpetual danger of extermination from its bloodthirsty neighbours; and Zionism is neither a racial nor an imperial but a cultural phenomenon. Of course, at the U.N. facts and realities do not matter. What matters is force, money and physical power.
>
> Indeed, the U.N. is rapidly becoming one of the most corrupt and corrupting creations in the whole history of human institutions. How many of the delegates were actually bribed by Arab governments to vote against Israel on this occasion is a matter of speculation; but almost without exception those in the majority came from states notable for racist oppression of every conceivable hue. . . .
>
> The melancholy truth, I fear, is that the candles of civilisation are burning low. The world is increasingly governed not so much by capitalism, or communism, or social democracy, or even tribal barbarism, as by a false lexicon of political clichés, accumulated over half

a century and now assuming a kind of degenerate sacerdotal authority. . . .

In some ways what is said and voted at the U.N. does not matter. There may be a case — not yet, I would say, an overwhelming one — for the United States government to cut off the U.N.'s money, and send the whole squalid circus packing. The slab of steel and glass on the East River might be then put to some useful purpose. But breaking up the U.N. would not end the problem, which springs not from paper votes but from the physical supplies of arms and money which certain states are prepared to pour into the terrorist cauldron. Russia, while ferociously executing dissidents in her own midst (those who hijack Soviet aircraft unsuccessfully know they will never emerge from the KBG interrogation cellars), equips a wide variety of terrorist gangs beyond her sphere of control.

And he ended by speaking of what was to be done:

Has not the time come to change our strategy? What I think the rest of the world is waiting for — indeed hoping for — is some positive sign that the civilised powers are going to uphold the standards of international behaviour set by their forebears; that they are going to do so in the most systematic, relentless and comprehensive manner, and if necessary — while they still possess it — with overwhelming force. All over our tormented planet, there are millions of decent, peaceable and intelligent men and women of all religions, complexions and races, who are praying that the resources of civilisation are not, indeed, exhausted — and that the Brezhnevs and the Amins, the Ghadaffis and the Maos, the Arafats and the O'Sadists will not be allowed to take over the earth.

I had first appeared in print in England in 1958, in a letter to *The New Statesman* protesting an article by G. D. H. Cole describing the American plans for world conquest, which had begun with the "invasion" of North Korea. The letter created a brief stir in London at the time. To have the former editor of *that* journal speak precisely to my purpose a quarter-century later was an event.

In Moscow Andrei D. Sakharov declared, "If this resolution is adopted, it can only contribute to anti-semitic tendencies in many countries, by giving them the appearance of international legality."

———◆———

But where were the Jews? In Moscow, certainly, they were heard from. On October 26, Soviet Jews from fifteen cities issued a public protest against the resolution, calling it "essentially anti-Semitic." But in New York there was — silence. So also in Israel, where the press paid little attention to the event. The first editorial on the resolution — so far as we in New York were aware — appeared only on October 16. I commenced to deplore this to Herzog, who assured me I was not alone. Ivor Richard had told him he was surprised by the lack of Jewish reaction. Von Wechmar of West Germany had told him it would have been helpful if the Jewish community had reacted somewhat more. I telephoned and harangued, but to no visible effect.

Finally Herzog had to take the matter head-on. On October 24 he made his first appearance before the Conference of Presidents of Major American Jewish Organizations. He made a formal speech. He asked, could Jewry be proud of its silence? It was the first major attack on world Jewry since the days of Hitler, and how had they reacted? In the greatest metropolis in the entire world, the greatest concentration of Jews in the entire world, there had been hardly a word of protest in the newspapers. Only on Friday the twenty-fourth, a week after the resolution passed in the Third Committee, did a weak editorial appear in *The New York Times*. In Israel the press was concentrated on the issue of the stevedore strikers at Ashdod Port, not having regard to the fact that there in the U.N. the world community was planning to eliminate Ashdod Port. El Al airline workers were striking against their own government, not realizing that in the United Nations Herzog was fighting for the right of a government in Israel even to exist. The essentials of Herzog's speech were reported in the next day's *Times:* "Herzog Says Jews Let Israelis Down during U.N. Debate." He was quoted at the end saying, "The lead on this issue was taken, to its eternal credit, by the United States delegation." This certainly was how he felt.

All hell broke loose for Herzog. He had insulted the American leadership; by implication affronted the Israeli Embassy in Washington. The matter was raised in the Israeli Cabinet, and the question of recalling him for an explanation was discussed. But he also suddenly found himself a hero with the rank and file of American Jewry and soon with the public in Israel. Sacks of mail arrived, overwhelmingly supportive, strikingly disapproving of the American leadership he had taken to task.

I went on telephoning, but still to little consequence. When I asked the United Nations Association to protest, and it produced a draft that began by deploring racial inequality in the United States, I more or less stopped telephoning.

The Western nations caucused and agreed that when the resolution came to the General Assembly we would try once more for a postponement.

———◆———

There is little trace either in Jewish doctrine or in Zionism of the idea that Jews are a race. The very idea was itself an invention of nineteenth-century anti-Semites such as Houston Stewart Chamberlain and Edouard Drumont, who saw the need for a new justification for excluding and persecuting Jews in a secularized age when the old religious grounds of anti-Semitism were losing force. One cannot choose the race to which one belongs. But in both the Jewish and the Zionist conceptions, any person of any racial stock can be or become a Jew by converting to the Jewish religion. Conversely, as the Israeli courts have said, any person born of a Jewish mother who converts to another religion is no longer a Jew. If one can join or resign from the Chosen People, it is scarcely a racially determined category.

It was equally striking to learn how recent the terms *racist* and *racism* were, not only new to U.N. vocabulary but to the language altogether. Chamberlain and Drumont may have been racists, or have preached racism, but there were no words in the French or English dictionaries of their time to describe who they were or what they were up to. As near as one could learn, the term first appeared in French, having both biological and nationalistic connotations, and made its way into English by way of a 1932 translation of Trotsky's *History of the Russian Revolution*. By 1936, according to the files kept by the *Oxford English Dictionary*, the word as used in English had acquired a definite biological meaning, which it has retained. I began to try to interest various Arab delegations in the problem of language entailed here, but with no success. In fairness, neither English nor French was *their* language; and with respect to the Israelis, the Arabs were pretty much determined that words would mean whatever they chose them to mean.

———◆———

Word of our linguistic explorations got around. The Kuwaiti ambassador asked me to lunch October 29 to talk about it. I arrived to find Dr. Abdallah al-Sayegh, a Palestinian Arab born in Tiberias, now a Kuwaiti citizen, also present. His life study had been Zionism, and his rage was clear at the people who had overmastered his own, and sent so many into exile. I nonetheless pressed my point that the General Assembly was about to brand the national liberation movement of a member country with a term that the U.N. had never defined. How could we know if Zionism was a form of racism if we had never defined racism?

Al-Sayegh fairly leapt. To the contrary! he exclaimed, the term "racism" is precisely defined in Article I of the International Convention on the Elimination of All Forms of Racial Discrimination, adopted by the General Assembly in 1965. This was a blow. I allowed that I had better learn my texts, and with that, luncheon in a nice town house overlooking the East River came to a close.

I returned to the Mission and told Reis of my humiliation. He replied that the Kuwaiti was quite wrong. Article I of the Convention refers only to "racial discrimination" and does not contain the other term, "racism," much less does it define it. Nor does any other article of the Convention.

I came to see that all this mattered not at all to the Arabs. What mattered was that the Israelis looked down upon them. They were prepared to hit back with any charge that came to hand. That an American might say that this charge was not just any charge, but the most awful accusation that could be hurled at Jews, and a matter for the gravest concern in other parts of the world, especially the Soviet Union, where Sakharov's fears would surely be realized — such argument made no impress whatever.

When the debate came in the General Assembly, al-Sayegh spoke for Kuwait, and picked up exactly where our luncheon conversation had left off:

> The United Nations definition of racism and racial discrimination is contained in the United Nations Declaration on the Elimination of All Forms of Racial Discrimination, Article 1 of which states that "discrimination between human beings on the ground of race, color, or ethnic origin is an offense to human dignity and shall be condemned"; and in the International Convention on the Elimination of All Forms of Racial Discrimination, which goes even further, in Article 1, by stating that "in this convention, the term 'racial discrimination' shall mean any distinction, exclusion, restriction or preference based on race, color, descent or national or ethnic origin. We accept no abridgement of this definition."

That the excerpt he quoted defined "racial discrimination" and did not contain the word *racism* would probably not have mattered, but in any event, almost certainly he did not notice.

———◆———

Charles H. Fairbanks, a young political scientist at Yale, a Straussian, prepared a long memorandum to the effect that words and their meanings do matter:

We have seen that the equation of Zionism with racism is absurd, that it involves a distortion of the meaning of words. We have seen how bad this is from the point of view of those who do care about human rights. We now need to raise the question whether this reversal of meaning will benefit the nations that voted for it in the [Third] committee. The hope behind this resolution is evidently to transfer our sentiments about racism to Zionism by linking the words. . . . In fact, one has to wonder whether the equation of Zionism with racism will not give rise in many minds to the following reflection: if racism is no worse than Zionism, just how bad is it?

This kind of outcome is a real possibility. To see how likely it is, we must step back and survey for a moment the history and the probable future of human rights language. Let us begin with the future.

The members of [the U.N.] cannot lull themselves into thinking that the official equation of Zionism and racism is an isolated act. It sets a precedent for future speech about racism and human rights issues in general. . . .

Even those who now care about human rights will become ever more cynical about the terms they now use to express this concern. The words will at length cease to stand for anything authentic or to evoke any feeling in those who hear them. . . .

The charge of racism will eventually become something that people laugh at. To call Zionism a form of racism makes a mockery of the struggle against racism as the emperor Caligula made a mockery of the Roman Senate when he appointed to it his horse.

Again, those who are utterly indifferent to human rights may wonder why this matters. It matters for three very important reasons. First, when the terms of human rights speech have lost their specific meaning it will be possible to use them in unforeseen and disturbing ways. . . .

Second, the language of human rights is being used to achieve many nations' foreign policy goals, such as change in international economic relationships and change in Southern Africa. If the Committee's path is taken, the words will soon be made useless for such purposes. When racism can mean anything at all, it will no longer make men indignant that the new government of South Africa is racist. . . .

The third important consideration is this . . . many of the members of the United Nations owe their independence in part to the influence of notions of rights, spreading from the domestic sphere to the international sphere, on colonial powers. Looking at the whole of earlier history, a disinterested observer would be compelled to predict that unless human nature has changed many weak nations will lose their independence in the next century. It is certainly hard to believe that this can be avoided without the help of ideas of rights. . . . To ignore this danger shows an optimism about human nature falsified by the last century's events in many of the very countries supporting the resolution. . . .

It might, finally, be said that when the old language of human rights has become meaningless through abuse there will appear new words expressing the same thing, as in other areas of language. *This is precisely what will not happen.* . . . Human rights is a concern of an unusual kind. Never in human history did the term or the idea of human rights appear before the seventeenth century. When the idea of human rights did appear, it was the product of a specific philosophic doctrine, the social contract school. . . . The question is whether any other philosophic school could produce a doctrine of human rights anew; certainly it is not an indigenous term in the vocabulary of the deepest forms of modern thought, such as existentialism and Marxism. . . . When the old language is worn out and destroyed, no new Jefferson or Woodrow Wilson will arise to renew it. The presuppositions of such renovators have been undermined. . . .

Our specific principles of human rights will not fall and rise again. Any damage done to them is *irreversible.*

To the nations that do not care about human rights I would therefore say: you are giving away real and enduring props of national security in idle skirmishes soon to be forgotten. For the rest of us, we should know what we see before us. What we are witnessing is not merely one of the routine degradations of the United Nations and its ideals. It is, unless we can stand in its way, the most crippling blow yet dealt in the irreversible decline of the concern with human rights as we know it.

The vote came on November 10. The General Assembly was tense, not with uncertainty of the outcome, but rather with the knowledge of it. A succession of resolutions were adopted amending the Decade for Action to Combat Racism and Racial Discrimination. Most of the resolutions were aimed at Israel. By a vote of 93 to 18, with 27 abstentions, the General Assembly established a Committee on the Exercise of the Inalienable Rights of the Palestinian People to insure that there would be resolutions to vote on next year. When the Zionism resolution was reached, Belgium moved to adjourn debate. We got a fair-size vote, including a good many African countries: Ethiopia, Ghana, the Ivory Coast, Kenya, Liberia, Malawi, Sierra Leone, Swaziland, Togo, Upper Volta, Zaire, and Zambia. But the Soviet-Arab coalition held, and we lost 67 to 55, with 15 abstentions. Herzog would later contend that this was the highest pro-Israeli vote in a decade, but it wasn't enough. The other side never dropped below 65.

The outcome was so predetermined that only two nations spoke in the formal debate prior to the voting. Afterwards Herzog rose. Like

Tiresias in *Oedipus Rex,* he began at a peak of intensity and sustained it throughout a superb text:

> It is symbolic that this debate, which may well prove to be a turning point in the fortunes of the United Nations and a decisive factor as to the possible continued existence of this Organization, should take place on November 10th. Tonight thirty-seven years ago has gone down in history as Kristallnacht or The Night of the Crystals. This was the night on 10 November 1938, when Hitler's Nazi storm troopers launched a coordinated attack on the Jewish community in Germany, burnt the synagogues in all its cities and made bonfires in the street of the Holy Books and Scrolls of the Holy Law and Bible. It was the night when Jewish homes were attacked and heads of families taken away, many of them never to return. It was the night when the windows of all Jewish businesses and stores were smashed, covering the streets in the cities of Germany with a film of broken glass which dissolved into millions of crystals giving that night the name, Kristallnacht, The Night of the Crystals. It was the night which led eventually to the crematoria and gas chambers, Auschwitz, Birkenau, Dachau, Buchenwald, Theresienstadt and others. It was the night which led to the most terrifying holocaust in the history of man.

As he concluded, he tore the resolution in two. In 1935, in the Yeshurun Synagogue in Jerusalem, his father had torn in two the British White Paper announcing the limitation of Jewish immigration to Palestine.

I spoke toward the end. It was our speech wholly, Washington having had the sense to leave us be. I began with words Podhoretz had written: "The United States rises to declare before the General Assembly of the United Nations, and before the world, that it does not acknowledge, it will not abide by, it will never acquiesce in this infamous act." I let it be understood how seriously we took this matter:

> As this day will live in infamy, it behooves those who sought to avert it to declare their thoughts so that historians will know that we fought here, that we were not small in number — not this time — and that while we lost, we fought with full knowledge of what indeed would *be* lost.

I recounted in detail the argument we presented against the resolution itself: "In logic, the State of Israel could be, or could become, many things, theoretically including many things undesirable, but it could not be and could not become racist unless it ceased to be Zionist." I then turned to the yet larger point we wished to make:

> It is precisely a concern for civilization, for civilized values that are or should be precious to all mankind, that arouses us at this moment to

such special passion. What we have at stake here is not merely the honor and the legitimacy of the State of Israel — although a challenge to the legitimacy of any member nation ought always to arouse the vigilance of all members of the United Nations. For a yet more important matter is at issue. . . .

The terrible lie that has been told here today will have terrible consequences. Not only will people begin to say, indeed they have already begun to say, that the United Nations is a place where lies are told. Far more serious, grave and perhaps irreparable harm will be done to the cause of human rights. The harm will arise first because it will strip from racism the precise and abhorrent meaning that it still precariously holds today. How will the peoples of the world feel about racism, and about the need to struggle against it, when they are told that it is an idea so broad as to include the Jewish national liberation movement?

As this lie spreads, it will do harm in a second way. Many of the members of the United Nations owe their independence in no small part to the notion of human rights, as it has spread from the domestic sphere to the international sphere and exercised its influence over the old colonial powers. We are now coming into a time when that independence is likely to be threatened again. There will be new forces, some of them arising now, new prophets and new despots, who will justify their actions with the help of just such distortions of words as we have sanctioned here today. Today we have drained the word "racism" of its meaning. Tomorrow, terms like "national self-determination" and "national honor" will be perverted in the same way to serve the purposes of conquest and exploitation. And when these claims begin to be made — as they already have begun to be made — it is the small nations of the world whose integrity will suffer. And how will the small nations of the world defend themselves, on what grounds will others be moved to defend and protect them, when the language of human rights, the only language by which the small can be defended, is no longer believed and no longer has a power of its own?

There is this danger, and then a final danger that is the most serious of all. Which is that the damage we now do to the idea of human rights and the language of human rights could well be irreversible. The idea has not always existed in human affairs. It is an idea which appeared at a specific time in the world, and under very special circumstances. It appeared when European philosophers of the seventeenth century began to argue that man was a being whose existence was independent from that of the State, that he need join a political community only if he did not lose by that association more than he gained. From this very specific political philosophy stemmed the idea of political rights, of claims that the individual could justly make against the State; it was because the individual was seen as so separate from the State that he could make legitimate demands upon it.

That was the philosophy from which the idea of domestic and international rights sprang. But most of the world does not hold with that philosophy now. Most of the world believes in newer modes of political thought, in philosophies that do not accept the individual as distinct from and prior to the State, in philosophies that therefore do not provide any justification for the idea of human rights and philosophies that have no words by which to explain their value. If we destroy the words that were given to us by past centuries, we will not have words to replace them, for philosophy today has no such words.

But there are those of us who have not forsaken these older words, still so new to much of the world. Not forsaken them now, not here, not anywhere, not ever.

I closed as I had begun: "The United States of America declares that it does not acknowledge, it will not abide by, it will never acquiesce in this infamous act."

Garment and I then went off to be interviewed on television. For the first time now we were tired, even depressed. All that was left was not to appear so. We made our way back to the Assembly chamber. There, sitting in our row, unannounced, unabashed, outraged, bearing witness, was Hubert H. Humphrey. *Ha-mavin yavin;* those who understand will understand.

10

The OK Corral

THE WORLD WOKE to what it had done. The Soviet press set about exploiting a great propaganda victory. Tass praised the resolution, which, it said, reflected the true state of affairs in Israel. The U.N. decision, according to Tass, was "a legitimate and just condemnation of the militant Zionist doctrine of racial superiority, an ideology which finds its practical expression in the aggressive, expansionist policy of Israeli ruling circles."

The American press became no less engaged, though a bit more reluctantly. An hour or so after the Zionism resolution was adopted, *The New York Times* went to press with its standard editorial for such occasions. Entitled merely "The U.N. Vote," it described the vote as "offensive, spiteful and futile — and stupid as well." But then: "Pressure will now be great in the United States Congress, and among broad segments of the population, to have done with the United Nations. If the Arab states have cut off their nose to spite their face, the United States must beware of committing the same folly." The next day James S. Leonard, a sometime Foreign Service officer and now president of the United Nations Association of the U.S.A., spoke to *The Times* in similarly routinized terms:

What I really hope is that this will wake up people on both sides of the aisle to the real dangers and evil consequences of using that place as a political battlefield to score on the other guy instead of trying to bridge and reduce differences and find a solution.

But by the time this waffle appeared in the paper, *The Times* had realized that routine wouldn't serve. Something awful really had happened. On Thursday the lead editorial was entitled "Shame of the U.N." It was surely the strongest comment on the United Nations that had ever appeared in the nation's first newspaper. The words were bitter and scornful toward the "Arab-Communist bloc" and yet more so to those whose votes had been "purchased either with gold or oil." Prime Minister Indira Gandhi. Brazil's "conscienceless military dictators." Greece. Mexico. Japan. (Noting that Japan had "at least voted for deferral, but — in deference to Arab oil — abstained in the vote on the resolution.") Jamaica, which "lives on the American tourist trade" and "helped to defeat the deferral motion by abstaining on that vote as well."

The Times noted, though, that the majority was "narrower than it appears" from the 72–35 vote: "If abstentions are counted, fully half of black Africa refused to support the resolution." The paper was beginning to fight; to put the best face on defeat in order to do battle again.

In Washington the *Post* observed that "Zionism in its most fundamental sense is Jewish nationalism, the doctrine that holds that Jews, like a hundred and more other groups, have a right to political self-determination." Yet "Israel has become the first United Nations member to have its doctrine of nationalism and its national liberation movement defamed by brother states." The U.N. had given in to anti-Semitism; the charge began to appear across the nation.

In the Midwest, the Chicago *Daily News* noted a "philosophical kinship" between anti-Zionism at the U.N. and Nazism, and the Detroit *News* charged the resolution "encouraged more ugly anti-Semitism all over the world." In the East, the Philadelphia *Evening Bulletin* branded the resolution "grotesque." In the South, the Houston *Chronicle* remarked that Hitler "would have felt at home," and the Dallas *Times-Herald* termed the U.N. vote an "anti-Semitic act." The Minneapolis *Star* called the resolution "a blatant attempt to give an appearance of international legality to anti-Semitism"; the Boston *Herald-American* declared that it "offered carte blanche to bigots." The Anti-Defamation League of B'nai B'rith reported that for the first time in the five years that it had maintained a "Big 50" survey of the nation's leading newspapers, there had been a unanimous press reaction to a major issue, and the reaction was altogether condemnatory of the Zionism resolution.

The reaction in Congress was as unanimous. A week earlier, Donald M. Fraser of Minnesota, a member of the House International Relations Committee and one of the two Congressional members then serving on the General Assembly delegation, held a press conference at U.N. headquarters and spoke to this point. On October 28, the Senate, by unanimous vote on a measure introduced by Senator Humphrey, had in effect given warning that we would not abide this thing. In the House a similar resolution had been cosponsored by 436 members. In the memory of the House bill clerk, no resolution had ever drawn so large a number of cosponsors. On November 11, the House and Senate unanimously adopted identical resolutions which not only condemned the action of the General Assembly but went further:

> . . . the Congress strongly opposes any form of participation by the United States Government in the Decade for Action to Combat Racism and Racial Discrimination so long as that Decade and program remain distorted and compromised by the aforementioned resolution naming Zionism as one of the targets of that struggle. . . .

In the Senate debate, Robert Packwood, Republican of Oregon, said, "I can't think of anything in the last 30 years as odious. Wherever Hitler may be I am sure he drank a toast to the devil last night. . . ." In the House Benjamin S. Rosenthal, Democrat of Queens, said: "Hitler would have been proud of those 72 delegates. . . ."

Yet for all its intensity the reaction lacked the depth that would have come from a greater understanding of what had actually happened. The charge of anti-Semitism, and the evocation of Nazism, did not require much thought. (Especially as Anwar Sadat had appeared at the National Press Club on October 27 and recalled that in his youth all the Egyptian economy was "in the hands of the Jews"; and that when he sought to buy a radio set he was refused on "orders from Zionism, from Israel . . . because I am an officer in the army who has fought Israel.") But this amounted almost to avoidance of what the General Assembly majority had charged. The charge was that Jews had in effect *become* Nazis.

Most American Jewish leaders would have nothing to do with this deeper, harder reality. Probably it was beyond their emotional resources to do so. They were in any event too confirmed in their own liberalism to conceive that any such charge could be taken seriously.

A young scholar, Eric Breindel, has suggested that those active in American Jewish institutions were living in a time warp, unaware of the profoundly ideological character of the assault on Israel's legitimacy. This time lag made them slow to adjust to the change of adversaries. They tended to think that the left supported the establishment of the State of Israel as a result of sympathy and pity for the Jewish people in the wake of the Holocaust. In Breindel's view, this was always a profound illusion. The USSR and its satellites supported Israel in the early days in pursuit of the plainest strategic purpose of expelling Great Britain from the Middle East. Further, by 1975, this strategic objective had long been achieved, and its exigencies removed. By 1975 the time was in fact quite a bit past when Israel had been a favorite of the Western European and American left, when the kibbutz had been the epitome of socialism in action, Histadrut a genuine "workers' collective." Israel was no longer a socialist "experiment"; it was now being called a "racist, colonialist, settler state." But this new depiction of Israel was so dissonant and threatening that American Jews were hardly aware of it and thus singularly unprepared to deal with it. By this time, for example, the proposition that Israel was a principal ally of South Africa was an established theme of anti-Israeli propaganda, but Americans had scarcely heard it. The effect was that of a curious, self-imposed censorship. Such "nonsense" was not reported. Or, as happened when *The Times* reported the Soviet campaign linking Zionism with Nazism, it was set down once for the record and left at that.

Failing to grasp what actually had happened, there were rather too many who were entirely too willing to accept the explanation that it would not have happened at all save for my abrasiveness. As I have not the least rancor about it — the turn of events was, if anything, *too* natural — I offer the following as a lesson, possibly a warning.

◆

Within seven days of the passage of the Zionism resolution, the British Permanent Representative to the U.N. would denounce me at great length in a speech to the United Nations Association of the U.S. In nearly two centuries of diplomatic relations, of war and peace and various states intermediate, nothing remotely like this had ever occurred between us and Britain. But, then, in nearly two centuries the United States had never had a Secretary of State remotely like Henry Kissinger. If one knew this, events as they unfolded were not especially surprising. And I did know it. I knew, for example, that in 1970 Kissinger had sent an emissary to New York to ask Golda Meir to denounce William Rogers, then Secretary of State, whose "Rogers Plan" for the Middle East was not at all to his liking. (Nor to the Israelis'.) Mrs. Meir obliged; recognizing, one assumes, that Kissinger was the stronger man

and would eventually displace Rogers, at which point it would be useful
to have been of service to him in doing so.

In truth, such goings-on had by now become so much a routine as
not even to cause much resentment. Rogers would cheerfully enough
describe Kissinger's infidelities. It was the way he was, and everybody
accepted it. Even I accepted that he had to have *some* explanation of
what had happened in the General Assembly.

The basic thesis would be that I had somehow "lost" the vote by
antagonizing other delegations, especially those of black Africa. This
construction had the virtue of going directly to my two weakest points:
that I had already been charged with being antiblack, and that I was
widely supposed to have gone to the U.N. for the purpose of "raising
hell." (Even though, till now, I had in fact done little of that.) Kissinger's first comments in this key came in a press conference in Pittsburgh on Wednesday morning, November 12, two days after the
resolution had passed. He would say only "that the linkage of Zionism
and racism smacked of some practices that it would be better for mankind to forget." He would not say what, if anything, the U.S. would do.
He recalled his Milwaukee speech, but added, "We must not now swing
to the other extreme of not realizing some of the benefits that the
United Nations — with all its failings — still has for the United States."
Bernard Gwertzman, in *The Times,* noted that the Secretary "seemed
determined to persuade Congress and Administration officials not to
take any steps in haste," and the headline ran, "Kissinger Warns of
Haste on U.N.: Assails Zionism Resolution but Cautions Against Any
'Extreme' Reactions." He probably did fear this somewhat, and probably it also crossed his mind that I might try to lead such an effort. The
press sensed something was on his mind. The next questioner asked
if Kissinger feared he was losing influence in the White House, having
just been relieved of his position as Assistant to the President for National Security Affairs, his original White House post and one that he
had continued to hold after becoming Secretary of State. No, he replied,
he did not feel he had been "diminished." Then the subject of my behavior came up:

> Q: *Mr. Secretary, would you associate yourself with the remarks made
> by Ambassador Moynihan about General Amin, . . . and can you tell
> us what the reaction to that has been?*
> A: Ambassador Moynihan makes so many remarks in the course of a
> day that it is not easy to keep up with all of them. [Laughter.] This one
> I kept up with.
> I would share his displeasure with General Amin, though I might
> express myself in a more restrained manner, given the differences in our

temperaments. I do not associate myself with identifying Amin with the Organization of African Unity. I believe the Organization of African Unity contains states that are attempting to pursue a responsible role, and therefore — his chairmanship reached Uganda by rotation — I would not consider him a typical representative of the organization.

Q: Mr. Secretary, speaking of Ambassador Moynihan, he said on television this morning that the countries which pushed through this Zionism resolution would suffer for it. Was he speaking of the afterlife, or do you or did he — have anything concrete in mind?

A: Well, I am seeing Ambassador Moynihan later today, and I will find out exactly what he had in mind.

———◆———

The same morning Kissinger held his press conference in Pittsburgh, I spoke in the Third Committee on behalf of a resolution the United States had introduced the previous day calling for amnesty for political prisoners throughout the world. Coming, as this did, the day following the Zionism resolution, it was almost necessarily depicted in the press as a retaliation, which it was, but only in the most general way. The idea had come much earlier, as resolutions condemning Chile and South Africa were being maneuvered through the same committee. Each specifically called on the government concerned to release its political prisoners. The United States had voted for both; the jujitsu principle decreed that we now try to use the momentum of the majority against the majority. Kissinger knew of this plan and had raised no difficulties. Our proposal was simple enough. The General Assembly, it declared,

> appeals to all Governments to proclaim an unconditional amnesty by releasing all political prisoners in the sense of persons deprived of their liberty primarily because they have, in accordance with the Universal Declaration of Human Rights, sought peaceful expression of beliefs and opinions at variance with those held by their Governments or have sought to provide legal or other forms of non-violent assistance to such persons. . . .

My speech was no more complicated, if somewhat less innocent. It began by noting that the General Assembly had now, with United States support, called for amnesty for political prisoners in South Africa and Chile. But,

> . . . even as South Africa and Chile are obliged by certain standards concerning prisoners . . . so equally are all other members of the United Nations. It is implicitly acknowledged, however, that it is for

governments themselves to conform to international standards. And if some governments, then all governments.

Hence, at this moment, the singular appeal of amnesty. A moment of peace and of peace-making, and a mode which allows governments to do what they ought without the appearance of coercion. All governments.

Universality in this matter is of special concern to the United States government — and we would hope to all governments. There are two grounds for this concern which strike us with special force.

The first is that the selective morality of the United Nations in matters of human rights threatens the integrity not merely of the United Nations, but of human rights themselves. There is no mystery in this matter. Unless standards of human rights are seen to be applied uniformly and neutrally to all nations, regardless of the nature of their regimes or the size of their armaments, it will quickly be seen that it is not human rights at all which are invoked when selective applications are called for, but simply arbitrary political standards dressed up in the guise of human rights. From this perception it is no great distance to the conclusion that in truth there are no human rights recognized by the international community.

A generation ago the British poet Stephen Spender came to this perception in the course of visits to Spain during its long and tragic civil war. He had first come to Spain out of sympathy for one of the sides in that heart-rending conflict. He had returned to England to report what he had seen of atrocities committed by the other side. Thereafter he made several trips to Spain, over the course of which he was forced to realize that atrocities were not a monopoly of one side only; they were indeed all too common on all sides. At which point, to his great and lasting honor, he wrote: "It came to me that unless I cared about every murdered child indiscriminately, I didn't really care about children being murdered at all."

This is what the United States proposal is about. Unless we care about political prisoners everywhere, we don't really care about them anywhere. It is something else altogether, that is on our minds, something we conceal with the language of human rights, in the course of which we commence to destroy that language, much as George Orwell, who fought in the Spanish Civil War, saw that it would be destroyed.

And then, to emphasize our concern for universality, I said what to many was unforgivable — that the Chilean and South African governments which had become objects of international excoriation might rank lower in the scales of tyranny than some of their accusers:

> Our concern about discriminatory treatment is not eased by scrutiny of the list of cosponsors of the draft resolutions on South Africa and Chile. These are, to repeat, resolutions calling attention to the plight

of political prisoners. The South African draft resolution has 60 co-sponsors. The Chilean draft resolution has 33. The United States has broken down these respective lists according to "The Comparative Survey of Freedom," that great contribution to clear thinking and plain speaking which is the work of Freedom House, an American institution of impeccable credentials, which traces its beginnings to the first efforts in the United States to win support for the nations then engaged in the mortal struggle against Nazism and Fascism in Europe. "The Comparative Survey of Freedom" ranks the levels of political rights and civil rights in individual nations on a scale of 1 to 7, and then gives a general summary "Status of Freedom," by which nations are classified as Free, Partly Free, or Not Free. One of the melancholy attributes of a nation judged Not Free is that, in the opinion of the distinguished political scientists who carry out this survey, the nation is one in which individuals are imprisoned for political beliefs or activities of a non-criminal nature. In other words a nation with political prisoners.

What does "The Comparative Survey of Freedom" tell us about the cosponsors of these resolutions? It tells us that in its judgment, no fewer than 23 of the cosponsors of the draft resolution calling for amnesty for South African political prisoners, have political prisoners of their own. In the case of the draft resolution calling attention to the plight of political prisoners in Chile, it would appear that 16 of the cosponsors fall into the category of nations which have political prisoners of their own.

This leads to a particularly disturbing thought about the processes by which the United Nations has come to be so concerned about human rights in some countries, but not in others. This is that we tend to know about violations of freedom — know at the time and in detail — only in those countries which permit *enough* freedom for internal opposition to make its voice heard when freedoms are violated.

Is it not the case that the freedom of the press in South Africa — such as it may be, for we do not assert it to be complete — contrasts sharply with that of its neighbors? In the *Monthly Bulletin* of the International Press Institute of June 1975, Mr. Frank Barton, Africa Director of IPI, is reported as having told the Assembly of that impeccably neutral and scrupulous organization:

> The unpalatable fact is — and this is something that sticks in the throat of every self-respecting African who will face it — is that there is more press freedom in South Africa than in the rest of Africa put together.

And what of Chile, a troubled land, where at least one estimate states that there are some five thousand political prisoners, and which is rated "Partly Free" by the Freedom House Comparative Survey?

And what of Israel, a country rated Free by Freedom House, with high if not perfect scores in Political Rights and Civil Rights? Is it not enough to say that much of the case being made against Israel by other nations today, is made in the first instance by the fully legal opposition parties within Israel, including Arab-based parties, many of which have been quite successful in electing members to public office, and that this opposition is given notable expression in the Arabic language press in Israel, which has been described as the freest Arab-language press in the world?

Thus we come to the second of the concerns which animate the United States at this point. This is the concern not only that the language of human rights is being distorted and perverted; it is that the language of human rights is increasingly being turned in United Nations forums against precisely those regimes which acknowledge some or all of its validity. More and more the United Nations seems only to know of violations of human rights in countries where it is still possible to protest such violations.

Let us be direct. If this language can be turned against one democracy, why not all democracies? Are democracies not singular in the degree to which at all times voices will be heard protesting this injustice or that injustice? If the propensity to protest injustice is taken as equivalent to the probability that injustice does occur, then the democracies will fare poorly indeed.

To those members of the United Nations who would allay our suspicions we make this simple appeal: Join us in support of our draft resolution calling for amnesty for all political prisoners. The list of known prisoners, a list assembled by organizations such as Amnesty International, is a sufficiently long and harrowing one. But there is far more horror to be felt at the thought of the names we do *not* know. It is time to free these men and women. The time for this amnesty is past due, and the path is long. Let us take the first step here and now.

———◆———

That evening the President gave a White House dinner for Gaston Thorn, in the latter's capacity as Luxembourg Prime Minister. Thorn had made plain his disgust at the Zionism resolution, and of Ford's view there was no question. Even so, the toasts were routine, the U.N. hardly touched upon. Kissinger did not want a fight with the U.N. majority.

After the dinner Kissinger and I wandered back to his old office in the West Wing, it being evidently his view that he had acquired a kind of usufruct domain. We talked of nothing in particular. He offered me a drink, but could find nothing but *mao t'ai*. He was back on diet cola. There was not a word to suggest any differences.

Five days later *Newsweek,* in its lead story, reported that at this meeting "Kissinger raked Moynihan over the coals . . . for his behavior at the U.N." The article, written in Washington, described the passage of the Zionism resolution, and in the third paragraph went to the business at hand:

> . . . The Zionism resolution made it easier to attack the concept of a secular Jewish state and thus furnished the first new philosophical framework for anti-Semitism since World War II. It also maneuvered the Western democracies into their sharpest confrontation with the Third World countries since the Arab oil embargo. That dispute could do profound damage to the U.N. and to the search for peace in the Middle East, and some Western diplomats complained that Moynihan's outspoken performance only aggravated the problem. Moynihan insisted that he had acted properly and that low-keyed opposition to the resolution would have been appeasement. "Did I make a crisis out of this obscene resolution?" stormed the ambassador. "Damn right I did!"

Then, explicitly, to the argument that I was responsible for the resolution passing:

> Many U.N. delegates and several experienced American diplomatists cited Moynihan's speech last month in which he denounced Uganda's President Idi Amin as a "racist murderer" and criticized the Organization of African Unity, of which Amin is taking a turn as chairman. These critics claimed that Moynihan's linkage of Amin and the OAU had cost him African votes on the deferral issue — perhaps enough votes to have won. . . . That may have been. But many of the other nations that voted for the Zionism resolution were embarrassed by it and may have been using Moynihan as a convenient scapegoat.

Finally, to the woodshed:

> Beyond the deferral vote, some diplomats, including friends of Moynihan, complained that his policy of talking tough to the Third World (outlined last March in a *Commentary* magazine article) has led to intemperate language. . . .
> Moynihan also seemed to be at odds with his boss. The ambassador insisted that he and Secretary Kissinger "are very old and close friends — and continue to be." But two highly placed sources in Washington said that Kissinger raked Moynihan over the coals at the White House last week for his behavior at the U.N. and for his independent efforts to stir up Congressional reaction to the Zionism resolution. Kissinger "really took Pat to the woodshed," said one of *Newsweek*'s sources.
> Moynihan fervently defended his outspoken ways. "When you fight, you do better than when you don't fight," he insisted. "The alternatives were to lose quietly or somewhat noisily — and arouse people to

what was happening." Moynihan reiterated his denial of a popular piece of gossip that he was using his position to run for political office, possibly against New York Sen. James Buckley next year. "I would regard it as personally dishonorable to leave this place and run for office," he declared.

The charge that struck home, of course, was that I had lost votes. *Newsweek* did allow me to reply:

> If you take the Black African vote and leave out the Muslim sub-Saharan countries, the outcome was that we had eighteen countries with us and only twelve against. . . . We have never had so many African votes. Never.

This was an accurate statement, but not an especially meaningful one. On the key vote to postpone, thirteen sub-Saharan African countries had been with us, three abstained, and three were absent, so that altogether nineteen either were with us or not against us. Only one of these, Upper Volta, had a significant Muslim population. Of the twenty-one sub-Saharan states that voted not to postpone, nine had significant Muslim populations — Chad, Gambia, Mali, Mauritania, Niger, Nigeria, Senegal, Somalia, Sudan — leaving twelve non-Muslim votes against us. Hence my count of eighteen to twelve, of which the most charitable thing to be said is that it was the most I could think of to say at the moment.

The reporting officer at the U.S. Mission made much the same point. On November 11, the day following the vote, a routine cable, cleared by Bennett as there was no need for me to see it, went out from the U.S. Mission to all African posts. (A similar cable would have been sent to European, Latin American, and Asian posts.)

On the final vote, as against the Third Committee vote, "improvements" were recorded with respect to five countries: Central African Republic, Gabon, Malawi, Mauritius, Swaziland. "Deterioration" was recorded with respect to five others: Burundi, Equatorial Guinea, Gambia, Rwanda, São Tomé and Príncipe. If I had lost votes by speaking out between the Third Committee vote and the final tally, no one ever found them. The reporting cable noted that the Mauritius Permanent Representative "was the only speaker to imply — in obnoxious terms — that he had been pressured by USG." And Mauritius was among the five "Improvements." The plainest fact was that the normal, huge anti-Israeli majority had *not* materialized. The *Times* editorial of November 12 pointed to this as the most significant aspect of the vote as such. Herzog would say so at the least opportunity. But this is not what was

being said in the upper reaches of the Department of State. There it
was being said that we somehow "lost" the Zionism resolution because of
"confrontational" tactics.

This is neither as mysterious nor as malign as might be supposed.
The Department of State is an old, even venerable, institution. But it
is entirely new to voting as a means of resolving disputes, especially
voting in a deliberative body characterized by extensive debate between
fairly fixed blocs. In such a quasiparliamentary setting, our rhetoric was
by no means extreme. Far stronger speeches are given on the floor of the
U.S. Senate, not to mention the House of Commons. Certainly far
stronger speeches were being given by other U.N. delegations. Yet just
as clearly this is not the language of private negotiation. The Department, an institution almost wholly attuned to private negotiation, had
not learned to make the distinction.

The Zionism resolution was adopted by 72 votes to 35, with 32 abstentions. One year less one day later (there being a season for such
things at the United Nations), on November 9, 1976, the General Assembly adopted a resolution *"strongly condemning"* the continuing and
increasing collaboration by Israel with the racist regime of South Africa
by 91 votes to 20, with 28 abstentions. To my knowledge, the only
notice taken of this was in an editorial in *The Wall Street Journal,*
which observed that in the debate Ambassador William Scranton had
"held his tongue," pursuing the established wisdom "that the U.S.
would have fared better if Mr. Moynihan hadn't alienated Third
World nations with his public protests" against the Zionism resolution. Now, by a vote of 91 to 20, Israel was condemned for a trade
which, the *Journal* said, was far more active between South Africa and
many African, Arab, and Communist states. Scranton soon had enough
of this, and gave a tough speech declaring: "The only universality that
one can honestly associate with the Universal Declaration of Human
Rights is universal lip service."

––––––◆––––––

When the rumor, now elevated to the level of *Newsweek* speculation,
began to circulate that I was running for the Senate from my seat in
the General Assembly, I assumed it to be Soviet disinformation. (Do
such assumptions verge on the overdramatic? I would suspect that, to
the contrary, in diplomacy the assumption of constant hostile activity
by adversaries makes for peace of mind. One is never surprised to be
surprised.) This may have been, but I see now that it was by no means
a necessary explanation. An election year was coming up, and the season had commenced to speculate about candidates. It seemed to me a

problem to be got rid of, which I had tried to do on *Face the Nation* on October 26. Before the program I asked George Herman if he would ask me about this. He was an old enough friend to do so, and put the question in the closing moments. I had memorized an answer, and rattled it off with milliseconds to spare:

> HERMAN: Is it fair to ask an ambassador to the United Nations a political question? As you know, there is a lot of talk that you are running for political office, specifically the Senate in New York State, from the podium —
> AMB. MOYNIHAN: Can I just speak right quickly to that? It is — it is not so. It might very much please some of the people in the UN who see us as enemies to think that this is — that it is so, to explain positions we are taking on matters of principles as in fact having some squalid personal ambition. I am not. I would consider it a dishonorable thing, this charge having been made, I would consider it dishonorable to leave this post and run for any office, and I would hope that it would be understood that if I do, the people, the voters to whom I would present myself in such circumstances would consider me as having said in advance I am a man of no personal honor to have done so.

That *Newsweek* article about Kissinger dressing me down appeared on Monday, November 17. On Tuesday Kissinger came to New York, actually to have lunch with Lou Harris & Associates (the kind of favor he knew how to do very well, and for reasons he very well knew), but nominally to meet with the Secretary-General of the United Nations to talk about Cyprus or the Middle East or something. I met his plane, and on the way into the city he asked how the people at *Newsweek* could be so stupid as to write that he had taken me "to the woodshed" when we had had the friendliest possible conversation, and why were the editors of *Newsweek* such incompetents.

———————◆———————

I went off to lunch with Godfrey Hodgson of *The Sunday Times* of London, who, with an instinct in such matters, knew something was going on and had come over to find out what. At three o'clock I joined a gaggle of reporters and officials at the entrance to the Secretariat building, awaiting the Secretary of State. A reporter handed me a copy of a speech Ivor Richard had given the previous day to the United Nations Association. It went:

> There is I believe an ancient Chinese curse which runs — "may you live in interesting times." We are living through interesting times at

the United Nations. Recent events here — particularly the appearance of President Amin of Uganda, and the vote last week on Zionism, have caused a furore, the like of which has not been seen in years, at least here in New York and in parts of the press. How much of the fury was self induced and how much was deeply felt and spontaneous indignation, I find it difficult to judge — not being a New Yorker.

I must say to you however that the issue has not received the same attention in Europe. In my own country it has been received partly with contempt and after a closer analysis of the votes cast, partly with a welcoming realisation of the fact that if there ever was an automatic majority at the UN it is no longer automatic now. The alliance between the Arabs and the Africans upon which such a majority depended is clearly breaking down. The cracks are deepening, and the divisions becoming more apparent. There has not been the same outburst of public expression in Europe as there has been here. This is not due to any lesser feeling on our part about the issue of anti-semitism. It is more due to the fact that we have managed to avoid reacting to the vote in purely ideological and emotional terms.

As I see it, my function at the UN is two-fold — it is to try and represent my country to the best of my ability but also it is to try and make the organisation work a little better. Britain sees the United Nations as a major instrument of her foreign policy. We regard it as a place in which and from which we can extend British influence, and defend British interests. I do not see it as a forum in which to argue my own particular brand of political theology. Certainly I do not see it as a confrontational arena in which to "take on" those countries whose political systems and ideology are different from mine. I spend a lot of time preventing rows at the UN — not looking for them. Whatever else the place is, it is not the OK Corral and I am hardly Wyatt Earp. There is nothing whatsoever to be gained by ideological disputations of the most intense sort which one is probably going to lose anyway or at best end up with a rather unsatisfactory intellectual statement. My function is to use the United Nations not to purge it particularly if in order to purge it the chances are I would end up by encouraging my enemies, irritating my friends and isolating my country.

Let us therefore try and place the Zionist vote and the events leading up to it into this perspective. That Zionism is racism is an absurd proposition, rejected by most of the world, which I trust could now safely be seen in that perspective and in that context. I suggest that we all, your country and mine, do precisely that.

My first response, not especially professional, was to think Richard had done this on his own, and to make as little of it as possible. I put out a three-sentence statement: "I know of course that these are Ambassador Richard's views, and he has every right to state them. We are the best of friends."

◆

He so enjoyed being at the U.N. "Don't you find it fun!" he had remarked early on, standing at the bar off the Security Council lounge. Fun was about all there was left for a Briton at this point: a certain jollity about being good losers. Amin was a sensitive subject. In June a British lecturer in Uganda, Dennis Cecil Hills, had been arrested on charges of having described the President, in an unpublished manuscript, as a "village tyrant." He was found guilty of treason by a military tribunal and sentenced to death. Amin, in the brilliantly *épatant* manner he had acquired in such escapades, announced that unless the British Foreign Secretary, Mr. Callaghan, presented himself personally within ten days, Hill would face a firing squad. The British sent Lieutenant General Sir Chandos Blair, "armed [as the press put it] with a letter from Queen Elizabeth, pleading for clemency." Amin took Sir Chandos to his tribal home in the northwest and gave him spears and bows and arrows as gifts. He then announced, through Radio Uganda, that the General had been "undiplomatic, hot-tempered and disrespectful." Callaghan solemnly told "a crowded and silent House of Commons" that he would never visit Uganda until Amin had first granted amnesty. No, never! Amin then announced that the British were preparing an invasion. "Alert the army," he shouted to members of his defense council. "Alert the air force! Call Libya and tell Libya to begin sending airplanes here!" Callaghan flew to Kinshasa, where President Mobutu assured him that General Amin had reprieved Mr. Hills while on a two-day visit to Zaire. Callaghan flew to Kampala, where no one was at the airport to receive him. The next day, July 10, before receiving Callaghan, Amin told newsmen that he had not yet decided Hills's fate. Then in the course of the meeting the prisoner was produced and the President pronounced him free: "He is free. This proves that I am not mad, as British newspapers said." Flanked by Callaghan and Hills, he was photographed in a blue open-necked general's uniform with Israeli paratroop wings and the red-and-white Glengarry of Britain's Seaforth Highlanders Regiment. "I am pro-British," he declared. "I want to strengthen my ties with the British." He personally escorted the Foreign Secretary back to Entebbe Airport, and so lived on to murder Dora Bloch in her hospital bed after the Israeli raid of July 4, 1976, and to butcher the Anglican Archbishop Janami Luwum the following February.

◆

At a State Department briefing on November 20, after Richard's speech had become public, a journalist asked whether it was not "un-

seeming" for Richard to attack an American ambassador who had criticized the Ugandan President, representing as Richard did "the country
whose officials crawled before General Amin. . . ." The Department
press officer had nothing to say. There was nothing *to* say. Except, perhaps, that Mr. Hills, on his repatriation to England, rather apologized
for his harsh description of the Ugandan President, and announced that
he would revise his manuscript.

At lunch on Thursday, at the Soviet Mission, Richard came up to
say that my reply to him was being taken to mean I thought he had
made the speech on his own, and that it did not represent official British policy. This took most of the afternoon to sink in. At dinner at the
residence of the Iranian Ambassador, I went up to Richard and engaged him in a not especially deft exchange. Ivor, I said, there are
people in the Department of State who are saying that your speech
represents formal British policy. Quite right, said Ivor.

The Friday morning *New York Times* was at the Waldorf by the time
we returned from dinner. Hofmann's story was direct:

Moynihan's Style in U.N. Now an Open Issue

Critical whisperings here about the performance of Daniel P. Moynihan as the chief American delegate broke into the open this week, but
the State Department said today that Secretary of State Henry A. Kissinger had full confidence in the outspoken diplomat.

What many had been saying privately in what has amounted to a vir-
tual campaign about Mr. Moynihan's "confrontational" style was expressed publicly on Monday by Ivor Richard of Britain in an address to
the board of directors of the United Nations Association.

At breakfast I told Elizabeth I would be resigning at noon, and that
she might want to come to the press conference.

———◆———

What I did was defensible, but not reasonable. Defensible in the
sense that there were genuine issues at dispute here, which went to the
heart of the question of how liberal societies deal with the hostility
and aggression of totalitarian societies, and how liberalism is to survive
in a world in which its ideological force seemed largely spent. I did
genuinely believe that Kissinger was trying to negotiate another "decent interval," in this case for the West itself. He was doing this, as I
saw it, out of despair that the West would ever come to its senses and
realize the imminent danger of its being overmastered. There was, I
judged, a touch of personal resentment in all this. Congress, he felt, had

let him down on Vietnam. But his pessimism, even disgust, with the West was deeper than anything that could be touched by events. Else he could not have behaved at once so nobly and so ignobly.

I had wanted to speak to the issue of language: to say that to preserve the meaning of words is the first responsibility of liberalism. I knew that I had at least one audience, by virtue of the biting word *racism* that had been thrown like acid into the face of a whole people. But I wanted to speak more broadly, to the proposition that it was no longer possible, at this point in the twentieth century, to be truly a liberal *without* enemies on the left. The first lesson Orwell taught, the second we learned from what his teaching brought him.

Once Richard went out of his way to impress upon me that his speech was official, I had no choice but to assume that Kissinger was behind it. Large events followed from this, including, it could be argued, the outcome of the 1976 presidential election. Which is poignant in its way, for it now appears that what Richard was saying was not so. But at the time one had to suppose otherwise. I knew what Kissinger had done to Secretary of State Rogers. It was all rather impersonal, and even at times rather cheerful: certainly Helmut Sonnenfeldt had been so in welcoming me back to the State Department. But it certainly was believable.

John F. Kennedy had done as much to Adlai Stevenson. The episode had taken place thirteen years earlier, but to someone who had been in the Kennedy administration in 1962 the memory was much alive. In December of that year Stewart Alsop and Charles Bartlett published an article in the *Saturday Evening Post* describing the inner circle at the White House during the Cuban missile crisis. The account was brilliantly compressed — opening with Dean Rusk's "We're eyeball to eyeball" — and gave "hawks" and "doves" to the language. In the process, however, it nearly destroyed Adlai Stevenson, who was described as having been "soft," as having proposed a "Munich," as being the one man who did not meet the test of the crisis. "Adlai on Skids over Pacifist Stand in Cuba" ran the New York *Daily News* headline when the article appeared.

John Bartlow Martin, Stevenson's biographer, describes the effect as "devastating." He recounts the endless — private — assurances that Stevenson received from the White House on the matter. Kennedy himself had told Schlesinger: "Will you tell Adlai that I never talked to Charlie or any other reporter about the Cuban crisis, and that the piece does not represent my views." Pierre Salinger solemnly assured the press that the White House had not seen the article in advance, and that Bartlett (who was perhaps the President's closest friend) had never used any inside White House information. The President himself called a friend to say: "Goddamn it, why would I leak a thing like that? What the hell would I want to have trouble with my own Cabinet for?"

Washington knew better. For a brief moment, Martin writes, Stevenson "more than half believed the conspiracy stories" that went about. When the *News* headline appeared, Clayton Fritchey, then handling Stevenson's press relations, reported that he might even resign. But the President told Arthur Schlesinger, "This goes on all the time. Why should Adlai get so upset? Just tell him to sit tight and everything will subside." And so Stevenson decided to be reassured, and what was left of him stayed at the U.N.

But of course he was being lied to. Martin does not mention it, and, perhaps more understandably, neither do Sorensen and Schlesinger in their studies of Kennedy, but the President had not only seen the article in advance, he had edited it. Sorensen recollects that Kennedy was "mistakenly charged with authorizing, encouraging or providing the erroneous information in a Bartlett–Stewart Alsop article on the Cuban missile crisis. . . ." But there was no mistake. Alsop, in his book *The Center: People and Power in Political Washington,* wrote: "Kennedy read the piece for accuracy, and proposed a couple of minor changes." The most important, conveyed to Bartlett through the President's military aide, "was that we eliminate the name of Theodore Sorensen from our list of 'doves.'" In a *Newsweek* column in 1971 Alsop further commented that not only had Kennedy read the article and edited it, but that he had done so "rather badly."

And this was the point. With only the slight change that comes with experience, *to all appearances* what was happening to me was no different from what had happened to Stevenson. If I were to pretend that nothing was happening, how would I escape any better than he?

I was not alone in these concerns. At the moment I was deciding to resign and in the several days that followed, three writers of quite different politics were putting down their own thoughts. Looking back, there is a rather striking agreement among them as to what was at issue.

First, in a syndicated column that appeared on Sunday, November 23, and would have been written before I even began to think of resigning, John P. Roche predicted that if James Schlesinger had "walked the plank without a splash," I would do nothing of the sort. The President had not sent me "to Turtle Bay to say, 'Tut, tut.'" And yet my speech on the Zionism resolution had brought out in Kissinger, in his Pittsburgh press conference, just that:

> The Pittsburgh statement . . . contained a most peculiar formulation, especially from a man who seems to believe in choosing words carefully. Referring to the General Assembly vote, Kissinger observed that

equating Zionism and racism "smacks of some practices it would be
better for mankind to forget." Maybe I am suffering from hardening
of the categories, but it strikes me that the vote smacks of some practices mankind should never forget.

Not without a certain symmetry, the next issue of *Newsweek,* which
appeared on Monday, November 24, carried an essay by Meg Greenfield, who has seemed to me the best political mind of that particular
sensibility — an unconcern with class, a conviction that whatever happens in politics happens singly to individual men and women — to appear since Rebecca West. She would have written the column the
previous week, and in response to the *Newsweek* account of the various
goings-on between me and Kissinger. Her article was titled "U.N. Chic,"
with the clear reference to Tom Wolfe and the assorted confusions of
the 1960s. She addressed the issue of language:

> The mere fact that it takes so much doing to straighten out the
> semantics has suggested to some — in the State Department, among
> other places — that Moynihan's strategy of forcing the issue was faulty.
> Why not, after all, make a virtue of practicality? Why insist on giving
> the charge of "racism" a meaning it has all but lost thanks to a decade
> of mindless invocation?
> It is certainly true that Moynihan has chosen to dramatize the issue.
> And it is also true that he has made much of both the fundamentally
> sinister meaning of the term "racism" and the Assembly's failure to de-
> fine it properly. . . .
> It seemed to many people around Washington that the wiser course
> would have been to take advantage of the muzziness of the term "rac-
> ism" and its declining capacity to arouse either much passion or
> thought. But there was Moynihan, hollering up a storm with citations
> from dictionaries and historical references. . . .
> I think Moynihan was right to raise the roof — and not just because
> the resolution itself was so clearly a substitute for an earlier abandoned
> move to expel Israel from the U.N., if not in fact a preliminary step to
> expulsion at some later date. The insistence of the U.S. Mission in-
> spired and/or obliged a number of member states to confront the mean-
> ing of what they were doing, and that is something of a breakthrough
> in itself. Beyond that, the corruption of language in our national and
> international political life is not, in my view, a phenomenon worthy
> only of the attention of doctoral candidates and amenders of the dic-
> tionary. History — ancient and modern — offers more examples than
> one wants to contemplate of the intimate connection between corrupt
> national, racial and political rhetoric and the subsequent brutalizing
> of whole societies. It is not harmless.

In an essay, "Henry & Pat & Ivor," which appeared in *The New York Times* the same day, Monday, November 24, William Safire raised the question of why Kissinger, and not just Richard, was going about deploring me. Safire recognized the nice touch of getting friendly foreigners to do one's deploring, noting that the Secretary had spent November 15–17 at an economic summit meeting at the Château de Rambouillet, with Callaghan present also. Kissinger was failing, and flailing about in the process. "As power ebbs," the essay began, "the sense of humor sours and the hatchet hand loses its skill":

> His campaign to undercut . . . Moynihan, lacks the surgical skill he used to practice on William Rogers. The finesse is gone.
>
> At Rambouillet, he had a private breakfast and other talks with his friend, British Foreign Secretary James Callaghan. With uncharacteristic vehemence, British and American spokesmen insist that at no time during those long talks was a single word mentioned about British dissatisfaction with the style or position of the American Ambassador to the United Nations.
>
> That's curious; immediately after Rambouillet, the British Ambassador to the United Nations — Ivor Richard, a Labor Party politician anxious to follow Mr. Callaghan up the ladder — launched into an oblique but savage personal attack on America's U.N. Ambassador.
>
> Since this denunciation was later described as "an informal reflection of official British policy," one might think that a friendly British Foreign Secretary would have tipped off his American counterpart that an attack of that magnitude was forthcoming. A quick "By the way, our chap is clobbering your chap tomorrow, first time this century" would be expected between allies.

Supposing Kissinger had *not* inspired the speech; neither had he protested it. Certainly if the Briton had attacked Kissinger, he would have heard from me. And there were passages in Richard — Roche spotted them — which got close to attitudes it *were* better for New Yorkers not to forget:

> Recent events here — particularly the appearance of President Amin of Uganda, and the vote last week on Zionism have caused a furore, the like of which has not been seen in years, at least here in New York and in parts of the press. How much of the fury was self induced and how much was deeply felt and spontaneous indignation, I find it difficult to judge — not being a New Yorker.

But not a word of remonstration had gone out from Washington. This had annoyed me, but at the same time made me less suspicious, for a true Kissingerian scenario would have called for him to deplore the assault he had incited. All that I knew for certain was that I could not let it pass.

On the Friday morning when this began, I called a press conference for noon, and then telephoned the White House and the Department to say I was resigning. Kissinger came out of a Congressional hearing to say I mustn't. Richard Cheney called from the White House to say I couldn't — not without first speaking to the President. This was true. I agreed to see the President on Monday. The press conference was called off, and I went instead to luncheon with Pearl Bailey, who, at the President's request, was joining the delegation. That evening we gave dinner in honor of Alexander Calder, who sat pleasantly at his table and drank three bottles of California red without the least suggestion that he was used to anything better. The next day I filled the trunk of the limousine with Guinness, and went off to the Harvard-Yale game in New Haven with the object of cheering on the Harvard Department of Government, which on these occasions played a much-analyzed touch-football match with the Yale Department of Political Science, and the further object of staying out of reach of telephones. James Q. Wilson, of rugged judgment in such matters, who knew our colleague Kissinger longer and better surely than I, said I should concede nothing. If I did, he said, the President would lose the most hopeful and popular turn in foreign policy in a decade, possibly in a generation.

This was something new. Until Wilson raised the subject I don't think that I, or Garment, or any of us had noticed. We were absorbed with what we were doing, and if anything troubled by the absence of response in some circles. But in the nation generally, in a matter only of weeks, a huge response had come forth. We had touched something in what, lacking a more precise term, we tend to call the national spirit. The country had had enough of defeat, enough of evasion, enough of worldly acceptance of decline. Suddenly we had appeared speaking of confidence, of strength, of the meaning to us of human rights and the price we *would* pay to ensure their survival. In an article in *The Times* that Friday, Hofmann had noted that "press editorials are vastly favorable. . . ." He had dug up a fact of which I don't recall I was aware: The U.N. Mission was receiving the heaviest mail at any time since the Cuban missile crisis. It was running 80 to 1 favorable.

———◆———

Kissinger called Leonard Garment in great distress: terribly hurt. I was the closest friend he had in the Cabinet; he had brought me back into the administration; how could I possibly suppose he had had anything to do with Richard's speech; it was essential that I stay.

This was true. And there was the sorrow of it. He had *not* set out to undo me. But everybody in Washington, and now everybody in New York, myself included, thought that he had, because that was the way of the world.

Two years later I know more without understanding the event any better. Kissinger did not think he inspired the attack, and certainly he did not request it. Callaghan evidently did not know it was coming, and was infuriated by it. Probably the British embassy in Washington did encourage it, but how much I shall never know. It doesn't matter that much, for at the time no one thought the British were acting on their own, including the British. As for Callaghan, he cannot have supposed the Secretary of State was unhappy, else he would have said so. As for the Secretary of State, he later explained that not then knowing the kind of a person Richard was he had to assume I had behaved outrageously, as nothing else could have provoked such a response. Hence his silence. But he should not have let it go at that. At very least, without too much defending me, he should have attacked the British. Events had given him, really, no choice.

But he was not really on top of events any longer, at times not even abreast of them. He was worn out. His power, as Safire put it, truly was ebbing, and he was in some ways losing his skills. The Ford Cabinet had just then gone through its first convulsion, and no one had come out the better for it. On November 2, the President had discharged James Schlesinger as Secretary of Defense and William E. Colby as Director of Central Intelligence, and relieved Kissinger of his position as National Security Advisor. The move was widely seen as Ford's getting rid of Schlesinger at Kissinger's behest, but then half getting rid of Kissinger himself as the price for removing his rival. Just before these maneuverings, the Vice President had removed himself from the coming presidential campaign.

So of a sudden, Nelson Rockefeller — who, as James Reston commented, had made Kissinger a world figure in the first place — was on the way out. Kissinger's White House office and staff were gone. Persons who were no special friends were taking competing posts. And the Reagan wing of the Republican party was blaming him for all manner of things. On November 9, Ford, in a television interview, acknowledged that it was "tension" between the two Secretaries that had led him to dismiss Schlesinger. This statement had left Governor Reagan "shocked," and lost Ford much of the benefit on the right of having removed Rockefeller. In point of fact from this moment on Ford's presidency was in great trouble. And this was as much Kissinger's doing as anyone's. If Ford did not think so, the White House staff did, and Kissinger was no longer in the White House.

It was time to lament a sea of troubles, which Kissinger did at goodly length, bringing me into the litany, positioning me as a hawk of the Schlesinger camp. It was no surprise that the Washington columns began to reflect Kissinger's distress. In an Op-Ed article written at this time for the Washington *Post,* entitled "Aiming Arrows at Henry Kissinger," Marquis Childs listed me among the Secretary's tormentors and told why those tormentors must not succeed:

> A further complication is Daniel Patrick Moynihan, the U.S. delegate to the United Nations. His critics among Western Europeans and some Americans say that if it had not been for his intemperate language, trumpeting through the halls of the U.N. like an avenging and self-anointed angel, a vote to put off the inflammatory resolution on Zionism and racism could have passed. It failed by only a few votes.

At the risk of further trying the reader's patience, it must be said once more that in Kissinger's Washington, it was to be assumed that when such a passage appeared it was Kissinger himself speaking. Eight times in ten it would have been, and only innocents bet the exceptions.

———◆———

Garment and I flew to Washington Monday morning, November 24. He would do the negotiating; prepared, if it came to it, to argue that if someone had to go it would have to be the Secretary of State. We were much in the news. Each of the television networks that morning, each that night. The *CBS Morning Show* stated on Daniel Schorr's authority that "the President will tell Moynihan that, as a Cabinet-level officer, he reports to the President, and not to Kissinger."

The President and I met alone by the fire in the Oval Office. In the first thirty seconds I said that of course I would stay, and went on to talk of the difficulties getting the bureaucracy to see the issue of human rights. Weaver had prepared a bill of particulars, the gravamen of which was largely a matter of desk officers who, not wanting our issues to impinge on their bilateral relationships, enlisted support higher up in the Department. Just days after we had barely fought off the Cuban resolution on Puerto Rico, for instance, the Department of State had lifted a whole set of restrictions on U.S.-Cuban trade, citing the great improvements in our relations with Castro. After the Zionism vote, to take another example, I had given it out that the Chilean junta had sold its vote — which it had done — to the Communists or at least to the

Arabs. The object, of course, was to point out the developing links among these diverse dictatorships. But the Chilean desk was appalled: just when relationships were improving so.

It was not, probably, what the President had in mind to talk about, but I wasn't going to talk about the Secretary of State. All Ford said, really, was that we had to try to get along together, even if we didn't agree; that it was because Schlesinger wouldn't that he had had to leave. I asked did he think I had started the row, and he knew the answer was that I had not. He then asked Kissinger to come in. He had been waiting outside almost the whole of the time and his face when he came through the side door was terrible. He assured me of his complete support; I assured him of mine; the President assured us both.

Ron Nessen, the press secretary, thereupon gave out a statement. The President and I had met, it said. We were later joined by the Secretary. I had their strong support for the effective job I was doing and had been "encouraged . . . to speak out candidly and forcefully on major issues coming before the U.N." Daniel Schorr promptly reported that I had been alone with the President for half an hour, and only thereafter was Kissinger allowed to join us for ten minutes. Kissinger, he said, had already gotten the administration in trouble "with the right-wing and some others, for the snub of Solzhenitsyn. . . . Kissinger, whose past . . . keeps coming up in Congressional investigations." And there was I, in Schorr's description a "ranking hero" of the moment:

> It no longer mattered very much whether Kissinger had anything to do with the implied attack on Moynihan by the British delegate to the United Nations. What matters is, that the White House desperately wants to keep Dr. Moynihan, and that Dr. Kissinger was perceived as a problem, and so, Dr. Kissinger had to be put down . . . just as others had to be put down in the days when Dr. Kissinger, his star then brighter, threatened to resign because of what was being said about him and wiretapping.

That was the White House staff talking. Their interests, properly, were the President's, not mine. My own interest — now — was to make the meeting seem as little a personal defeat for the Secretary as possible. I avoided the press in Washington, and when I got back to New York gave out a four-line statement saying that I was staying on. But the damage was done. Three days later Reston commented on the happenings. I had been given "a phony vote of confidence by Ford and Kissinger," he said, "who didn't think the issue was worth another political flap."

II

Theatre of the Absurd

RESTON MISSED WHAT was happening. As did most people in Washington — a capital, he wrote, "almost hopelessly lost in the tangles, personalities and controversies of the past" — because it wasn't happening in Washington. For that matter, it wasn't happening in New York. East New York, which is in Brooklyn, yes; but not in Manhattan. It was happening in the country, and in a sense, to the country. There was a rallying. Writing from Washington, Reston took it as given that there would be no "major new domestic or foreign policy developments out of here in the next twelve months." Technically, he was right. Nothing would happen in Washington. But in the nation at large the American people were discovering, on their own, that human rights was for them a fundamental concern in foreign policy.

This is too crucial to be left to indirection. The positions we were taking at the U.N. proved to be enormously popular. On November 22, Clarence Mitchell wrote to the President to say that he had been speaking (continuing his N.A.A.C.P. duties) in Illinois, Massachusetts, New York, and Texas, and that the "mere mention" of what I was doing "evoked spontaneous and prolonged applause." This began to be evident on the streets. Neither Garment nor Mitchell nor I had anticipated any such response. We had assumed a narrow audience of persons who read *The Times*. Suddenly we realized much of the nation was watching. (Or listening, as I now suspect. There were, as I have said, few print journalists at the U.N., and not much television, save on special occasions; but the halls swarmed with radio correspondents, waiting outside meeting rooms, recording events hour by hour and sometimes minute by minute. Almost anonymous, some — notably Moses Schonfeld of Mutual Broadcasting — were immensely skilled.)

The difference between the response in Washington and that in the country at large may be explained, I believe, by sharply different energy levels — for want of a better term — and sharply contrasting attitudes toward the U.N. Elites were exhausted, but the country was not. The country, moreover, was very much interested in what was going on at the U.N., while elites had quite lost interest. Thus while to Washington we seemed to be causing useless trouble in a setting best left dormant, to the country, evidently, we were saying the right things in the right place to say them.

This, at least, is an explanation suggested by the striking contrasts that show up in the survey research for this period. In the Chicago Council on Foreign Relations poll, the public, by a nine-to-one margin (27 percent against 3 percent), was more disposed than the leaders to assign a "very important" role to the U.N. in determining foreign policy. Sixty-eight percent of the leaders thought the U.N. "hardly important," while exactly the same proportion of the public held the opposite view that the U.N. was "very important" or "somewhat important." Hence the audience we had suddenly gained.

———◆———

There was also, however, an audience we had lost. In the aftermath of the Zionism resolution, President Thorn of the General Assembly had commented:

> . . . It is unfortunate that unanimity on social questions, consensus on economic issues and the political climate should have been destroyed by yesterday's vote which is the unhappy product of pressure by those who wanted to impose a point of view which is historically and philosophically false.

The political climate created by the Seventh Special Session had been destroyed. This in turn threatened to destroy the argument of those in the United States whose position on foreign affairs rested heavily on the proposition that the behavior of other nations, especially the developing nations, was fundamentally a reaction to the far worse behavior of the United States. But here, in the immediate aftermath of a great achievement of multilateral cooperation, an achievement for which the United States was primarily responsible, these very nations had associated themselves with the most appalling anti-Western position to date. With Disraeli, it could be said of most of these persons that they had only one idea and that was wrong, but it should not be supposed that this limitation did not have its advantage. Faced with this newest outrage, they came forth with their all-purpose explanation. This, too, had been caused by American behavior. In this instance, unhappily, mine.

On November 26, Oakes produced a *New York Times* editorial called "The Moynihan Affair." However one judged "the flamboyant performance" of the U.N. ambassador, *The Times* said, his responsibility was to remain at his post. But this was "not to imply blanket approval of some of Mr. Moynihan's tactics at Turtle Bay or of his well known oratorical excesses in extramural activities." Some African delegates, the editorial continued,

> privately say that their resentment . . . influenced them to vote for the anti-Zionist resolution. . . . Others say that Mr. Moynihan's pressures on them for this and other roll calls were so intense that they had to vote contrary to the United States to maintain their self-respect. . . . It surely required great provocation for such an old and trusted friend of the United States as British Ambassador Ivor Richard to ridicule the verbal gymnastics of his American counterpart.

From Washington came word that Averell Harriman was telling dinner parties that I was a charming fellow, but that I had "lost us" Africa. This spread about, and soon was generally agreed upon in such circles. I regarded all this as more of the pattern of avoidance to be expected from an elite losing its nerve, which was, after all, what I had been writing about. This is also a matter too crucial to be left to indirection. It was normal enough to be defensive about my own conduct, and not to agree with those who were critical. But the criticism revealed its own purposes, its ·hidden agenda, in an unmistakable way. Without (to my knowledge) exception it focused exclusively on Africa. But nothing had happened in Africa. The pattern of voting there had been, if anything, rather more favorable than we might have expected. The disaster came in Latin America. But no one mentioned Latin America; it was not one of those regions about which it was the fashion at this time to feel guilty, or, more important, to assign guilt to others.

The most insightful commentary on the Zionism vote appeared on the *Today Show* on Monday, November 24. Barbara Walters, noting it was two weeks since the vote had been taken, suggested that the most meaningful pattern of much of the Latin American vote was that it had been "more anti–United States than anti-Israel." Tom Streithorst then summed up the essentials better than anyone else had done in the press:

> There are no great surprises in the Afro-Asian-Communist votes on the General Assembly's Zionism equals racism resolution. But many observers were taken aback by the way Latin America cast its ballots. Only eight countries followed the lead of the United States or Israel. . . . World powers in hemisphere affairs, Brazil and Mexico, went with the Arabs. Those two countries alone represent more than half the population of Latin America. Traditionally they've been regarded as allies and friends of the United States, a view some have begun to question.
>
> Latin America has no vital interests in the Middle East. Its votes have little to do with the substance of the resolution. What it reflected was power, political and economic. It demonstrates how much the United States has lost south of the border. . . .

This surely was much more to the point than the "oratorical excesses in extramural activities" wherein Oakes had found an explanation. (At this point, I had made precisely three speeches outside the U.N. One was to a closed meeting.)

On the same day as the *Times* editorial, another comment appeared: Max Lerner, by now the dean of American political columnists and the one with far the widest intellectual horizons, spoke of the event with a perspective that even now suggests the muddle and waste of it all:

> The flap raises a question that goes beyond the relationship between the UN Ambassador and the State Dept., strained to the breaking point despite President Ford's effort to patch it up. It is the question of how well or badly any foreign office manages to combine two kinds of diplomacy — the open brand and the behind-the-scenes brand.
>
> . . . Kissinger's talent for maneuver and persuasion makes him a master of the second kind of diplomacy, which takes place backstage. Moynihan is a virtuoso of the first kind and he prefers the overt to the covert. By selecting Moynihan for the UN post five months ago, Kissinger seemed to agree that the U.S. had not fully used its effective resources in the General Assembly. The idea was to play the old game the detectives use in questioning suspects — that of the tough guy and the nice guy plying him in succession.
>
> Clearly, a Secretary of State cannot play both the tough and the nice guy roles himself. He must delegate one of them, but orchestrate both. . . . Somewhere Kissinger's orchestration broke down, and with it came the threat of Moynihan's resignation.

"Alas," he wrote, my arrangement with Kissinger hadn't worked, and there was reproach enough for both of us. True.

◆

By long arrangement, Social Democrats, U.S.A., was to give a reception for me on the evening of the day I met with Ford in Washington. This now turned into a rally of sorts. Bayard Rustin and Lane Kirkland spoke. It is the unenviable circumstance of social democrats that they have much experience of enemies. Quicker than I, they knew what was afoot; more readily than I they accepted the challenge. The speeches were powerful: they understood, they approved, they were with me. Kirkland ended with the assertion that the guest of honor was deserving of praise in nothing more than in "the enemies he has made."

Nothing like this had happened to me. These were the people — the class of people, if you will allow — whose good opinion, one had learned in the city high schools and in the City College, truly mattered. Whose opinion lasted. Midge Decter, James T. Farrell, Irving Kristol, Martin Mayer, Theodore Draper, Carl A. Wittfogel, Hilton Kramer, Walter Goodman. In our New York, not the other one.

"Socialist Group Fetes Moynihan," announced *The Times* next day. And truly they had, with all their singularity. Rustin, nature's aristocrat, had purchased a silver julep cup at Tiffany's. Carl Gershman, rather in the role of the youngest subaltern in the regiment, presented it to me, saying it would be ideally suited to hold pencils and pens. He had been in charge of the arrangements, and earlier had come with great hesitation to ask if they might use the reception room of the Mission. Here they were: an organized party for nearly a century; they had known influence, but never power. Their manners were those of a more circumspect time. They did not know much of the government. But they knew a Stalinist when they saw one. And they always fought. They hadn't much to show for it all, but by the end of the evening I had resolved that for a while at least they would have an ambassador.

Washington was now closing to me; what the President wanted would not make that much difference. So was the U.N. Michael J. Berlin reported on the New York *Post* reception and noted: "The American Social Democrats had invited those few Social Democrats remaining at the U.N. to help celebrate . . . , but only five of them showed up — from Austria, Barbados, Israel, the Netherlands and Singapore." I would not have expected Ivor Richard. In theory the Labour Party and the Social Democrats, U.S.A., were equal members of the Socialist International, but the Labour Party had changed. A month earlier, it had arranged for Boris Ponomarev, head of the International Department of the Communist Party of the USSR, to come to London on a "fraternal" visit, where he was received by the Prime Minister and by Mr. Callaghan. Ponomarev had been a member of the executive committee of the Comintern during the treason trials of the 1930s. His hands still dripped blood. The American socialists, innocent of power perhaps, could never be guilty of such a lapse. I would stay with my own.

———◆———

The amnesty resolution had died even before the encounter with Richard, but not before playing a part in events. We had not consulted with the West Europeans before introducing the measure in the Third Committee on November 12. Put this down in the largest measure to inexperience, although there were true constraints on what we could have done. It wasn't until the United States had finally voted in favor of amnesty in Chile and South Africa that we were free to propose a universal amnesty. By the time these votes had been taken, the period in which new resolutions could be introduced at the committee level had almost expired. Hence the hurried arrangements and the speech on November 12.

The amnesty proposal was not a response to the Zionism resolution. But just as it served the purposes of avoidance to believe that American "oratorical excesses" had lost the vote on November 10, it was equally useful to treat the amnesty proposal as an act of pique. This was conspicuously so with the European Nine. Their formal response was that they hadn't been consulted and accordingly could take no part in the enterprise. More likely, their true feelings were that the Zionism resolution had shown that at the U.N., the forces of totalitarianism were in the ascendant and only fools would try to resist the irresistible.

This was the point we had reached in November, 1975. Throughout the postwar years, as Stephen Haseler writes, European social democracy "was thought of as the political model of development" that would keep Western Europe free, affluent, stable, and forever linked to the United States and the liberal system in general. For the longest while it was seen to do just that. But somewhere in the 1960s, in a manner not yet explained, the conviction faltered and the perception changed. In 1974, the quintessential social democrat Willy Brandt left office, trapped by the Soviets in an espionage coup. As he did he was reported to believe that "Western Europe has only twenty or thirty more years of democracy left in it; after that it will slide, engineless and rudderless, under the surrounding sea of dictatorship; whether the dictation comes from a politburo or a junta will not make that much difference."

It was agreed that the "Vinci group," the informal group of democratic countries first assembled by Ambassador Piero Vinci of Italy, would meet for lunch at the U.S. Mission on Monday, November 17, to hear our case. I left the champagne off the menu. With coffee served we went directly to the matter at hand. Whether by prior arrangement or not, all agreed that the key difficulty lay with Article 1 of the American resolution, whereby the General Assembly "Appeals to all governments to proclaim an unconditional amnesty by releasing all political prisoners. . . ." What was the intended meaning of the term *political prisoner?* I answered that in our view a definition was not necessary and might not even be useful. The resolution was only an appeal to governments; it was not binding on them. No one would know better who was a political prisoner than the government that had put the person in prison in the first place. The Europeans were not moved. The Ambassador from Malta proposed that what needed to be done was to establish a working party to develop an agreed definition of "political prisoner." I asked if he had in mind the procedure by which a U.N. group developed a definition of "aggression." He said that he did. I asked if he was aware that that had taken seventeen years. He said that he was. The meeting broke up. Richard, who was present, gave his "OK Corral" speech to the United Nations Association later that same day.

The refusal of the Europeans to support the resolution left us on our own resources, but these were few. William F. Buckley, Jr., apart, no columnist came to our aid. The sense of defeat and guilt in so many of the others was numbing. On the day the amnesty resolution was introduced, Anthony Lewis wrote of the Zionism resolution that "this country has a share of responsibility for the disaster." A generation ago, he said, "the United States was in a position to talk of moral standards in world affairs," but no longer:

> A superpower that drops 500,000 tons of bombs on Cambodia is in rather a doubtful position to lecture others on morality. So is a Secretary of State who asserts the right to upset the constitutional government of a friendly country by covert means.

James A. Wechsler in the New York *Post* did us the courtesy of taking the amnesty proposal seriously, but said he could not support it. He commented on the general response:

> The deadly silence was predictable. Despite many eloquent Moynihan phrases about the indivisibility of justice and freedom and the "selective morality" practiced by too many U.N. members, the exercise

was fatally flawed by his avoidance of any reference to the fate of Vietnam war resisters in the United States.

If he had used the occasion to proclaim that the demeaning terms of the now dormant Ford clemency program were being transformed into full-fledged amnesty for our anti-war dissenters (some still in jail, many others in exile, and still others stigmatized by dishonorable discharges), the resolution . . . could have assumed authentically historic dimensions.

Garment wrote to the *Post* that while it was "perfectly proper" to raise the issue of a broader Vietnam amnesty in the context of our resolution, the resolution itself "was not intended to pass judgement on every disagreement that exists — within this country and among the countries of the world — over what a nation may deem to be a crime." Wechsler responded by saying that this attitude made the resolution even more "transparently barren. . . . Without amnesty at home, our message to the world will soon be filed and forgotten. It might even have better been left undelivered."

If Wechsler's response was disappointing, his observation was all too accurate. The silence *was* deadly. (Save from Moscow, where Tass leaped on us, charging that "the United States does not intend to stop aid to . . . repressive dictatorial regimes.") By the week's end the proposal was dead. The Non-Aligned in particular had responded with no inconsiderable deftness. Instead of opposing the resolution, as the Soviets might do, or proposing to postpone consideration, as the Europeans had done, they moved instead to amend it to death. The Saudis proposed an additional paragraph calling for amnesty for those "detained for having been effective activists for the right of self-determination of their people." For "effective activist" read terrorist. Ghana proposed a first operative paragraph identifying those imprisoned for "their struggle for self-determination and independence against colonialism, foreign occupation, alien domination, racism and racial discrimination as the persons for whom the resolution was being adopted." As no such struggles were deemed to exist in any of the Communist or "left" dictatorships, the resolution would thus have applied only to the democratic nations and the remaining dictatorships of the "right." Byelorussia proposed to delete altogether the preambular paragraph on the plight of persons detained for nonviolent opposition to their governments. In its place it proposed a reference to a resolution of the Twenty-Eighth General Assembly that attempted to legalize the use of violence to promote self-determination. The Russians proposed a reference to "combatants struggling against colonial and alien domination and racist regimes." They further proposed a substitute for our first operative paragraph that removed entirely the appeal for amnesty and in its place put language taken from the resolution on the use of violence to promote self-determination. Curiously, of all the countries in the world, only Rumania offered an amendment that would have strengthened the American text.

There was no hope. If the matter reached the full General Assembly, we would be alone and unavailing against the majority. We decided to withdraw the resolution, which was done as suddenly as we had introduced it. On November 21 Garment announced this in the Third Committee, stating that the fifteen-odd proposed amendments would make a "travesty" of the resolution. He spoke to the condition of liberty in the countries of the majority, and expanded on the theme we had begun in the Zionism debate, that the small nations of the Third World would come to regret the day they had helped debauch the language of human rights, the language that protected their sovereignty as well as their citizenry:

> What disturbs us is . . . consequential. It is not the United States interest that may be violated today; it is the interest of the rule of law to which we appealed in our resolution, and the interest of the central idea of the United Nations itself. . . . We began with a call to the nations of the world to free prisoners of conscience; we could well end with a measure that asks amnesty for political terrorists — and only for political terrorists. We presented a measure that would have given individuals at least some small measure of protection against the state; we are about to be given back a document that states can use as an excuse to assume still more power over individuals. We asked this body to show its concern for human rights in every nation; but in response, some could not resist the temptation to use this measure as a weapon in their battles against particular enemies. We spoke of universality; we are given parochialism. We sought consistency and were presented with a radically inconsistent treatment of peoples and circumstances. We asked for precision and are answered with slogans. So it is not surprising that the measure we seem about to end with today will lack as well the most important requirement for a proper law: It cannot command the respect, that sense of obligation, which is the only alternative to force among human institutions.
>
> There are particular people who will continue to suffer because the United Nations has not proven capable today of demanding their release in words that command universal respect. Throughout the world today, men who led their countries to freedom are suffering in the jails to which they were committed by their political rivals. Men of distinguished careers in the service of their governments have been removed from society for no reason other than the threat they posed

to the political security of their opponents; such men have been imprisoned or worse. Labor union leaders have been jailed for organizing workers. Religious leaders are jailed for speaking and teaching their doctrine. Writers and artists are in jail because they will not turn their work to the service of state propaganda. Leaders of opposition parties are in jail for the sin of posing an alternative to those who are in power. Huge numbers of citizens sit in jail after mass arrests that catch in their net those who hold the vaguest connection with a country's active political life.

They are in jail — but that is not the worst of it. They are detained in prisons without being told why. They are held incommunicado. They are beaten and tortured, to extract confessions or to instill terror among others or to provide even more perverse satisfactions. They are tried by courts which show not a shred of respect for the due process of law. They are sentenced to detention facilities that will kill them slowly, they are given food which will not sustain life, they are sent to psychiatric hospitals where the skills of medicine are used to increase their pain. They die prisoners, or worse — for there are those who do not reach prison at all.

It is a shame, but there is a shame which is perhaps even worse. It is that this body at this time seems not to care. It cares to condemn violations of human rights in those countries that it chooses to make pariahs, but it will not permit a universal, precise, consistent, and clear appeal to free political prisoners everywhere. It professes a concern for the rights of man, but it will not join in an appeal to give protection to people exercising these rights. It has given those men and women sitting in the prisons of the world no cause for hope.

And so we are now withdrawing our motion. . . . It might have become a travesty upon the pain of political prisoners and upon the United Nations itself.

———◆———

Silence greeted the withdrawal of the resolution as it had the introduction, with one squalid exception. From Washington Clayton Fritchey wrote a column that all but exulted in our failure. He began with the Zionism debate, where my "rhetorical overkill," as he put it, had been calamitous: "After all, a motion to pigeonhole the hateful resolution by postponement lost by only two votes [67 to 65]. . . . [*sic*]" He went on to praise the courage of Ivor Richard, whose audience, "composed of American supporters of the U.N., reportedly gave the British envoy a big hand." He then turned on the amnesty resolution:

At about the same time, Moynihan introduced, with trumpets, a sweeping resolution calling for amnesty for all political prisoners everywhere in the world. It was so obviously a stunt that not even America's allies took it seriously. Although Moynihan first said his proposal was of supreme importance, he abruptly withdrew it a few days later when it was clear it was going to be a dud.

In launching this counterproductive initiative, however, Moynihan righteously denounced "the selective morality of the United Nations in matters of human rights." It could hardly have been more embarrassing to the State Department, for at that instant, it was refusing to give Congress a list of those countries receiving U.S. military aid that have engaged in "gross violations" of human rights.

He noted that Tass had denounced me. He recorded that Kissinger's "quiet diplomacy" had resulted "in Moscow increasing the Jewish émigrés from a few hundred to more than 35,000 a year." He warned: "When Congress took a hard line and tied the question to trade with Russia, Moscow cut the number of émigrés in half."

This was the man who was Adlai Stevenson's press secretary at the U.S. Mission in those last years when the Kennedys were increasingly murderous toward their vanquished rival, using every device — the leaked story, the faked evidence, the whispered calumny designed not to kill the man but to destroy his self-respect. Which they may or may not have done; but if they didn't quite succeed, it was not because of Clayton Fritchey. Stevenson gone, he soon enough found new masters.

◆

The most puzzling disappointment was the social democrats of Western Europe. They too had been faithless, but why? Out of a failure of understanding? Could it only be that? In some the failure was surely of the spirit. At about this time Prime Minister Olaf Palme of Sweden paid his visit to the U.S. I had not in my life seen so much hate in a man's face, a mouth contorted with the venom within. But the others? Was it not the same old infirmity of which Rebecca West reflected in *Black Lamb and Gray Falcon* on the eve of the Second World War:

> "If this be so," I said to myself, "if it be a law that those who are born into the world with a preference for the agreeable over the disagreeable are born also with an impulse towards defeat, then the whole world is a vast Kossovo, an abominable blood-logged plain, where people who love go out to fight people who hate, and betray their cause to their enemies, so that loving is persecuted for immense tracts of history, far longer than its little periods of victory." I began to weep, for the left-wing people among whom I had lived all my life had in their attitude to foreign politics achieved such a betrayal. They were always right, they never imposed their rightness.

In something of this mood I went off to Cambridge for Thanksgiving, where the Bells gave dinner and the Glazers and others gathered. I needed to talk. The Center for the Study of Democratic Institutions and the Fund for Peace were to convene the fourth of their *Pacem in Terris* convocations the following week in Washington. Kissinger had been asked to speak, paired with Senator Edward M. Kennedy, on the theme "American–Soviet Détente, Peace and National Security," but was required to be with the President on a trip to Peking and other capitals in Asia. I was to speak in his stead.

This was to be my first speech on a general foreign policy theme since the A.F.L.-C.I.O. I wrote a careful paper that took advantage of the Catholic associations of the name of the convocation to tell the Protestant audience rather more about papal encyclicals than probably it needed to know, and drew a good deal as well on Leo Strauss. It had come to me that Strauss's idea of the collapse of "the Modern Project," by which he described the world system that grew out of the political philosophies of the sixteenth and seventeenth centuries, and which by 1914 seemed on its way to triumph, was a considerably more profound way to describe the crisis of democracy that occurred later in the twentieth century than the standard explanations of the moment. Certainly the *Pacem in Terris* conference — a huge affair — met in the atmosphere of this crisis.

In his introduction to the proceedings, later published in three volumes, Fred Warner Neal suggested that "the confusion and uncertainty" evident in the audience and in the speakers "reflected the almost unbroken series of unhappy events which transpired earlier — the Watergate scandals, the disgrace and forced resignation of a President, the highest offices in the land filled by men unelected by the people, revelations of gross wrongdoing by the FBI and CIA, and, finally, defeat in an unpopular war." He was clearly including me under the heading of the confused — but largely, I believe, because he so much disagreed with what I had said, which was that while détente was made necessary by the technological imperative of controlling nuclear conflict, it would in doing so almost necessarily lead to an *increase* in ideological conflict.

Where necessary, I said, military force would continue to appear, used as an extension of ideological war: "At this moment, as an example, the Soviets in effect have landed Cuban troops — but Soviet withal — on the Southwest coast of Africa, even as they are consolidating military facilities on the Northeast coast of the continent." This was my first public reference to Angola, and was the only passage in my paper to attract attention from the press. Although it was taken as another one of my "oratorical excesses," it was precisely what the Secretary of State wanted me to say, or was willing to have me say. I had cabled him the text, which returned without change save for two refinements: in my original text, I had had "Russians," rather than "Cuban troops," landing on that Southwest coast, and I had had the Soviets establishing "bases" rather than "facilities" on the Northeast coast of the continent.

I put it to the audience later in the text that inhibitions had arisen in the American polity which prevented us from responding to ideological conflict. A situation such as that in Angola had happened in the Congo fifteen years earlier and the United States had supported a military response. How many, I asked the audience of three to four thousand, thought we should send troops to Angola? Perhaps two dozen hands were raised. There is the measure of it, I said. There has been a change. I "was not necessarily trying to defend or deplore these inhibitions. I was trying to be analytical about them." I went on to make the thesis explicit:

> The Soviet leaders have repeatedly stated that *détente* does not mean an end to ideological competition. They have not perhaps stressed that it means an *increase,* but surely that is something for us to perceive, not for them to proclaim. . . .
>   . . . Why do we have such difficulty with such a notion? I will suggest three clusters of influence, ranging from the temporary to the persisting.
>   The first, and temporary, condition arises from what I have elsewhere called a failure of nerve within the American élites that controlled and directed foreign policy in the postwar period. . . . The Vietnam war was quintessentially an élite decision, made by a confident, essentially coherent, and to that point undefeated foreign policy establishment.
>   Then it was defeated.
>   Time heals such hurts. Time and the circulation of élites of which Pareto wrote. What it means for the moment however, is that in the area of ideological encounter our responses are much slowed. Where we had been quick to sense danger — even, sometimes, quick to perceive opportunity — we are now slow to do so. . . .
>   An intermediate cluster of influences which retard our responses to Communist aggression may be simply stated as the superior capacity of Marxist argument to induce guilt. Observe that this is stated as a relative relationship. Liberal democracy makes great claims on nonliberal societies, and has done so for some time. There is probably not now in the whole of the world a totalitarian state which does not have a constitution guaranteeing individual liberties. On the other hand, there is not a liberal society which does not contain a real Marxist or neo-Marxist movement dedicated to its overthrow on grounds of insuffi-

cient liberality. Nor is there any liberal society which is not torn by doubts on this score. Yeats sensed the mood:

> Come fix upon me that accusing eye.
> I thirst for accusation . . .

It is said that if a Communist regime were to take over in the Sahara there would in time be a shortage of sand, and we shall doubtless in time have tested that hypothesis, but we can be fairly confident that to the very end there would be those in the West convinced that the sand had gone to build swimming pools for the rich — in the West. . . .

More specifically, guilt is a weapon which our adversaries contrive to have us use against ourselves. This technique was much in evidence not long ago at the United Nations when, on the 30th anniversary of the U.N. and in a moment of relative peace in the world, the United States introduced a resolution — which had been readied a month earlier — calling for a general amnesty for political prisoners. . . .

The first American press accounts written in New York suggested that the resolution had been introduced in retaliation for the anti-Zionism resolution; . . . the general effect of such accounts was to distract attention from the measure we had proposed to the question of what motives we had in doing so. A classic mechanism for inducing guilt. Soon American commentators all but apologized for what we have done. . . .

. . . There is an element of guilt in our relations with many of the newly leftist nations in the world, which is not to be accounted for by older concerns. . . . Part of it may be accounted for the continuing success of Marxist doctrine in inducing guilt in the West, part by a separate but related sublimation of aggression. . . .

. . . The third cluster of influences . . . is the long term ideological drift away from liberal democracy, the influence of which . . . crested in 1919, at the end of the First World War, and has declined ever since. In a lecture given at that worthy Jesuit institution the University of Detroit, just weeks before the appearance in 1963 of *Pacem in Terris* . . . [Leo] Strauss . . . spoke more generally of the failure of what he called "the Modern Project." This was a world system that grew out of the political philosophies of the 16th and 17th centuries and which in, say, 1914, seemed well on the way to triumph. The West, at this time, was certain of its purpose, a "purpose in which all men could be united." It had a clear vision of its future "as the future of mankind." All went well enough, for a bit thereafter, until Communism, which had been seen as a parallel movement to the modern project — part of it really, "a somewhat impatient, wild, wayward twin" — revealed itself, as Strauss puts it, to "even the meanest capacities" as something else, as Stalinism and post-Stalinism. Oriental despotism was once again a major force in the world; such that it came to pass, in Strauss' words: "The only restraint in which the West can put some confidence is the tyrant's fear of the West's immense military power." For the rest there is a decline. Specifically, the purpose of a universal society, "a society consisting of equal nations, each consisting of free and equal men and women, with all these nations to be fully developed as regards their power of production, thanks to science" — that purpose is no longer sustainable. In its stead political society in the foreseeable future reverts to what it always has been, what Strauss called "particular" society — "society with frontiers, a closed society, concerned with self-improvement."

One must accept this as a long-term condition, but also see in it the essence of what might be our long-term security. For a particular society is a society that can be defended, and, I think, will be.

It comes to that. Out of the decline of the West there will, I sense, emerge a rise in spirits. We have shortened our lines. We are under attack. There is nothing in the least in the culture that suggests we will not in the end defend ourselves successfully.

We shall do so as we have in our armamentarium the incomparable weapon of liberty. We are the party of liberty, all of us. . . . Always have been, even when least true to it. And as the lights go out in the rest of the world, they shine all the brighter here. . . . In the United Nations today, *half* the nations have had a violent change of government within the past eleven years. What it requires, most of all, is truth-telling: to one another, and to the rest of the world. We are not merely advised in this matter, to those who would lend some authority to *Pacem in Terris,* we are commanded: "The first among the rules governing the relations between States is that of truth. . . ."

Surely we must see this. Just as we must see the persistent attempt to dissuade us from speaking out for what it is: the assertion of their weakness and our strength. The night the American amnesty resolution was introduced, a German newspaper woman called on me. . . . As we sat down she said, "Before beginning, let me just tell you that already the news of what the United States has proposed will be whispered from cell to cell in East German prisons. You would think such news would never reach such places, but it does; it is what keeps you alive. I know. I spent four years in one of them." On the heels of our initiative, one American commentator, having declared us unworthy to do anything decent, gleefully predicted that our effort would be met with "a deadly silence." Which in retrospect might to many seem to be the case. But is it the case? Or is it only that we have not learned to hear the whispers? *Sursum Corda.*

———————◆———————

In the course of a panel discussion that followed, George F. Kennan gave the most emphatic endorsement to what I had said "about our relations with the Third World and with the many new left regimes there. . . ." And I was suddenly struck by the extent to which I was being misread. It was no surprise to have someone such as Neal ask,

"Does rousing rhetoric, like that of Ambassador Moynihan . . . make so much noise that we can't hear what other nations are trying to tell us?" It was another thing altogether to have Kennan suppose that I shared his view, which was that the new nations were of no consequence, and disagreeable as well, such that, as he once put it, quite the best policy toward the new nations would be to pay them no attention of any kind for three to four decades, after which they could be told that if they were ready to behave like grown-up countries they would be admitted to grown-up society.

Still more difficult was to be caricatured as a mindless interventionist. On the second day of the *Pacem in Terris* conference this task fell to Kenneth W. Thompson, in a paper titled "Too Much Shouting, Too Little Quiet Diplomacy." His was the first half-professional treatment of the thesis I had been presenting, and it was hard to accept. Thompson, who had spent much of his career at the Rockefeller Foundation, knew as much as or more than I did, but was immobilized by guilt. He had become the quintessential executive of a giant foundation, some product of predatory capitalism in its primal acquisitive stage, now devoted like a medieval foundation — same word, come to think of it — to beseeching Heaven's mercy on the soul of the departed founder. In place of masses and plainsong, there were lunch at the Century Club and weekend conferences at Colonial Williamsburg.

In Thompson's traditional view the U.N. was a place where, behind the scenes, dedicated men and women, recognizably products of Rockefeller Foundation fellowships, shaped the green revolution and eradicated smallpox. Now, however, the American ambassador was spoiling it all. This was why in the aftermath of my A.F.L.-C.I.O. speech,

> African leaders had no alternative but to strike back. Flamboyant and ill-considered Irish wit rent the delicate political fabric of coalition of African moderates. Overnight the leadership of some African states that had been elements of restraint within the Arab-African bloc in votes on Israel at Kampala and Lima turned against us. Given African domestic politics, American political rhetoric fashioned in part for American domestic politics left them no alternative.

No one asked him to name such a state. This kind of foreign policy analysis was hopelessly nonempirical. Its object was not to sort out facts, but to assign blame.

Thompson's own position seemed to me defensible, yet without truly responding to the needs of that time. Thus his central accusation of me:

> The trouble though with all-out and indiscriminate confrontation at the United Nations is that it is bad timing and doubtful tactics, bad

historical and political analysis, and bad social and political philosophy
— whatever its other virtues. It is bad timing because the United States
has recently abandoned one ideological crusade against the Soviet
Union and China. Having substituted the hard and realistic impera-
tives of foreign policy for a worldwide anti-communist crusade there is
a deep pathos in our embarking on a second Cold War, this time as
the leader of North against South. Yet the conceptual basis is remark-
ably similar: a monolithic rival which we uncompromisingly oppose,
an alien ideology which in its original London School of Economics
and British socialist version or its derivative forms of the seventy-seven
or more so-called socialist states of the less developed countries, has
identified us as the enemy, and our messianic urge to convert others to
our form of absolute truth.

This leads to the second indictment — bad historical and political
analysis. . . . Schumpeter three decades ago spoke of the tendency of
Marxists to portray the world in overly simplistic terms offering a
fairyland account of vast complicated social forces. Those who have
worked in Africa and Asia question whether the political and economic systems of seventy or eighty countries are all cut from the same
cloth, however similar at times their rhetoric and social organization.
Moreover, descriptions of any one may quickly become outdated. Ambassador Moynihan, writing in March 1975, sought to qualify his
rather dogmatic judgments of Third World countries by explaining
that "Half the people in the world who live under a regime of civil
liberties live in India." The qualification proved as premature as the
original premise. Whether we praise or condemn Third World states,
we ought to be more discriminating lest the patterns we describe change
before the echoes die away. Indiscriminate anti-socialism is as misleading as the sole criterion for a foreign policy for the Third World as indiscriminate anti-communism has been in the Cold War.

Finally, it is bad social and political philosophy to maintain that
moral and political choice involves choosing a single value, casting it in
absolute terms and blindly defending it whatever the consequences.
Unfortunately, this is essentially the position we have taken in the
present United Nations Assembly. Our goal, we say, is "speaking for
and in the name of political and civil liberty" [Moynihan in "The
United States in Opposition"]. Liberty is held superior to all other
values because those who pursue it not only are right but rewarded
in having done better economically and socially — a defense all too
reminiscent of that of Norman Vincent Peale's justification of Chris-
tianity. The rather shrill appeal that America shouts to the heavens,
that it alone is the party of liberty, carries us back to the call for the
defense of freedom everywhere in the world by a young President a
decade and a half ago, followed all too closely by the Bay of Pigs. As
President Kennedy learned, and his successors after him, wise choices in
foreign policy, as in politics, are more than standing for a single, if
estimable, value.

The caution about elevating a single value, especially the Western value of liberty, was Niebuhrian and surely legitimate. But the rest was intellectually disgraceful. This charge, that I was starting a new Cold War based on "indiscriminate anti-socialism," was at one level merely false. But at another level it was a reflection of intellectual corruption. This was 1975. If you had spent most of your career as a servant of the Rockefellers, a fixture of the Council on Foreign Relations, a giver of grants, and a member of panels associated with the foreign policy "establishment" that had superintended the Cold War with Russia and extended American business enterprise to the farthest reaches of the globe in the booming years following victory in World War II — then you could conceive of nothing more shocking than another Cold War based on "indiscriminate anti-socialism," and would accuse others of advocating just that, even if they had done nothing of the kind.

◆

In spite of all this, I received the 1975 Human Rights Award of the International League for the Rights of Man. I took heart from the occasion, a crowded affair at Marietta Tree's; the closest I had got to the world of Adlai Stevenson. I took for my theme a passage from Justice Robert H. Jackson's Godkin Lectures for 1955:

> Our forefathers' conception of a liberal legal order had been the dynamic ideology of most of the nineteenth century. But the twentieth century has seen the depressed masses in nearly all backward countries abandon it as their hope and turn to a militant Communism radiating from the Soviet Union, which Clement Attlee once described as merely "an inverted czardom. . . ." Revolutions in our time, whether by Communists, Fascists, or Nazis, have not pretended to overthrow or moderate the power of the state over the individual, but, instead, have each aspired to concentrate in the state a more absolute power over every activity of life and leave nothing but tatters of the "rights of man." Paradoxical as it may seem, we are in an age of rebellion against liberty. . . . Civilization is still threatened by forces generated within and perhaps by itself.

Morris Abram presided, insofar as was possible given the occasion, and said that if there was going to be a great debate, he should be understood as being on our side of it. This in its way was an event. The breaking up of old alignments that Podhoretz had foreseen seemed to be coming about.

Old friends rallied. Stephen Hess, in a long letter to *The New York Times*, put my case better than I had done. The criticism by foreign diplomats indicated, he said, "the degree to which these gentlemen have lost sight of the purpose of diplomatic representation. It is not the papering-over of basic differences, although this is sometimes a useful diplomatic technique. Rather, its purpose is to avoid misunderstanding between nations. This is exactly what Moynihan has been doing."

———◆———

We now proceeded to "avoid misunderstanding" with South Africa, in a dissertation on the legal and political regime there. This was the first time any presentation of this kind had been made, and it set a standard of argument and evidence in such matters that any institution might be proud of. Yet even this enterprise ended on an uncertain note. The United States invoked the doctrine of natural rights in a devastating critique of *apartheid*. And yet when it was over, we wondered whether anyone in the General Assembly even knew what we were talking about, much less cared.

It began October 23, when Clarence Mitchell addressed the Special Political Committee. *Apartheid,* he declared, was an "odious and abhorrent" system, to which we had stated our opposition in numerous debates in successive sessions of the General Assembly. The United States had maintained an arms embargo against South Africa since 1962. Further:

> The United States Government has pursued a policy of seeking to encourage in South Africa a peaceful change from the policies of apartheid to policies which will provide for the attainment of basic human rights by *all* South African citizens, regardless of race. To this end, we have adopted a policy of communication: to impress upon the Government of South Africa our opposition to apartheid; to signal our unequivocal support for changes in the political and social system in South Africa, and to maintain contacts with all members of the South African population, including those not permitted to participate in the governing of that country. It is the belief of my government that South Africa should be exposed to the relentless and unceasing demands of the world community to eradicate the apartheid system.
>
> The U.S. deplores the detention of persons whose only act is outspoken opposition to the system of apartheid. The South African Government is courting disaster when such repressive measures have the effect of closing off all avenues for peaceful change.

This brought forth a long, rambling, emotional speech from the South African Prime Minister, Balthazar Johannes Vorster. He forgave "Mr. Mitchell" his misunderstandings. He reminded Mitchell that the United States "had *apartheid* laws from 1946 when UNO was formed until 1954 when it was outlawed by the Supreme Court . . . [and] it wasn't their parliament who changed it, it was the Supreme Court." He chose not to comment on the assertion that *apartheid* was "odious and abhorrent." But he would not accept Mitchell's charge that people were being detained for their opposition to *apartheid:*

> What I do take exception to is this — that is the whole point of my argument. When he used those words: "The U.S. deplores the detention of persons whose only act is outspoken opposition to the system of *apartheid.*"
> I don't blame Mr. Mitchell for using these words because presumably, he was briefed by one of the lower echelons of the State Department. . . . I want to say . . . in all fairness to my country . . : , that is a downright lie. . . . I am entitled to issue this challenge to the State Department, which wrote this speech for Mr. Mitchell, name me one individual in South Africa who was arrested and detained, only because of his outspoken opposition to the system of *apartheid.* No man has ever been arrested or detained in South Africa because he has spoken out against *apartheid.* Good heavens . . . there are forty-eight of them in parliament. They walk the streets of Johannesburg by their hundreds and thousands. They sit in editors' offices. . . . People will continue to play with fire and will continue to try and undermine and subvert the state of South Africa. People will continue to be detained and arrested in South Africa for as long as this situation goes on. Make no mistake about it.

The American ambassador in Pretoria, William G. Bowdler, immediately cabled us Vorster's speech. (As the United States does not approve of the South African regime, our ambassadors there feel free to report that the regime does not approve of *us.*) The response was everything we could have hoped for. Vorster did not much reply to such charges when made by African governments. But it was clearly, to him, a different matter when such criticism came from the United States. I responded to his challenge in a brief statement on October 31:

> Prime Minister Vorster's statement about Clarence Mitchell is completely unwarranted. Mr. Mitchell had his facts right. South Africa has its policy wrong. The Prime Minister has challenged Mr. Mitchell to name persons who, in Mr. Mitchell's words, are detained for their "outspoken opposition to the system of apartheid." Mr. Mitchell will respond in an appropriate manner.

It took November to do so, but in the end Mitchell was ready with a six-thousand-word reply, accompanied by three pages of names of persons, whites and nonwhites, in detention in South Africa for opposing *apartheid.* It was a brief worthy of the man who helped bring about every civil rights act of the twentieth century. His reply went precisely to the point that Vorster considered unassailable. Mitchell, for the United States, asserted that the legal system of South Africa was behaving illegally:

> The South African system of detention and repression is built into the legal structure itself. There is a system of political laws which are designed to stifle and intimidate political opposition, laws which make criminal acts which are not criminal in any free society. . . . Acts which form the rough give-and-take that is the life blood of democracy are considered criminal in South Africa.

There followed a closely reasoned, carefully documented argument that what was legal in South Africa was illegal by the standards of a liberal society.

It was a moment we were immensely proud of, and yet it was spoiled. No one in the General Assembly listened. The session was coming to a close; there had been so many speeches already. But it was more than that. Apart from Gambia's and Malawi's, there was not an African delegation on the floor of the General Assembly who represented a government which would have met the standards of natural law and natural right that Clarence Mitchell was propounding. Throughout Mitchell's speech the chairwoman of the *apartheid* committee, Madame Cissé of Senegal, fresh from receiving her Lenin Prize, roamed about gossiping with other delegates. Next to us the Tanzanian delegates talked at the top of their voices about their plans for the weekend. (I later complained to Salim of Tanzania, who decently responded that this should not have happened.) When Mitchell finished no one rose to acknowledge what he had accomplished.

We had introduced a wholly new method of argument to the General Assembly. The equivalent, I was to contend, of the "Brandeis brief" in the American legal system. But no one listened; no one cared.

———◆———

A theme of our speeches throughout November had been that to corrupt the language of human rights — the language, that is, of Leo Strauss's "Modern Project," the language of "a society consisting of equal nations, each consisting of free and equal men and women" — would soon enough imperil the language of national rights also, and soon enough it did. In December, two fledgling nations were conquered or partitioned by their neighbors, while a third was invaded by Communist forces from half a world away. It would be gratifying to report that there were those who made some connection between what we said would happen and what now did happen, but there were none. This perhaps only confirmed our charge that the Charter was being drained of meaning. In any event a short recounting seems in order, in the manner of the small memorials in old graveyards which record the brief existence of children who died at birth.

◆

On December 8 Dili fell. A place of no great importance, it was the capital of Portuguese Timor, a colony of Portugal since 1586. On July 12, Portugal had announced that the territory would probably remain under Portuguese rule until October, 1978. Early in August, however, a coup took place, mounted by a centrist party seeking immediate independence. This was followed by civil strife between the centrist group and the left-wing Revolutionary Front for the Independence of East Timor, known by the acronym *Fretilin.* By early September the leftist group had evidently prevailed, and was soon recognized by the People's Republic of China. On December 8 the forces of neighboring Indonesia seized Timor's capital of Dili, and soon took over the whole of the colony. Indonesian Foreign Minister Adam Malik said that this was done in response to a request from the centrist rivals of *Fretilin,* and that a plebiscite would soon be held. President Ford had been in Jakarta just two days before the invasion. The White House press secretary, when asked, stated that Indonesian President Suharto had raised the subject in "very general terms," but had no further comment.

Portugal broke diplomatic relations with Indonesia, insisting on the right of the people of Timor to self-determination. Portugal requested a meeting of the Security Council. *The Times* declared: "By any definition, Indonesia is guilty of naked aggression. . . ." China, acting for a group of nations, introduced a draft resolution in the General Assembly's Committee on Dependent Territories calling on all parties to work for independence, and on the Indonesian troops to withdraw "without delay." On December 22 the Security Council unanimously approved a resolution calling on Indonesia to remove its military forces from Portuguese Timor — also without delay. There were many suggestions as to what the Secretary-General might do. Fighting went on for a bit. A U.N. special envoy, Vittorio Winspeare-Guicciardi, was appointed. In February the deputy chairman of the provisional government forecast that the Indonesian forces would complete their takeover in three to four weeks, and estimated that some sixty thousand persons had been killed since the outbreak of civil war. This would have been 10 percent of the population, almost the proportion of casualties experienced by the Soviet Union during the Second World War. The three-to-four-week estimate must have been correct, as the subject disappeared from the press and from the United Nations after that time. A dispatch from Canberra in the *Christian Science Monitor* of January 26, 1978, began: "In a move seen here variously as premature, unnecessary, realistic, and even tragic, the Australian Government formally has acknowledged that Indonesia has sovereignty over East Timor."

———◆———

Spanish Sahara was a place of somewhat greater importance in itself — as Spanish Sahara was the fourth largest producer of phosphates in the world, a commodity whose value had quintupled when the price of oil had been quintupled — and of vastly greater importance to the rule of law and the authority of the United Nations Charter. In December of 1975, the territory was partitioned. Eight weeks earlier, the International Court of Justice, in an advisory opinion requested by the General Assembly, had solemnly affirmed the right of self-determination of the people of this, the last Spanish colony.

Twelve months earlier, December 13, 1974, the General Assembly, "reaffirming the right of the population of the Spanish Sahara to self-determination," had requested an advisory opinion by the court on whether this area had been, at the time of Spanish colonization in 1884, "a territory belonging to no one (*terra nullius*)," as asserted by Spain. Both the Kingdom of Morocco and the Islamic Republic of Mauritania were making claims to prior suzerainty over the region, and whether Spain would actually leave the place was still an open question. No one might have cared — there were at most seventy thousand inhabitants of the bleak territory, and of these almost all were nomads — save for the discovery that its northern region was pure phosphate. The opportunity to win yet another victory over colonialism now combined with the prospect of profit. There was talk of invasion. Generalissimo Franco was adroit to the last. He would not have a war, no matter how miniature. In May, 1975, he announced that Spain would grant independence to the territory in the shortest possible time, and thereupon asked the Secretary-General to send U.N. observers to be on hand for the transfer. On October 17 the International Court of Justice issued its opinion. The Court found that at the time of colonization by Spain, Western Sahara "was not a territory belonging to no one (*terra nullius*)," but neither did the information and materials presented to it "establish any tie of territorial sovereignty between the territory of Western Sahara and the Kingdom of Morocco or the Mauritanian entity." Thus, the decision concluded, independence should go forward "through the free and the genuine expression of the will of the peoples of the Territory."

With that, King Hassan II of Morocco announced that he would lead a peaceful "march of conquest" of a quarter million of his subjects into Spanish Sahara. Algerian President Houari Boumédienne announced that if Morocco did this Algeria would go to war. Secretary-General Waldheim called for the "utmost restraint" to "avoid tragedy." The Security Council appealed to all "concerned and interested parties" to avoid any action that might heighten tension. The marchers went forward. Then they went back. Franco stepped down and Prince Juan Carlos de Borbón succeeded him. As Acting Chief of State he flew to the colony and declared that Spain would protect the "legitimate rights" of the people of Spanish Sahara and the "honor and prestige of the Army of Spain." He thereupon turned the territory over to Morocco and Mauritania to divide between them. Algeria, which also bordered on the territory, was outmaneuvered. The General Assembly passed two resolutions. One sided with Algeria; the other sided with Morocco.

The two events spoke to the nature of the new world system. It was not so different from the old. It was for the moment more stable, but a reasonable forecast would be that Africa in particular had a century of border wars ahead of it. On the other hand, such was the power of the anticolonial idea that great powers from outside a region had relatively little influence unless they were prepared to use force. China altogether backed *Fretilin* in Timor, and lost. In Spanish Sahara, Russia just as completely backed Algeria, and its front, known as *Polisario,* and lost. In both instances the United States wished things to turn out as they did, and worked to bring this about. The Department of State desired that the United Nations prove utterly ineffective in whatever measures it undertook. This task was given to me, and I carried it forward with no inconsiderable success.

———◆———

It is difficult to say precisely when Luanda fell. Or to whom. But by December it was clear that the capital of Angola was occupied by Cuban troops dispatched by the Soviet Union, with Soviet personnel also on hand.

Now came the U.N. response to Angola. This ought to have been our finest hour at the Thirtieth General Assembly. It was not. If soon thereafter it was time for me to go, the events of December argued with equal force that Kissinger's time had come as well. He could now only repeat himself. There were no surprises left in a man whose entire technique had rested on surprise, or had done when Nixon was the President making the decisions.

Angola was declared independent on November 10 by the departing Portuguese High Commissioner. His proclamation transferred power to the "Angolan people" rather than to any government, negotiations with different factions having failed to produce an agreement. The Popular Movement for the Liberation of Angola (M.P.L.A.), a Marxist group, and the National Front for the Liberation of Angola (F.N.L.A.) thereupon issued declarations of independence of their own. A third group, the National Union for the Total Independence of Angola (U.N.I.T.A.), also asserted itself. These were true ideological conflicts in that the M.P.L.A. was genuinely Marxist and the others were not, but at root divisions were tribal. The Bacongo in the north (F.N.L.A.), the Kimbundu in the middle (M.P.L.A.), and the Ovimbundu in the south (U.N.I.T.A.) were as different as French, Germans, and Poles, and their lands were at least as extensive. Anyone who had thought much about the subject would have probably predicted a long period of negotiating and skirmishing ending with some kind of accommodation, of the sort that Zaire, Nigeria, and others had managed.

Then suddenly in early October, it was learned that five Cuban merchant ships with weapons, ammunition, and Cuban troops had arrived in Luanda. Next, South African troops entered the territory from the south. Finally, on November 14, three days after independence, Russian troops, pilots, and tank crews joined the Cubans.

It was a brilliant move; as startling in its way as the appearance of Soviet missiles in Cuba in 1963. The Rand Corporation at its peak of performance could not have invented a Third World weapons system the equal of the Cuban army. A white army, or at very least an army with white officers; a European army in the sense of an army speaking a European language, using European weapons, paid for by a European power; yet a white, European army able to go anywhere in Africa and kill black men with ideological impunity. Devastating.

The reaction in Africa was terror. The states bordering on Angola were panicked. And this was the point as I saw it. The Soviet move was *too* brilliant. It had startled Africa. It had seized the attention and imagination of governments around the world. It was our moment for an equally devastating countermove.

Russia had invaded Africa. White troops were killing black men and women. In the name of Communist expansion. With but one tiny European enclave still left on the continent, of a sudden the blue eyes were back; recolonization begun. I felt we should take the issue to the General Assembly and to the Security Council and never let the argument fade until the last Cuban was out of Africa, and the pro-Soviet governments of that continent permanently labeled as apologists for what was truly a neo-colonialism.

Kissinger wouldn't. I never learned why, which led me to suppose that it was nothing more complicated than now at last a running down of energy, combined with a now settled distrust and even dislike of what we were up to in New York. He had, it will be recalled, revised and approved my remarks on Angola to the *Pacem in Terris* conference, including the allusion to the Chinese, whom I counted on to join us in attacking the Soviets. I had declared:

> It is fair to assume they [the Soviets] mean to colonize Africa and manifest that they are already partially successful, their main problem being opposition from another Communist power and also from the fact that the United States will call them [to account] in instances of open military operations, as indeed the Secretary of State has done.

Now this was much exaggerated. There was no evidence that the Soviets meant to "colonize Africa." They were out for what they could get, but probably were quite uncertain as to what that might be. Bases in Somalia; facilities in various West African ports. Leverage here; leverage there. But there was scant evidence that they were intent on reconvening the Congress of Berlin. Still, *they could be made to appear so.* They could be forced to deny such intentions. They could be required to face the charge and the fact that Russia had an army in Africa that was fighting Africans.

For the first time since the Soviets had become involved in the Congo in 1961 (in not different circumstances), the United States faced a major foreign policy decision in which the U.N. was likely to be not only a useful resort, but an essential one. Word had begun to filter out that South African troops were supporting what was now a coalition of F.N.L.A. and U.N.I.T.A. Any American support for that coalition would in the end be depicted by the Soviets, and their greatly superior numbers in the General Assembly, as an American army in Africa fighting Africans.

I appeared on television Sunday, December 7, and raised a somewhat clumsy alarm. The Russians, I said, had invaded southern Africa. If they succeeded, they would control the oil shipping lanes from the Persian Gulf to Europe. They would be "next to Brazil." (In extenuation, may I say that James Schlesinger had seriously hoped to get a naval base in Angola from the Portuguese.) The world, I argued, would thereupon "be different." There was no way we could intervene, for this would be taken as support for South Africa, and would defeat any other purpose we might have. I now began to plead with Washington for permission to call for a meeting of the Security Council. No instructions came. Assistant Secretary Buffum was in his final days in the American government in charge of U.N. affairs. He would soon be an Under-Secretary-General at the U.N. itself. Kissinger was traveling, repeating an old and by now worn formula, missing the moment.

On December 8 the General Assembly debated the omnibus condemnation of South Africa, which by tradition came toward the end of the session. Seven African countries, conspicuously pro-Soviet and distinctively distant from Angola itself, had introduced an amendment which added armed intervention in Angola to the list of Pretoria's many misdeeds. The Organization of African Unity itself had denounced all foreign intervention, without naming names. Zaire had submitted a resolution to this effect. Having no instructions one way or the other, I went to the rostrum and spoke the bluntest, plainest truth I could summon. Two white armies had invaded Angola. If the General Assembly were to go along with the big lie that there was only *one* army involved, then let it be plainly understood that the General Assembly would be on record as having found that invasion of African countries by *some* white armies was perfectly acceptable. And this was how the delegates would be seen to have used their heritage of national independence which the United Nations had done so much to establish. It was a curiously impressive occasion, for the delegates knew what I was saying and knew what they were doing.

The press reported that in the strongest attack on Moscow made by an American in many years I had described the Soviets as "a new colonial, imperialist power," had accused them of attempting to "recolonize" Africa, had asked the General Assembly to take up the issue of Russian involvement in Angola and Somalia, and had urged African nations to demand the withdrawal of Cuban forces.

The next day, December 9, a *Times* editorial entitled "'Big Lie' in Angola" backed me completely, and for good measure included a passage about Angola's "1,000-mile coastline with deep-water ports and Portuguese-built airfield [which] could provide the Soviet Union with a dominant position along the South Atlantic." Both the opening and closing paragraphs called ón the U.N. to act:

> The civil war in Angola confronts the United Nations with one more moment of truth. Cuban troops and Soviet arms, brought in by a large-scale Russian air-and-sea-lift, appear to be turning the tide in favor of the Communist-led Popular Movement for the Liberation of Angola (MPLA). This blatant military intervention by white powers from distant continents in the internal affairs of a black African country is the kind of aggression that the United Nations was created to oppose. . . .

The Soviet Union, meanwhile, has unleashed its controlled press in defense of its action as support of a "national liberation struggle" and, therefore, not "incompatible" with detente. According to Izvestia, "the process of detente" does not rule out armed intervention in Angola or require "the cessation of anti-imperialist struggles . . . against foreign interference and oppression."

This double-thick sham is far from compatible with the principles of co-existence signed by Soviet leader Leonid Brezhnev in 1972. Its exposure is within the capability of the United Nations, even if military action against a superpower is not.

———◆———

It worked. On December 10 the Soviets and Cubans, in something like panic, attacked me personally in the General Assembly; Malik accused me of "slandering the Soviet Union with the big lie." Alarcón Quesada, describing me as a "pseudo-professor," asserted that his country was "proud" of its support for the M.P.L.A., although he made no mention of troops, or of what kinds of support Cuba was providing. But on the same day the Soviets were forced to drop the amendment that the seven African nations had put forward. We had outmaneuvered them. *The Times* reported, "Diplomats in touch with the sponsors of the amendment, which was supported by the Soviet Union and opposed by the United States, said that it had been withdrawn when it became apparent that it could not win a majority of votes in the Assembly."

This was the first time in the Thirtieth General Assembly, the first time in a decade at least, that the United States had managed to deprive the Soviets of a General Assembly majority on an issue of colonialism and imperialism. The jujitsu principle had worked. Far from resisting the condemnation of South Africa, we had joined it, and then proposed to condemn the other white aggressor as well.

Now was the moment to go to the Security Council and demand that the invaders leave Angola. But Kissinger could not see the opportunity. Unforgivably — for he was certain to fail — he had got himself involved in trying to channel CIA money through Zaire to the F.N.L.A. and U.N.I.T.A. It was the same old pattern: still bombing Cambodia, still planning a deal with Le Duc Tho. But now every "secret" mission, every concealed maneuver, was reported in the next day's press. *The New York Times* of November 7 had Sisco and Colby telling the Senate Foreign Relations Committee that they needed congressional support for sending arms to Angola through Zaire, Ethiopia, and Kenya. This prospect would be used as a "bargaining chip" with the Soviet Union. But no one would play that game any longer. The Senate saw the opportunity to prevent what it chose to construe as the threat of another Vietnam.

Senator John Tunney, Democrat of California, introduced an amendment cutting off all further covert military aid to Angola. Ford thereupon tried to make this an issue of patriotism, or whatever, and failed ignominiously. Cuban forces continued to build up, and by early 1976 had more or less decisively prevailed.

On January 19, 1976, a *New York Times* article reporting on the assumption of emergency powers by Zambian President Kenneth D. Kaunda quoted him as warning of "a plundering tiger with its deadly cubs now coming in through the back door." I took the occasion, at a Security Council meeting shortly afterward, to ask the Zambian Ambassador just what country or countries he thought the President might be referring to. But already it was too dangerous to speak openly of the matter, and the Ambassador made no reply. By February 13 *The Times of Zambia,* a newspaper owned by Kaunda's party, published an editorial calling on the Soviets and Cubans to prove that they were ready to sacrifice yet more for the world socialist revolution by pushing on south in Namibia and even farther into South Africa itself. Only such a step, the editorial argued, could "justify, sanctify, and glorify" Soviet and Cuban intervention in Angola and the deaths of thousands of Angolans in that fighting.

One thought back to the summer of 1975, and the calculations the Soviets must have been making. On the one hand, their wheat crop was poor. They would need to import a great deal from the United States. In the spirit of détente the Americans would oblige. On the other hand, opportunity beckoned in Angola. Given such a gross violation of the spirit of détente, the Americans might not oblige. Surely the Soviet calculated they could exercise one option or the other. Wheat or Angola. In the end they got both. Ernest W. Lefever wrote,

> If detente has any substance, Angola is certainly a test case. No American troops are needed. Why does not Mr. Ford, hopefully with the support of Congress, inform Mr. Brezhnev that U.S. grain shipments to the Soviet Union will be suspended and the strategic arms limitations talks broken off until Moscow withdraws its Cuban expeditionary force from Angola?
>
> This would take courage in these troubled times when the earlier "illusion of American omnipotence" is giving way to an even more dangerous malady — the paralysis of power.

This went to the heart of it. What was needed was courage, and that was what was lacking. Kissinger was exhausted and everybody else was afraid. I was to learn that the decision not to make a diplomatic issue of Angola was taken by the President on June 27, 1975, just before I arrived at the U.N. Soviet intentions (with assistance expected from the

Yugoslavs!) were by then known to us. As early as April, Kenneth Kaunda was fair to begging us to help Savimbi, whose region bordered Zambia. (As time passed, Houphouet-Boigny of the Ivory Coast, Senghor of Senegal, and Mobutu of Zaire were to plead for American intervention in various forms, including, in the case of Mobutu at least, an appeal that we should persuade the South Africans to remain involved.) Kissinger settled for driblets of CIA money: just enough to cause scandal. His position in June was that before starting a diplomatic row with the Russians, one had to know what would happen if the challenge failed. His reasoning remains a mystery to me. There was a sense in which a diplomatic challenge could *not* fail: no nation in southern Africa wanted the Soviets to have an army there. We would have been supporting the same position. Somehow Kissinger feared to demonstrate that words could not stop tanks. But this is not necessarily so, or not necessarily the point. There we divided.

———◆———

The General Assembly was coming to a close now, and I took to enjoying it. On December 11 the Decolonization Committee submitted its annual report, wherein, *inter alia,* United States military forces on the Virgin Islands were described as a threat to the peace of the region. I went to the rostrum and explained that said forces consisted of fourteen Coast Guardsmen, one shotgun, one pistol, and an 82-foot vessel used for emergency rescue assistance. I speculated that this would not normally be seen as much of a threat to other nations in the region. But then it must be allowed that there was in truth a neighboring island that had evidently so denuded itself of its own forces in pursuit of colonialist, imperialist adventurist goals elsewhere that it might indeed feel threatened by fourteen Coast Guardsmen. Even so, I went on, the Committee's report was "riddled with untruths." The General Assembly was becoming a "theatre of the absurd." (Not, I might have added, in precisely the sense that Martin Esslin had first used the term, but close enough.)

Salim, chairman of the Committee, seemed hurt that I felt his report was filled with lies. It was not clear whether he didn't believe they were lies, or whether he didn't believe that mere lies should come between friends.

———◆———

As host country, the United States gives the penultimate speech of the General Assembly, followed by the President of the Assembly. I prepared a long statement to the effect that the Thirtieth General

Assembly had been "a profound, even alarming disappointment." It had been "repeatedly the scene of acts which we regard as abomination," events "which the United States will never forget." The General Assembly had been "trying to pretend that it is a parliament, which it is not." It was merely a conference made up of delegates from sovereign governments that had agreed to listen to recommendations that were in no way binding. I speculated that the reason why so many delegations had difficulty with the distinction as to what had been consented to and what had not was that "most of the governments represented in the General Assembly do not themselves govern by consent." This made it hard for their representatives to understand principles, such as the delegation of power, that are peculiar to democracies. There were, unhappily, only "28, possibly 29, representative democracies in the world," and one of them, Switzerland, was not a member of the U.N. I suggested that the General Assembly might function better if it organized itself into parliamentary caucuses that reflected the forms of government of the member nations. The democratic caucus would not have many members, but perhaps it might have some success in explicating the Charter to the delegations of nations that, having forsaken democratic procedures themselves, had difficulty grasping that the Charter assumes democratic procedures.

The Assembly sat in silence, save for the Permanent Representative of the Soviet Union. The text of my address had been delivered to the press in the late afternoon. A copy made its way to the Soviet delegation. Shortly before I was to speak, I was told Malik urgently wished to speak to me. We met alone in the delegates' lounge at the back of the Assembly chamber. The Russian was shuddering in agitation. A passage in my text quoted Andrei D. Sakharov. He asked, did I not know that this man was "an enemy of the Soviet people." I replied that I knew nothing of the sort, that I supposed that the Soviet people would be proud of this great physicist who had developed the Soviet hydrogen bomb, and gone on to win, in the very year 1975, the Nobel Peace Prize. Malik asked that I leave out the quote. I said he would see what I would do.

I came to the passage in question, and read it with as much deliberation as I could summon. The United States at the Thirtieth General Assembly had proposed a resolution calling for amnesty for political prisoners everywhere. Perhaps some delegations had not grasped the significance of our proposal; they would be enlightened in the matter by the views of the great Soviet scientist Andrei Sakharov, who had expressed his hope that the principles of peace and human rights would eventually triumph, and who had said on the subject, "The best sign that such hopes can come true would be a general political amnesty in all the world, liberation of all prisoners of conscience everywhere." He had concluded, "The struggle for a general political amnesty is the struggle for the future of mankind." The United States, I declared, had not abandoned that struggle, did not despair of that future. We would be back with our resolution on amnesty.

By this time Malik had walked out.

They, for once, had quit the field. In the final week of the General Assembly the Soviets had had to withdraw a resolution in the face of our scorn, and had to walk out of the Assembly itself as they could not bear our contempt. Two days later Tass denounced me as "a very eccentric person capable of shocking even diplomats who had seen a lot in their lifetime." For which read Yakov A. Malik, who having lived his life in a world of lies, had fled before the truth.

———◆———

If he had known the half of it. It may well have been, as Adam Ulam would write a few months later, that "the Soviet Union . . . under Brezhnev achieved . . . the leading, if not yet the dominant position in world politics." Yet this was more the consequence of failures on the part of the democracies than of any success of the Soviet Union. Malik's land had become a vast prison in which escape had become the principal object in life for extraordinary numbers of persons who might be assumed to be the most loyal to the regime. The grandchild of Malik's patron Stalin had been born a citizen of the United States after Stalin's daughter herself had escaped. As is now known, before I left the U.N., Shevchenko, in effect Malik's second-in-command, had begun to have doubts. How ideological was his defection I could not then tell. But it should have been no occasion for "consternation" in the U.N. Secretariat.

During World War II, inside information was making its way around Bloomsbury that the American troops then arriving in Britain had been sent in anticipation of a general strike, rather than for purposes of invading the continent. Orwell remarked that one had to have gone to a university to believe that; that any taxi driver knew it wasn't so. By 1975 ordinary people around the world knew the Soviet Union was a hateful and hated regime: only persons of privilege could avoid this uncomfortable reality.

12

Time to Go

AND SO, in a sense, it did not end badly. Over the months we had developed a technique of making it more costly to attack the United States than had been the case. Two days before the end of the session the Ambassador of Mauritius, R. K. Ramphul, said of me that the other delegates "lived in positive dread of his manners, his language and his abuse." Allowing for a certain defensiveness on my part, I suggest that this translates as a protest that we had made the General Assembly a somewhat dangerous place for *them,* a place where an unexamined routine of going along with the Non-Aligned while the Non-Aligned went along with the Russians could get an ambassador in trouble. Ramphul was cited that evening by Robert MacNeil in a television interview with Thorn and Richard. MacNeil asked: "Is the approach to the U.N. based on what is called combative rhetoric actually hurting the institution . . . ?" Thorn took the reference, of course, and said that like (the now somewhat chastened) Richard, he did not wish to comment about me personally, "But I think Mr. Moynihan gave a certain signal: Stop there, and let's discuss, let's face the truth. I think that was helpful."

If the delegates lived in "positive dread," some managed even so to overcome it. As the session closed there was a succession of overtures from various Missions suggesting that it would be helpful if the United States kept more closely in touch in the coming year with a view to a more harmonious Thirty-First General Assembly. On the day after Thorn's statement, this being now the next-to-last day of the Assembly, the Chinese made something of a point of giving a luncheon for me at their Mission. Huang Hua, as far as I could tell (which was not far), was troubled that the Chinese seemed never able to best the Soviets in any direct encounter at the U.N. Nations such as Tanzania, where the Chinese might have expected to have influence, routinely backed the Soviets against them. If the Ambassador of Mauritius dreaded my performance, the Ambassador of China rather welcomed it. ("Not bad," he later said to Theodore H. White. "Apart from the Africans, not bad.")

We never sided with the Chinese. My object was simply to use every possible occasion to draw attention to what the Chinese said about "that power which styles itself socialist." In doing so I was not always up to the rigors of the Chinese postrevisionism. In August, first in a Peking newspaper and then in the Party's theoretical journal, *Red Flag,* Mao had launched a campaign against one Sung Chiang, hero of the sixteenth-century novel *Water Margin,* an account of a peasant rebellion. For reasons none could divine then (nor any since), Sung Chiang was criticized for "capitulationism," and a great agitation ensued. In this spirit, I tried to make my own contribution. In the Security Council one evening, Malik, replying to a discourse I had delivered on totalitarianism, warned against the dangers of "gangsterism." I replied,

> Mr. President, it is time for an element of seriousness in this proceeding. Totalitarianism is bad, gangsterism is worse; but as my distinguished colleague and friend from the Soviet Union must no doubt agree, capitulationism is worst of all, a prospect which one must be careful to avoid and in fact which I do not propose to succumb to.

A solemn second secretary of the Chinese delegation thereupon waited on me to explain that I hadn't grasped the essentials of "capitulationism." When I asked what these were, he would not say. But when I asked whether he did not agree that the Soviets were guilty of capitulationism, he quite agreed. Even so, I slacked off criticism of Sung Chiang.

If Ivor Richard was muted by this time, it was not just the humiliation of having been exposed as a running dog of American imperialism. We had begun to make an impression on public opinion in Europe. It was hard to measure, but letters and clippings began to come in, many sent by Foreign Service officers in various capitals. (Some came from the U.S. Foreign Service itself. Four young men in the Moscow Embassy signed a letter of remarkable good cheer and encouragement.) In Norway and Holland especially, there seems to have been some public stirring, while in Britain our cause was taken up by Tories on the one hand and social democrats on the other, a combination very like that in New York.

◆

Things in Washington got better. In a letter of November 5, the Secretary gave notice of our intention to withdraw from the International Labor Organization. The letter, which I drafted, was explicit in saying that we had no expectation of actually doing so, nor had we any illusion that we could ever "restore the world of 1919 or 1944." But on the matter of pretending that a government-controlled trade union or employers' association was not in fact government-controlled, we would not yield. On this point, we felt, the I.L.O. simply had to keep to the obligations of its Charter. By giving notice, we would be able to resume our payment of dues (the Congress would agree to that) while at the same time setting a two-year period in which the organization could reasonably be expected to respond.

It seemed to me that the one critical advantage we had over the totalitarian powers in these matters was that all the basic charters of the international organizations to which we belonged were, in this sense, with us and against them. The more we insisted on the integrity of these charters, the less we might expect to see such organizations turned against us.

In mid-December the President nominated Samuel W. Lewis, a career officer of the first quality, as Assistant Secretary of State for International Organization Affairs. A small office was created in his division to carry out the matching of bilateral relations with activities at the U.N. along the lines we had proposed in our paper the previous August. Lewis took hold directly, and the new year looked bright enough.

Our argument was in fact making itself felt in the Department better than we knew. Early in January a front page story by Leslie Gelb in *The New York Times* reported, "U.S. Linking Aid to Votes at U.N. Kissinger Reported to Aim Punitive Cuts at Nations Aiding Hostile Stands." This was described as a new policy arising out of my *Commentary* article and out of Kissinger's "long held belief that when nations acted against important interests of the United States on issues that were extraneous

to their own interests, the Administration should take a stern line." The
Secretary, it was reported, had already postponed aid agreements with
Tanzania and Guyana. Other nations such as Malawi and the Ivory
Coast would be given additional aid. Gelb made clear that the Department official who "disclosed this information to The New York Times
very much disapproved of the new policy." He called the policy "no
more than a 'zap list' to punish small countries and do nothing about
others like Egypt that were also voting against the United States." Not a
man one would want to be with in an alley fight. Still, another official
got it straight. Gelb quoted him as saying, "If bilateral concerns aren't
overriding like Middle East peace talks we have to do something tangible
to them to show that their opposition to us is not cost-free." This is all
we had asked in our August paper.

A few days after the Gelb story a cable from Khartoum reported that
at an Afro-Arab symposium on liberation and development, Tanzania
had stated that the United States had suspended $28 million in aid
because of Tanzania's "unhelpful" voting record at the last General
Assembly. The Tanzanian representative urged the meeting to take a
stand specifically condemning the United States for such "pressure
tactics." But seemingly other Africans wanted no direct confrontation.
A final communiqué condemned pressure exercised by "any power"
against countries confronting "colonialism, Zionism and racial discrimination." Again, this was all we wished. Let the Tanzanians get
their aid from the same capitals from which they got their politics. Let
the Ivory Coast know that we valued friends.

This development hugely upset Father Theodore M. Hesburgh. In an
article on *The New York Times* Op-Ed page, he ascribed the new policy
to me, and condemned it as "both immoral and counterproductive."

But even *The Times* could see our point. A long lead editorial of
December 21 talked of "the First World's future." It began by recalling
the optimism of the time when Woodrow Wilson had proposed "to make
the world safe for democracy," and when Americans had thought that
"government of, by and for the people was so irresistibly contagious that
the oppressed in other nations would readily throw off their bonds and
join in the benefits of life, liberty and the pursuit of happiness. Whilst
this rhetoric survives, it is clearly no longer pertinent to global realities."
The editorial then recalled my statement at the close of the Thirtieth
General Assembly that there were now only some twenty-nine representative democracies still functioning. From there on it all but repeated,
one by one, the arguments I had been making all year long:

> The future safety of the democracies does not depend on their ca-
> pacity to convert other nations but on the realistic recognition that

they will constitute a minority among the community of nations for the foreseeable future. The collapse of democracy in India underscores this unpleasant reality. So did the impotence of the democracies to stem the tide of the fraudulent anti-Zionist resolution in the United Nations General Assembly. . . .

That democracy is neither the dominant ideology today nor likely to be the wave of the immediate future is cause neither for despair nor for surrender. The democracies need to act effectively as a purposeful minority with common goals and forge a stronger coalition of mutual support than any now existing if they are to retain their vitality and assure their survival.

The only visible cloud, no bigger than a man's hand, was a James B. Reston column in *The Times*. Around Christmastime before a presidential election, he observed, the political world of Washington begins to turn over. Now once again the old order was collapsing. Mansfield and Scott were leaving the Senate; Albert was leaving the House; the President had dismissed his Secretary of Defense and the director of the CIA; and, "it is not at all sure that Secretary of State Kissinger, faced with a charge of contempt of Congress, will agree to go on and allow himself and his policies to be issues in the Presidential campaign." The President was not controlling his people, and officials were arguing their own personal views in public, as Schlesinger and Colby had done:

> So the Ford Administration is in trouble, not only with the Congress but with its own colleagues, and with its own policies in the United Nations. It appointed Pat Moynihan as its ambassador to the U.N., because Pat insisted that the time had come to defend America's interests against the unfair and even outrageous anti-American challenges of Moscow, Peking and the third-world spokesmen. And Moynihan has been faithful to his promises.
>
> He has not only defended the interests of his country, but in the process has provoked the Soviets, affronted the European allies, and outraged the Secretary General of the United Nations and the new nations of the third world.
>
> This troubles the President and Secretary of State Kissinger. They think he has gone too far, but they are not in control in an election year. After firing Mr. Schlesinger for being too tough on the Soviets, they couldn't be too hard on Mr. Moynihan, without giving Ronald Reagan of California a compelling argument in the coming Presidential election.

The view attributed to Waldheim occasioned the thought that the Secretary-General had not felt free to reveal his true feelings until after I had voted to give him a new term. But the remark about the President

and Kissinger had to be taken seriously. It was too familiar. The
Secretary wondering whether he should not resign. The Secretary worrying that I had outraged the Secretary-General. The Secretary regretting
to the liberal columnist that he faced such unfair opposition from conservatives that liberalism itself might be in danger.

———◆———

The new year began with a Security Council debate on the Middle
East that went on the whole of January. It was an intense period of late
nights, hurried meetings, urgent telephone calls, and painfully con-
structed texts, which at the same time was all rather impersonal. I
became once more the representative of the Secretary of State and the
President, acting upon, having first insisted upon, minutely detailed
instructions. It was not an especially happy time. Things did not go well
for Israel, and, except for the United States, all the world seemingly
combined to make them go worse. This left the Israelis with only us to
turn to, and we were never able to do all they wanted.

The January debate had been agreed to on the previous November
30 in the course of a Security Council session devoted to renewing the
mandate of the United Nations Disengagement Observer Force on the
Syrian-Israeli border. The Israelis always agreed to renewing these
arrangements. In the hope of extracting some advantage, the Arabs
always held them up until the last moment. This time the Syrians insisted as a condition that the Palestine Liberation Organization participate in the debate. The Israelis were alarmed, as they might have been.
At the same time the U.N. was chipping away at the legitimacy of the
State of Israel, all but declaring it an illegal entity, the P.L.O. was beginning to be treated as a legal government.

I grew apprehensive myself as Washington began to be steadily more
vague as to just how I should respond to the Syrian demand. Kissinger
chose the moment to leave town, pleading the necessity (as I saw it) to
accompany the President on a visit to Peking. For the first time I was
asking for instructions and not getting them. Equally for the first time,
I began being difficult with the Department, insisting that I talk with
Kissinger. At midday on the thirtieth he called from Alaska, where the
President's plane was refueling. I explained that it seemed likely that we
could eliminate any invitation to the P.L.O. from the resolution itself.
He replied that in that case we could go along with a statement by the
Security Council President, but I should insist that this not be portrayed
as a consensus of the Council, and that we were not part of the majority
that supported it. I was to tell Herzog that at least we had eliminated the
references to General Assembly resolutions, which we had done. I was

further to tell him that there was no disagreement between the United
States and Israel, that we did not want the Security Council to become a
principal negotiating forum any more than they did. I asked that these
instructions be sent me in writing, and he duly sent a cable with the
extra notation that the instructions had been "reviewed" by the President. It arrived late in the evening and reached me at dinner with
Garment and Herzog. He, and Garment for that matter, felt we were
giving away much too much, and getting nothing in return. In his view
the Syrians were trying to discredit the Sinai agreement, showing that
they bargained harder than the Egyptians and got more. As midnight
came and the UNDOF agreement expired, the Security Council agreed
to its renewal and Malik said that it was the "understanding of the
majority" that the P.L.O. would be invited to participate in the January
debate. I responded that the United States "does not support the statement of the Council President," and that in any event the statement
"did not report a decision but was merely a summation of the view of
some members. . . ."

The question was clearly procedural and not substantive, and therefore not subject to a veto. Nor to a "double veto," that mysterious rite
of early Security Council procedure whereby the question as to whether
a question was substantive was itself considered substantive. But the
Israelis, seeing what was at stake, chose not to be reasonable. The reaction in Jerusalem was bitterness shading into panic. In the Knesset,
Prime Minister Yitzhak Rabin solemnly regretted that we had not
diagnosed the character of the Syrian proposal, which, he said, was
"incompatible not only with the needs of Israel, but with the declared
policy of the United States." Israel, he said, would not participate in
the January debate. In the United States anxiety began to rise that the
administration knew well enough what it was doing, which of course
was Rabin's intended message.

A shift was taking place in the focus of Arab-Israeli peacemaking
efforts. The issue of boundaries was receding, while the issue that had
been central all along, that of the future of the Palestinian Arabs, was
coming to the fore. Strictly speaking, this was a mark of progress, but
the appearance was of events worsening, and the United States could do
little to prevent this appearance, for American opinion was much less
supportive of Israel on this matter than it had been when the issue
seemed to be that of Israel's survival. A *Times* editorial on December 2
stated that the Israeli decision not to participate in the January debate
because of the P.L.O.'s presence was "short-sighted and contrary to
Israel's longer-term interests." An editorial of December 10 took comfort
in a joint communiqué issued at the conclusion of Yasir Arafat's then-
recent talks with the Soviet leadership in Moscow, and in the further

report that "At least eight members of . . . Rabin's . . . Cabinet . . . believe the time has come to ease into a more constructive and forthcoming posture."

———◆———

The Israelis did not despair too long. On the same day he spoke so regretfully in the Knesset, Rabin sent off Israeli planes to attack Palestinian camps in southern Lebanon, and killed fifty-seven persons in the process, the heaviest reported death toll in such a sortie in a year and one half. Egypt had to respond, and, with Lebanon, called for an immediate Security Council meeting, further insisting that the P.L.O. should participate. In the Council Guyana, Iraq, Mauritania, Cameroon, and Tanzania put forward this proposal. On their behalf, Richard, who was President of the Council, stated, as was required of him, that the five proposers wished to record that if their proposal was adopted the invitation to the P.L.O. would not be extended under the Council rule that provided for participation of Secretariat officials, private persons, and representatives of non-state entities such as "national liberation movements." Rather, "the invitation to the Palestine Liberation Organization to participate in this debate will confer on it the same rights of participation as are conferred when a Member State is invited to participate. . . ."

This was a blow. (Which the Israelis might have thought about before they flew off to bomb villages where the terrorists deliberately mixed themselves with completely noninvolved Palestinian refugees and plain Lebanese.) I spoke as strongly as I had ever done in the Council, pointing out that the P.L.O. categorically rejected Resolution 242 of the Council itself, which was the only agreed-on basis for serious peace negotiations, and that in such circumstances the invitation as proposed would repudiate the Council itself. I urged "all who share the hope for a just peace . . . to withhold their support from this egregious attempt to use this body to deal with an amorphous terrorist organization as though it were a concrete entity with the attributes of a sovereign government."

We lost on the proposal for P.L.O. participation. Under Council rules, nine votes (out of fifteen) constitute a majority. The United States, Britain, and Costa Rica voted "No." France, Italy, and Japan abstained. But Sweden abandoned us, and the proposal was adopted. I went over to the Swedish Ambassador and said that I did not envy him his Prime Minister. He did not disagree.

I stated that while the United States would "neither condone nor excuse" the Israeli air attacks, we insisted that any resolution denounce all acts of violence in the Middle East, and not merely those of one nation. The resolution of the five nations condemned only Israel, expressing a "solemn warning: that a repetition of such acts of violence would bring U.N. sanctions." I twice tried to amend it and failed, and we finally vetoed it. Costa Rica abstained, but every other Council member was against us. The *Times* editorial noted that on the final vote even Britain and France "cast all pretense of fairness aside." The same day, in the General Assembly, a similar resolution was passed by a vote of 97 to 3, with 27 abstentions. Only the United States and Nicaragua were prepared to vote with Israel against an utterly one-sided condemnation. The news event of the week was the photograph of Mr. Basel Amin Aql of the Palestine Liberation Organization seated at the Security Council table.

-----◆-----

The following January 7, Allon, who was Deputy Prime Minister as well as Foreign Minister, arrived in Washington to work out with us a strategy for the formal Security Council debate, which was to begin January 12. Allon, who appeared vague to some, seemed to me the most attractive of the Israeli leaders, a gentle man, an intellectual. Kissinger gave him almost the whole of his day and I tagged along, intermittently the center of attention, for it was I who would do the speaking, and not only for my own country but for the Israelis also.

Even so I felt a certain detachment. Whatever I said, it would be something the others had agreed to. More remarkable, however, was the sense of detachment Kissinger conveyed. He was not going to back the Israelis as they wished. He did not much want to talk about details. He did not, in fact, very much want to talk. Allon must have sensed this. At lunch, with about a dozen persons around the table, he asked about the situation in the world generally. Kissinger commenced a remarkable *tour d'horizon*, happy no doubt to leave the Middle East, but with the air also of someone who sensed that his own departure was now at hand. The fundamental question in the world, he stated, was the declining authority of the American executive. Vietnam and Watergate had done great damage to the presidency. And then there were the Jewish intellectuals who thought that a weak executive ensured support for Israel. (This was a repeated theme of his talk at this time, but also the familiar tactic; telling the Israelis that he would have to restrain their friends or, better, they should do so themselves, in order that he might better protect them from their enemies.) Power, he continued, is the basis of foreign policy; only a country with power can have a foreign policy based on morality, because only such a country has choices. (For which read, a weakened United States could not now behave as responsibly in the Middle East as it once would have done.) Assad had said to him: "You sold out Vietnam and Cambodia, why should we not suppose that you will also sell out Israel?"

Perhaps Kissinger wondered if he had overreached with the last remark, or perhaps the thought led him on. He began to talk of Nixon as I had rarely heard him do. Nixon had been the master of the use of force, which was to use it suddenly. *Never* to use it by increments, as his predecessors had done in Vietnam. Nixon could persuade the other side that *he* might go crazy, too. But all this was past. The American executive would never again be able to say to Israel, as it had said the first Tuesday of the Yom Kippur war: Use all your ammunition; we will replace it. The Soviets had clearly demonstrated our weakness by their move in Angola. They would follow it with a peace offensive. A sufficient number would be duped.

He commenced to talk of old battles. September, 1970. *There* was crisis management. Syria had sent tanks into Lebanon. Immediately, we sent a carrier plane from the Sixth Fleet to Tel Aviv to pick up targeting information. An airborne brigade at Fort Bragg was put on the alert. One of our divisions in Germany was moved to the nearest airport. The Israelis had said to us, remember that if *we* fight, we fight to win. Rogers had told him that if there was a war, "It is on your head." The Soviets were neutralized. The Syrians withdrew. All that was past now. Ambiguity was the essence of crisis management; but with the War Powers Act, for which Senator Jacob Javits was responsible, the President could never again be ambiguous.

At this point the Israelis interrupted. At very least they would have wished to forestall any further elaboration on the theme that the leading Jewish Senator was the man responsible for the fact that the United States could not now be of much assistance to Israel. They had, after all, been dealing with Kissinger for a full seven years now. But they also seemed absorbed by the technical point he had raised. Allon asked if, for example, the President would have to inform the Congress if he moved a carrier from one place to another in a manner meant to convey a readiness to fight, as Nixon and Kissinger had done in 1970.

I now resumed for our side. I said I was probably even more pessimistic about the West than the Secretary was, but that I was also more cheered than he was by the newly assertive movement in intellectual milieux, reflected by *Commentary* and other journals. I spoke as someone identified with and in the service of the Secretary's views. It seemed to me that far the greater intellectual force was with our position, but that unfortunately it would be at least a decade before this position would be accepted as a response to a new situation, rather than a discredited legacy of the past. At this point Kissinger evidently sensed that I was trying to identify him with my own views. Or else he remembered that he was not a hawk, but a peacemaker. He became challenging, even acerbic, insisting that the antidétente forces — *Commentary?* his U.N. Ambassador? — had no alternative policy to offer. So much for my attempted display of unity in the company of friendly foreigners.

This brought conversation to an end, and we got back to the Security Council. The Israelis had no serious proposals, no thoughts even. The U.N., as they might say, was dead to them. They confined their responses to a narrow range between indifference and defiance. I argued that the first fact was that we were going to end up vetoing any resolution that would conceivably emerge from the debate. Accordingly we should make this clear from the outset, to reduce any suspense, and to minimize the importance of the exercise itself. Then we should move directly to the central element of the issue the Soviets and the Arabs had introduced, which was the character of the Palestine Liberation Organization. As no one had a better idea, this was agreed to.

———◆———

It had seemed to me that this was something I *could* contribute to the Middle East debate. In the preceding months we had established an expectation that in U.N. debates we would make continued reference to the liberal principles of the Charter and would measure the performance of various governments, and the governments themselves, against those principles. The time had come to do this to the P.L.O., especially as it was commencing to be treated as if it were a government. I put this proposition to Podhoretz, who began documenting the case with a *furor scribendi*. For in truth this *was* the central issue. What was the P.L.O.? Who were its leaders? How did they get that way? The answer was that the P.L.O. was a group of well-financed leftist totalitarian terrorists whose claim to be the legitimate representatives of the Palestine people was based on the same antidemocratic theory of revolutionary elites on which the totalitarian governments of our time base their own claim to legitimacy. The P.L.O., however, suffered the disability of not controlling any territory, and the further onus of having rejected Security Council resolutions 242 and 238, to which even the totalitarian powers were committed as a basis for peace in the Middle East.

I warmed to the subject, but Kissinger cooled. We met again in Washington on January 9. He said we must give the Arabs hope that if the P.L.O. recognized and accepted Resolution 242, they would be accepted by the United States. He said the P.L.O. threat was the only incentive Israel had to deal with the West Bank issue. He began almost to rage against the Israelis. Four kilometers! he said, four kilometers would have got them a settlement with Jordan. Which four kilometers I did not know, and felt it would seem ignorant to ask. He then remembered himself, and allowed that the P.L.O. was a "copout" for Arab governments who could themselves move on the Middle East. His main concern in the debate was to support the Vladivostok formula. (This called for a settlement taking into account "the legitimate interests of all peoples in the area including the Palestinian people, and for the right of all the states of the area to independent existence." It envisaged that the Geneva Conference would play an "important" part in the establishment of a just and lasting peace in the area.) If I could get a resolution which reaffirmed resolutions 242 and 238 and called for the resumption of the Geneva Peace Conference, it would be all right to include the P.L.O. in the letter of invitation. It would be all right to have the P.L.O. take part in the debate under Rule 39, which provided for participation of national liberation movements. Better yet, was there any way to put off the whole thing?

This was Kissinger at the outset of his final year in office. Exasperated with everyone, but then catching himself, usually in time. He would rage against the Israelis one moment; the next moment declare that to force them back to the 1967 borders was to leave them in the condition of Czechoslovakia after Munich. Where I was concerned, the greater problem was inattention. He had only to give a very little thought to what was required to keep things steady; only to resist a very few temptations, which he'd already indulged sufficiently for a lifetime anyway. But he did not, and the point is that he probably didn't notice that he didn't.

On January 10, with Garment and Weaver on hand, I wrote a long, intense speech. The theme was the significance of procedure, not simply to the freedom of individuals but to the security of nations. When President Ford had spoken at the U.N. of the "tyranny of the majority," he spoke from two centuries of American experience of the tension between the rule of law and the rule of the majority. "Ours, we asserted, was to be a government of laws, not of men. And yet we also asserted that our decisions would be made by a majority of men." Thus had begun our concern that the majority, rather than sustaining the rules of the society, would commence to change them at random, and would end by depriving the minority of its rights. This made for injustice in the short run, but perhaps worse, in the long run it made for the collapse of the political system, "for sooner or later almost everyone would find himself in the minority and experience the reality that the system was not just, was not to be depended on." The number who could be depended on to defend the system would diminish and in the end the system would disappear. That is why Americans placed such importance on procedure, and why in our view the great issue before the Council was the integrity of its procedures. We had seen the decline of the authority of the General Assembly. We were beginning to see the same sequence in the Security Council. The majority of the Council was forcing its will on the minority in clear violation of our rules. There was no problem about the P.L.O. appearing before us. There were rules that provided for that. But for it to appear and participate with the same rights as are conferred when a member state is invited to participate would debauch both our procedures and the truth, and there would be consequences. The draft proceeded to elaborate them:

> It was the distinguished representative of Iraq, who . . . first advocated the formula for P.L.O. participation in this debate which is now cited as a precedent. Would the Representative of Iraq wish us to accord the same stature to representatives of the Kurdish National Movement, a band of brave men and women who defend with passion and conviction their assertion of claims to ancestral lands against the incursion and domination of wholly alien peoples representing governments which persecute them in horrendous ways, a struggle that has been waged since before there were Moslems in the Middle East, indeed since before there were Christians? . . .
>
> To suggest the chaos which would descend upon this organization, and the world which it represents, if the Security Council were to abandon the distinction as to what is and what is not a Member State is not at all to argue for an inflexible and frozen international system, dedicated to preserving the status quo interests of existing governments. The experience of the United Nations argues the very opposite. Through thirty years we have with tolerable consistency maintained the rule that this is an organization made up of sovereign and independent states, whilst at the same time this same organization has presided over the creation of an unprecedented number of new states. . . .
>
> . . . As the end of the First World War approached, . . . an American President proposed that the peace settlement be based on an entirely new principle, that of self-determination. It was he who proclaimed this Western concept, and at his initiative that it became enshrined, however imperfectly, in the Peace Settlement and in the Covenant of the League of Nations. It was from the vision of this American President that the state system of the Middle East arose. . . .
>
> What we understand by national self-determination may be achieved through a variety of political instrumentalities, but the one way it cannot be achieved is through the imposition upon a people of leadership

by outside forces. We would say, again not without hope of being heeded, that self-determination is a democratic idea. It is an idea based on law, on procedure, on consent. . . .

The Palestine Liberation Organization is not a state; it does not pretend to be a state. For the most elemental of reasons, only Member States can participate in our proceedings as Member States. Unless, of course, we change the rules, whereupon we shall look forward to welcoming the dissident factions and nationalities of half the world. . . .

———◆———

The text was cabled to Washington that Saturday afternoon. Sunday afternoon, Sam Lewis, the new Assistant Secretary for International Organization Affairs, called to say that Kissinger felt it was much too much of a blast to start off with. It was too soon in the debate to introduce substantive material. (Whatever that meant.) It was not wise to take on the majority/minority issue. Above all, I was not to "hit the Russians in any way, shape or form." On Monday morning Under Secretary for Political Affairs Joseph Sisco called to say that the Secretary felt my text would start a brawl with everybody, that he didn't want a broadside against the General Assembly and the Security Council, that it was not compatible with our long-range strategy of keeping a crack in the door for us. (Whatever *that* meant.) I was sent back the usual language, which I delivered dutifully enough that afternoon. Across United Nations Plaza, Herzog warned that the Council was laying the groundwork for a new Middle East war. On January twenty-sixth the predictable resolution came forward, and I cast my veto.

———◆———

There was not much point in all this. Had Kissinger and I been back in Cambridge we would have lived in cheerful disagreement, and in the process would have taught some graduate students a thing or two. But in government we were supposed to work together, not simply to argue. The problem was that we knew different things. What had Woodrow Wilson signified to the Europe in which Kissinger was born save a peace treaty that led directly to another war, and a doctrine of self-determination that aroused ethnic passions to the point where his own people, the Jews of Germany, were all but destroyed? How could he not admire what Metternich had done in the only comparable situation history had to offer?

A few weeks before this, in a talk to a closed meeting of American ambassadors in London, Helmut Sonnenfeldt, Counselor to the State Department, had remarked how much it was to be regretted that the

Soviets were still so inept in their role as an emergent "super power on a global scale." He explained, "They have not brought [to it] the ideological, legal, cultural, architectural, organizational and other values and skills that characterized the British, French and German adventures." Alas also, "the Soviets' inability to acquire loyalty in Eastern Europe is an unfortunate historical failure. . . ." Accordingly, we must help. "We seek to influence the emergence of the Soviet imperial power by making the base in Eastern Europe more natural and organic, so that it will not remain founded in sheer power alone. . . ."

So much for the Poles, the Hungarians, the Czechoslovaks.

This is what Kissinger knew, and Sonnenfeldt and men whose roots were still in Europe knew. I knew little of this. I was forty before I had any real idea what Burke was about; Kissinger knew in his cradle. On the other hand, I knew what Wilson was all about. I knew what Rebecca West had written of Versailles, that to the new nations it was deliverance. I knew that the world over, and especially in the new countries, it was a tie we had, a claim we had, that could be put to our purposes. And *at that moment* what I knew was perhaps more important than what Kissinger knew. If it were true that governments must proceed from the coldest calculations of power, then what was to become of the United States, whose executive power, by his own testimony, was shattered? What could be done? To commence to negotiate a decent interval for the West itself?

(The Russians gave nothing in return. Save contempt. In January of 1976 Kissinger and Sonnenfeldt arrived in Moscow to negotiate a nuclear arms pact. At a joint press conference Kissinger stated that this issue would be linked to Soviet withdrawal of Cuban troops from Angola. The Russians stated there would be no such item on the agenda, which had to be mutually agreed upon. Kissinger pressed. Brezhnev put him in the place reserved for the representatives of weak or foolish powers: "I have no questions about Angola," he said. "Angola is not my country." Kissinger interposed: "It will certainly be discussed." Brezhnev concluded the matter: "You'll discuss it with Sonnenfeldt. That will ensure complete agreement.")

In the midst of the Security Council debate I had lunch with Edouard Ghorra, the Permanent Representative of Lebanon, a man of great gentleness and transparent goodness, now in utter torment as the Russians, through the Syrians and the P.L.O., went about the destruction of Lebanese government and society. It was not that the Russians intended this; it was just that, as the Indians say, when elephants fight, the grass gets trampled. But our elephant wasn't even fighting. In October the first reports had come of significant amounts of Soviet aid to leftist forces through the Lebanese Communist Party. At the end of that month the State Department warned against outside interference in Lebanon, but the spokesman added that the United States was giving "absolutely no consideration" to military intervention. No carrier flights to Tel Aviv. No airborne troops alerted. Just a warning, which might as well have been an invitation for the Syrian invasion which would come shortly now. Ghorra asked if there was any hope of American help. I said there was none.

◆

This could read as if, were the choice mine, I would have been sending carriers into the eastern Mediterranean. I would not have. Even if it had been a good idea, it was beyond the range of any action the American public would any longer accept. Nor was I waiting for memories to fade and things to settle down so we could start up the shooting again. I had steadfastly (from 1965 on, not as early as Glazer and Riesman, but in time) thought that the Vietnam war was a calamity, and had said so to three Presidents. But I wanted us to show our colors even so, to argue back. This is a form of resistance, even of offensive. It is not the least dangerous weapon a nation can wield. But I suppose it seemed pale, after the *real* thing. After *real* power.

◆

Harvard had given me only a semester's leave, and that over the protest of Alan Pifer of the Carnegie Corporation of New York, who was an important overseer. My leave would be up February 1, and that would be it. When Pifer had first made trouble in the spring of 1975, he was opposed even to granting a semester's leave, and I had proposed to President Derek Bok that I depart then and there; but Bok thought he could handle the board, as indeed he did. This in itself was sign of change. At the end of Nixon's first term there was much talk of Kissinger returning to Harvard, but Bok would not have it for fear of the student reaction. Better by far that Harvard presidents should now be worrying mainly about their overseers. Even so, I had had more than my share of leave, and it was made clear that either I returned to Cambridge February first or not at all. I decided to stay in New York.

On January 9, in Washington, after finishing our talk on the Middle East debate, I told Kissinger I would leave Harvard. It had been a wrench for him to do so, and in truth his chair had been kept open far past the normal deadline. Next to great wealth, a chair in the Harvard Department of Government was possibly the most important security a man could have in Washington. There were few posts there with greater prestige, and a professorship had the advantage of being for life. It was a guarantor, also, that one's next book would be prominently enough published, and that a generation or so of young persons would in this manner come to know who had done well and who had done badly during those Washington years. My dilemma was that the only way to continue working for the Secretary of State was to give up the Harvard chair, yet giving up the chair would ineluctably alter our working relationship. I would no longer be an equal. I would have no real alternative to the job I held as his gift, or such at least would have to be his view. He knew that; and I knew it; and he knew that I knew. He would not be able to help himself. As if almost to acknowledge what would come, he said he thought I should run for the Senate. For he was a friend, and I think sometimes hated what he did. He was a good man, in a bad time.

So was Gerald Ford. There was more good in him than in any of the rest of us. But he was not a good butcher, as Kissinger knew a President must be.

I went off to dinner with John A. Dunlop, Secretary of Labor, who told me he was going to resign and go back to the Harvard Department of Economics. He had brought off an agreement between the building trade unions and the industry that had eluded other Secretaries of Labor for a generation. The A.F.L.-C.I.O. felt seriously in debt to the Republican administration for having achieved this. But now Ford, under pressure from the right-to-work lobbyists, was going back on his agreement to support the enacting legislation. Something in his background, too many years in the minority in the House of Representatives, too long a time with no thought of anything else, inhibited him as a presidential candidate. The support of labor, or even its neutrality, was far more important than the support of right-to-work committees. But Ford did not see this, and Dunlop was left with no choice save to resign, which he now told me he would do. John Dunlop, unknown to fear, secure in a lifetime's reputation, was leaving. An hour earlier I had told Henry Kissinger I was staying. I ended the evening feeling I had done something more appropriate to a twenty-year-old.

◆

Even so, on January 27, the first occasion thereafter that I saw the President, I said once again that I would stay at the U.N. I afterward wrote a memorandum of conversation that was considerably fuller than usual, attesting to the quietness of the time and also I think to a certain quietness in my own mind:

> I met with the President at 4:30 P.M. on January 27, 1976, for some forty minutes. General Scowcroft was present most of the time, and Mr. Cheney all the time.

The first business was filming a segment for a documentary on the Cabinet. I reported on the outcome of the Middle East debate in the Security Council, which, I said, was on balance quite positive, certainly civil. At the end of our meeting I said to the President that in my view it was now up to the Israelis to take some initiatives toward peace, and some resolution of the problem which the PLO now constituted for them. We had represented them well, even successfully, in the Security Council, but they could not let the matter drop there. It was their turn to show some movement. I would say so to Rabin this week. The President agreed but asked that I be careful in the way I put it. . . .

I asked if Angola should not be brought up at the Security Council. I said I feel like Carl Albert, who that day in the *Washington Post* was recorded as saying he knew nothing of Angola. The President said he was briefed on all covert matters. I said I knew all about covert operations because I read the papers, but otherwise knew nothing. The President said we had been winning there. I said that I did not believe this. That I had sat in that room and in the Cabinet room over too many years hearing people tell us that we were winning in some jungle war. No average citizen would believe it anymore. I said in any event no one was going to beat the Cubans there. Scowcroft agreed that once the Cubans arrived we stopped winning. I said the Congress simply had not been given an account of the event that could elicit its support. This was a misuse of the Presidency. It was like sending a carrier into Tokyo Bay in 1942 alone. He needed to have the case expounded. He said that when these Congressmen had voted against Angola their record would be clear. I said: "Mr. President, you want to attack Congressmen. I want to attack Russians."

I said to the President that my leave at Harvard expired this week, and that while it meant more to me than anything save my family, I would give up my professorship and stay on in the Administration through the primaries and the convention, as I did not want to do anything to hurt him. I said it may or may not be true as the *Wall Street Journal* put it that I was the most popular member of his administration, but I certainly didn't want to give any ammunition to Reagan who was constantly invoking my name. I noted that I had said I would stay on to Secretary Kissinger at a meeting we had on January 9. With Scowcroft out of the room I said that there really wasn't any other point in my staying on, as I was completely cut out of policy, and would remain so. There was nothing I could do about it and nothing he could do about it. The President did not disagree. . . .

———◆———

On leaving the President I was given a note to call Leslie Gelb at *The New York Times*'s Washington office, which I did from the White House lobby. Gelb had obtained a copy of a long year-end cable I had sent four days earlier, on January 23. Such cables are part of the routine of any embassy. In our case a half-dozen or so went out each January, summarizing the events of the previous twelve months with respect to various subjects and various regions. I had written a summary "brief essay" entitled "The Blocs Are Breaking Up." The previous spring Kissinger had set forth the policy of breaking up the Non-Aligned. The cable argued that we had had some success in this at the Thirtieth General Assembly, and would have more if we got more support from embassies around the world, to which I asked that the cable be sent. This was well enough received, in Washington at least. On January 24, Assistant Secretary Lewis had written to express appreciation for the "useful arguments." On January 26, Deputy Under Secretary Eagleburger had called to express his general agreement, and asked to make one small change before sending it to all capitals. (In February Lewis sent the Secretary a long memorandum that argued that indeed the blocs were breaking up, that the extraordinary solidarity of the Non-Aligned had reached its peak at the Sixth Special Session in 1974, and there was nowhere to go from there but down. *"The logic of the situation,"* he concluded, *"therefore is with us."*) I had not given the cable a high classification, as I wanted it to get around the government. What I did not anticipate was that anyone else would be that interested.

It was front page: "Moynihan Says State Department Fails to Back Policy against U.S. Foes in U.N." *The Times* printed the full text, of which two passages will give a sufficient flavor:

> The tactic, initiated at this mission on the instructions of the President and the Secretary of State, has been to respond to attack by counterattack. A recent article in the London *Times* described us as having "taken the war to the enemy." This was generous, but perhaps inaccurate. Save on a very few issues, such as the proposal of a worldwide amnesty for political prisoners, our position at the United Nations had been reactive. From a distance it may have appeared confrontational but this is simply because the United Nations General Assembly had become the setting of sustained, daily attacks on the United States, such that our counterattacks made it look like all hell was breaking loose up here. Actually we had a normal session which looked abnormal only because we had got into the practice of responding in ways which otherwise would seem quite normal and predictable.
>
> I recall a luncheon early in the fall at which I was asking the Yugoslav Ambassador to try to understand our concern that the Decolonization Committee (The Committee of 24), of which his country is a member, had seemed so determined to launch an insurgency in Puerto Rico by giving official observer status to the Puerto Rican Liberation Movement, which status had already been accorded by the "non-

aligned" at their Lima meeting in August. In the most placatory way I suggested that he certainly would not like the United States to start supporting some Croatian liberation movement at the United Nations. Well he sure wouldn't. He turned purple and started raving about Fascism. In no time our embassy in Belgrade was being asked for an explanation of this outrageous provocation. Fortunately our Ambassador there, Lawrence Silberman, was not about to be intimidated, but it is the fact that the Yugoslav reaction was generally speaking, normal, while our willingness to put up with vastly greater provocations has been singular. . . .

But we do fear that there necessarily remains in the Department a large faction which has an interest in our performance being judged to have failed. This faction has not hesitated to pass this assessment on to the press and to Congress, and to parts of the Department that otherwise would have no view one way or the other. This is bad. for the President's policy which the Secretary strives to carry out. At a time when we have so few allies, and so many of them are slipping into almost irreversible patterns of appeasement based on the assumption that American power is irreversibly declining, we would hope that some brave spirits in Washington and around the world would examine the evidence and that if convinced that things have not gone that badly up here, take some foreign diplomat to lunch and tell him.

The story was of conflict. In New York the next day, which was Wednesday, the President called to say I had his complete confidence. The *Times* headline Thursday, again front page, was "Ford and Kissinger Give Assurances to Moynihan." But this was not quite Gelb's story. There was an "uproar," he wrote. And what is more:

> The reaction from Mr. Kissinger and his department today ran counter to repeated private statements made in the past to numerous reporters by senior officials in the State Department. They have often said over the last year that Mr. Moynihan's outspoken style, which they have frequently characterized as demagoguery, and a campaign for personal power are seriously damaging United States interest in the United Nations.
>
> For example, one senior State Department official told several reporters that the United Nations resolution condemning Zionism as a form of racism would have been defeated if Mr. Moynihan had not "needlessly antagonized" most Africans.

The day went quietly at the Security Council. Then about midnight the Friday *Times* arrived at the Waldorf Towers. A vast editorial was not friendly, but nothing serious. Reston's column, however, was fatal. "What About Moynihan?" it asked:

His long diplomatic dispatch to Mr. Kissinger, complaining that the minor officials of the State Department, but not Kissinger, were opposing his outspoken attacks on the anti-American blocs was a little too clever, and the Secretary's public support of his mission was misleading.

Mr. Kissinger agrees with Moynihan's defense of American interests, but not with his style, his provocative rhetoric, his rambling off-the-cuff debating tactics, his self-concerning appeals to the rest of the U.S. Foreign Service, his vicious attacks on the State Department bureaucracy.

But in the process of Mr. Moynihan's strictures, he has . . . spread his opinions so widely that, wise as he is in the ways of the press, he risked the almost certain chance that they would be made public.

Even so, Mr. Kissinger, who served with Mr. Moynihan at Harvard and knows him well, can scarcely be surprised. Pat's idea of confronting the U.N. was not only defensible but long overdue; however, leaving it to Pat himself almost certainly meant that it would be overdone, and that's what has happened.

Now Messrs. Ford and Kissinger support him in public and deplore him in private. Having put him in the job, they can neither tame nor repudiate him. He has always been the enemy of his best ideas, always used the most provocative phrases, but Mr. Kissinger knew all that before and is now having to deal with the consequences and his own regrets.

———◆———

The next morning, Friday, the telephone buzzed; Teddy White without ceremony said, "You know you have to go, don't you?" I said I had just put a sheet of paper in my typewriter and had written, "Dear Mr. President."

It was as simple as that, and everyone knew it. In the Saturday *Times,* Russell Baker described it all in a grand spoof he called "Dangerous Case of English." "The newspapers are full of mystery this week," he began about my case. "Profusions of clues are scattered through the newsprint" — so copiously, indeed, that he suspected calculated distraction. The problem was, though, he could discern, that

> Moynihan spoke English, an ancient tongue which, though long fallen into disuse, still has the power to sway men's minds, and upon arrival at the United Nations, he outraged all humanity by speaking it aloud.
>
> Minute autocracies and tribal kingdoms, which wield a majority of the U.N.'s votes and one-and-one-half percent of its power, were appalled. Europeans were appalled. Washington was appalled, or at least that vast part of Washington that is the State Department and Henry Kissinger.
>
> This week, a sudden outburst of action. The newspapers bloom with

leaked reports that Moynihan is up to his old tricks. He has resorted to English again. This time he has written a memo and circulated it all over the State Department's wire system. It accuses the State Department of trying to undercut his attempts to carry out his assigned job at the U.N.

The newspapers play this leaked memo as a big story, but aficionados of mystery news instantly recognize that the papers are concealing the most interesting part: The real question is who leaked the memo and why.

If it was Mr. Moynihan, which is possible, was it to force a showdown with State and Kissinger? If it was State or Kissinger, was it to force a showdown that would at last rid them of this troublesome English speaker? The papers tell us nothing, although next day we have the customary White House declarations that Ford and Kissinger stand behind Moynihan.

The day after that, however, the papers begin to give us mysteriously unattributed reports that Kissinger and Ford can't say it aloud, but are actually at the end of their patience with Moynihan. Scolding editorials are written deploring Moynihan's inadequate diplomatic finesse. (His habit of using English.)

Something is going on here. What it is is a mystery. If the reporters know, why do they not tell us? One of the things that is going on is obvious enough. The papers are letting themselves be used by Government manipulators in return for a story that is a poor substitute for the story of what is really going on.

In The Week in Review on Sunday, *The Times* asked rhetorically: "Who leaked the cable to *The New York Times,* where it was first published? No one is saying. . . ." I wrote a letter to the editor to say that surely *The Times* knew: why did *it* not say?

———◆———

On Monday morning I called Henry Rosovsky at Harvard to say that I had sent my letter of resignation to the President, and that this would be announced at noon. He said he was disappointed. I said to the Dean that so was I, but it had become impossible to stay at the United Nations. The Dean said, "Oh, you mean *that* President!" Which sums up all I ever meant by a liberal society.

———◆———

This time the White House had not tried to change anyone's mind. The letters from the President, the Vice President, and the Secretary were lovely.

As I was to be President of the Security Council in February, it was agreed that I should stay on for that month. It went quietly. As did I.

Afterword

NOT UNTIL IT WAS OVER did it turn out that we had changed the language of American foreign policy. Human rights emerged as one of the organizing principles that define our interests and help to inform our conduct in world affairs.

It came suddenly, as such changes will. The nation was changing its mind. In the briefest period, hardly more than a matter of weeks, with a half-dozen speeches at most, we were a catalyst. It was too large a change to ascribe to any person or persons. But we were there — Garment, Mitchell, the others of whom I have written — and not many others were. It was too intense to last, but the intensity of the time was needed. *The Economist* thanked me for coming when I did, and for going when I did, which, looking back, seems fair enough.

The long postwar period during which containment had been the organizing principle of foreign policy, when American values had appeared to be secondary in importance to American power, had long since come to an end. As an organizing principle, containment gravely underestimated the importance of politics, and ideas, and values in the conduct of foreign policy. Its authors had thought of themselves as defending a line that separated the totalitarian from the democratic sphere, a separation that would endure so long as the line was defended.

But a generation passed and of a sudden it appeared that democratic values were under assault on both sides of the line. Unaccountably — it *must* be judged unaccountable — the Soviet Union retained a capacity to inspire commitment and belief in the most unexpected circles and places of what had been known as the free world. Further, containment in its strict military sense had not succeeded. The Soviet navy took its place on the high seas, while Soviet arms appeared, again, in the most unexpected places with the most improbable collaborators. Soviet strategic forces continued to strengthen.

Although détente was generally depicted as a conceptual breakthrough, a movement away from the rigidities of containment, it was never that. Détente was a diminished version of containment that followed from the fact that the primal doctrine was not succeeding. Rather than presenting the Soviets with no option about remaining within their own bounds, the authors of détente took the position that the Soviets could be persuaded where they could no longer be forced. The transition required that the Soviets be presented as having entered a new and more tractable phase. But there was little real evidence for this. At least as good a contrary case could be made. And this was the failing of détente: it drew its inspiration more from a sense of democratic weakness than of totalitarian strength. It *was* a form of disguised retreat, carried forward in a rapture of exalted dissimulation by persons whose assumption was that the American people would not face reality.

This was wrong. The electorate was quite capable of confronting the dangers of the time, so long as this was accompanied by some assertion of our strengths, some insistence that the political culture of the democracies was *superior* to that of the despotisms, left and right, all around us. It was hardly Henry Kissinger's fault that he did not sense this willingness. He later wrote me that our differences had been "perhaps due to the fact that I had to position our policy for a long haul in the midst of civil war conditions, while you were concerned with the immediate crisis." I would only reply that the immediate crisis was that of a public trying to get its government to recognize that if there had been a civil war it was over, and the nation wanted to be proud of itself again, and in ways to assert itself again.

———◆———

But, clearly, the changes of policy for which I was arguing were of an order that needed to be decided by an election, and especially so in the peculiar circumstances of 1976. Both the President and the Vice President had been appointed, not elected to office, after their predecessors had resigned in disgrace. The Secretary of State had been appointed by the President driven from office. No one had a mandate for the order of change that I was proposing. Nor did anyone in office have the energy.

It is odd that the issue of human rights, which came so naturally to him, nonetheless eluded Gerald R. Ford. Had he taken it up, it might have enabled him to win the 1976 election. That he did not, and his opponents did, almost certainly helped him to lose it. As the year wore on, the Reagan forces within his own party assailed him with charges of weakness on human rights and indecisiveness in the face of the totalitarian powers. He only barely gained the nomination. Had he, as President, been the proponent of an assertive human rights position in foreign affairs, he surely would have had a far easier time of that contest, and would have entered the general election as a President with a distinctive foreign policy that he had fashioned himself, and moreover a thoroughly credible one. Nothing would have seemed more appropriate for him as a person and as a public man. But he had not done so. Then, in the general election, Jimmy Carter kept after him on the issue in a generalized way: America was not asserting its goodness in the world. A soft theme, you might say, but far different from "Come Home, America." Then in a crucial debate, Ford said, "I don't believe the Poles consider themselves dominated by the Soviet Union." This was, of course, Counselor Sonnenfeldt's position, as presented to the Ambassadors in London, making its way out from the recesses of the mind where Presidents store briefings. To wit: If *we* took the position that the Poles were free and independent, then both we and the *Soviets* had the same position, inasmuch as the Soviets, also, held that the Poles were not under Soviet domination. Hence the "emergent global superpower" would feel less inept and more at ease in its new role, and détente would accordingly deepen.

This, too, was an epiphany of sorts. Of a sudden it was revealed that détente rested on a great many people's saying things that were not so to persons who knew them not to be so, and who they knew knew. It cannot have helped Gerald Ford. It enabled Carter to appear the more firm, straightforward candidate.

In the brutal reckoning of politics, this was Ford's choice, and hence his fault. The White House had been urged to seize the issue, and could have done so despite the Department of State.

Garment had stayed on as United States representative to the Human Rights Commission, and continued to press the case. In July he prepared a long memorandum for Assistant Secretary Lewis entitled "Human Rights/General Assembly." It urged that we not retreat to a passive role in the coming General Assembly:

> Democracy's bicentennial is beginning to generate excitement. Why not try to make some of it rub off on the United Nations? If this sounds theatrical, that is precisely the intent. There is an imperative need to dramatize the ideology of the West, to clarify our beliefs and intentions for our own people and for the world. Given a unifying theme and strong voices, the U.N. can be a magnificent forum. I repeat: This is a time when eloquent and reasoned expressions of our commitment to freedom may, like the tall ships, find a surprisingly warm response.

The memorandum made its way around Washington and even to the White House, but in the end nothing came of it. The head of Boys Town was appointed the public member of the U.S. delegation to the Thirty-First General Assembly.

———————◆———————

In the meantime, I had gone back to Democratic politics. In mid-February Senator Henry M. Jackson, campaigning for the presidential nomination, stopped by to see me in New York. No one so much as he had linked human rights issues to general foreign policy concerns. He had a politician's sense that a central advantage of human rights *as a strategy* in foreign affairs was that it could be pressed independently of the issue of political systems. A nation did not have to be democratic before it could be asked to consider the issue seriously. Thus, Jackson thought the Soviet regime could be asked to recognize the right of emigration without being frontally asked to change the nature of its regime. It was characteristic of the confusion of the time that Jackson, the most moderate of men, was routinely depicted as somehow extremist. In fact, he was working toward a resolution of the dilemma which Reinhold Niebuhr called the myth of a democratic universality; the idea that democracy is "a universal option for all nations." It may be it is not; certain liberties surely are.

On March 1, my first day out of government, I flew to Boston to campaign for Jackson in the Massachusetts primary, which he won. Next came the New York primary, in which he led the field, and I was elected a Jackson delegate. I went on to campaign for him in Wisconsin, Florida, and finally Pennsylvania, where his luck ran out, and Jimmy Carter took the lead he would never relinquish. In May, I was elected to the Democratic Platform Committee, and then to the Drafting Committee, where Ben J. Wattenberg of the Coalition for a

Democratic Majority served as Jackson's personal representative. When the Drafting Committee assembled in June I turned out to be the only member with experience in foreign affairs, and, with Wattenberg, I took the opportunity to write a foreign policy plank that combined the arguments we had been making at the U.N. with Jackson's more general views:

> We will reaffirm the fundamental American commitment to human rights across the globe. America must work for a release of all political prisoners, men and women who are in jail simply because they have opposed peacefully the policies of their governments or have aided others who have — in all countries. America must take a firm stand to support and implement existing U.S. law to bring about liberalization of emigration policy in countries which limit or prohibit free emigration. America must be resolute in its support of the right of workers to organize and of trade unions to act freely and independently, and in its support of freedom of the press. America must continue to stand as a bulwark in support of human liberty in all countries. A return to the politics of principles requires a reaffirmation of human freedom throughout the world.

On the Drafting Committee, and on the Platform Committee itself, there was the strongest perception that human rights should be at the center of our foreign policy, but for different reasons as between different groups. This needs to be made clear. The most *active* elements in the Democratic party at this time were associated with opposition to the Vietnam war, which had been the principal position of Senator George McGovern, who had led the party four years earlier. For these men and women, more than ordinarily concerned with morality in foreign affairs, the issue of human rights, curiously, was more tactical than otherwise. Put plainly, it was a means to discredit the policies of the previous and the incumbent administrations by establishing that the United States gave support to and was supported by regimes that ranged from the politically unattractive to the appalling. If we supported their regimes, we supported their politics. For some, this served only to prove further that it was best for America to come home. For others, it suggested an opportunity to change things for the better in situations where the United States surely had some influence. Obviously, motives varied. But there was one more or less uniform aspect to the views of such persons. They were far more concerned with the wrongdoing of the United States than of other nations that might be adversaries of the United States. In this, of course, they differed fundamentally from the positions we had proclaimed at the United Nations.

Fortunately, drafting committees are given to avoiding differences rather than emphasizing them. A motion was made to stop all military aid to nondemocratic governments. I countered that this should include economic aid as well; that there were just too many regimes that wished to get their machine guns from Czechoslovakia and their wheat from North Dakota, and that such a one-sided position by the Democratic Party would only help them maintain their well-stocked jails. There was a hesitation, and then a moment of recognition. Ours was the Democratic Party after all; there was room for George McGovern and Henry Jackson both.

In June, also, I entered the Democratic primary race for the Senate in New York. I was not, in my view, breaking commitment. I had not left the U.N. to do this. I had proposed to stay and would have stayed, and even after Reston's column the President could have kept me if he hadn't been inhibited by what he knew was being done to our position. My opponents in my own party were at near-polar opposites to me on the issues I most cared about, and in the end I barely won the primary. But I did, and went on to win the general election more easily.

Thus I came to be standing with the Senate on the platform in front of the Capitol when Jimmy Carter took the oath of office and in his Inaugural Address proposed to make human rights an essential element of American foreign policy. The President thereafter did not always see the issue as I would have done, and appointed almost none of the persons I would have appointed to pursue the issue. But the genius of the issue of human rights is that it is simple. It takes into account the incapacities of governments, a quality Richard E. Neustadt would commend. It is something Americans understand and share, no matter how they may differ in other matters.

At the end of President Carter's first year in office Anthony Lewis would write that for all its limitations, the new United States policy did do some good, and "the issue of human rights has been woven inextricably into the international dialogue." Freedom House would report that solid gains had been scored for political and civil liberty in 1977. Forty-four countries, with rather more than a third of the world's population, were listed as Free, now once more including India, which the President had just visited.

Among totalitarian governments, reaction to the new American policy was predictably hostile. In Hanoi, the official government newspaper denounced the President who, it said, "considers 'human rights' as the core of his policy. But his campaign for this issue has proved more and more to be an instrument of division against the socialist countries." Vietnam was then in the process of annexing a portion of Cambodia, or seeking to do so. Whether or not as an involuntary response to American policy, the Hanoi government was soon urging the soldiers of the Cambodian government to turn against their own government, and the internal contradictions of Communism seemed to be progressing nicely.

Halfway around the world, the Soviets had switched sides in the Horn of Africa, and had sent a massive force of Cubans to aid Ethiopia in a war with Somalia. The President of Somalia, General Mohammed Siad Barre, took to holding press conferences in which he begged assistance from the democratic nations against the "new imperialists," by which he had come to designate his former allies, the Soviet Union and Cuba. He pleaded that his small country was being attacked by brutal totalitarian powers of the Warsaw Pact and their allies, who pay no heed to the rights to independence and self-determination of small nations.

If the general or his ambassador at the United Nations recalled the American address given in the aftermath of the adoption of the Somali resolution on Zionism, they gave no indication. Nor evidently did anyone at the Department of State, which was busy devising ways to give aid to the Somali government. No one considered that this might be a useful occasion to remind the government in Mogadishu, and governments up and down that continent and indeed around the world, that the United States had tried to warn that the language that gives rights to individuals is the same language that gives rights to nations, and that to corrupt that language would threaten both.

And this was the problem. The failure of nerve so evident in the old administration carried over into the new one. If anything, the cadre awaiting its term of office, freed of any responsibility to defend the policies it had not made, became even more deeply persuaded that these policies were indefensible. From the very first a pervasive anxiety about the Soviet Union was in evidence. Before long, administration spokesmen were arguing that one accommodation or another had to be made as the Soviets were heading for strategic superiority in the mid-1980s. As for the late 1970s, one concession after another became necessary in Africa, or else, it would be explained, the Soviets would send in the Cubans.

In the circumstances, then, it was perhaps to be expected that on December 30, 1970, the President would be in Warsaw and in response to a question "How satisfied are you that your concept of the preservation of human rights is currently being honored here in Poland?" would reply, "I think that our concept of human rights is preserved in Poland. . . . There is a substantial degree of freedom of the press . . . a substantial degree of freedom of religions . . . and an open relationship between Poland and our country. . . ."

In these same circumstances, if not to be expected, it was perhaps not surprising that relationships between the United States and Israel worsened as never in the history of the two nations, and in Washington it was openly asked whether the United States was "switching sides." We became increasingly out of patience with the slowness of democratic procedures, the qualms about procedure and language, the caution in making commitments that the Israelis displayed, and that any democracy will display, given that procedures and language matter, and that commitments are to be kept. At times we seemed hardly to comprehend the asymmetry of negotiations between the Israelis and their adversaries, or if we did, to prefer the easy cynicism of the adversaries. For a moment it had appeared we would bring the Palestine Liberation Organization back onto the West Bank under Soviet auspices. Only the dismay of the Egyptian government, not that of our own, prevented the joint Soviet-American proposal from going forward.

Last, in such circumstances it is not surprising that the human rights initiative began to falter. Those seeking accommodation with rising Soviet power simply would not believe that in the end the Russians could be deterred by the threat to them of American argument and exposition. Those, now in the main outside of the Executive, who were prepared to confront the Soviets were increasingly troubled by the difficulties that American human rights policies were causing for non-Communist but equally nondemocratic nations, some of which would fairly be counted American allies. Our policy makers had yet to learn just how dangerous the world had become for a nation like ours, or to see that guarding the language of human rights would play no small part in our defense.

Index